Topological and Quantum Materials Explained

A Practical Guide for Engineers, Physicists, and Quantum Computing Practitioners

C. Louis-Charles PhD

Contents

Introduction

The growth chamber does not look like anything Marcus Webb has worked near before. He has spent twelve years at Cascade Microtech designing cryogenic control systems for semiconductor test equipment, and the equipment he knew was clean, orderly, and built around silicon. What Priya Nair is showing him in the basement laboratory of Axiom Quantum is a stainless steel cylinder trailing vacuum feedthroughs and cryogenic lines, its effusion cells loaded with mercury, cadmium, and tellurium. It is his first week at the company.

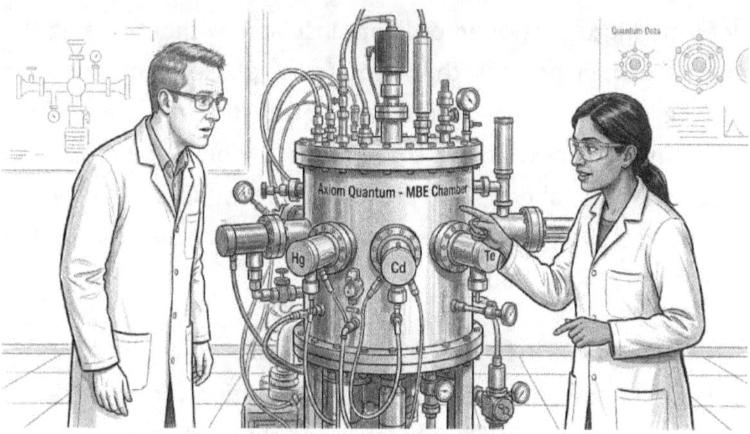

Priya explains. The chamber grows mercury cadmium telluride, written Hg1-xCdxTe, a compound semiconductor whose alloy composition can be tuned by adjusting the cadmium fraction x. At the right composition and temperature, the energy gap between valence and conduction bands inverts: states that normally live below the Fermi level end up above it, and vice versa. That inversion, she says, is not a defect. It is the physics axiom that Quantum is betting its entire qubit architecture on. Marcus listens. Then he asks the question.

"What does it actually mean for a material to be topological?"

Priya has heard some version of that question from every hardware engineer who has walked through Axiom's basement since the company was founded in 2021. It is, she tells him, the right question, and answering it properly takes thirteen chapters. The short version: topology classifies shapes not by their curvature but by how they are fundamentally connected. A coffee cup and a donut are topologically identical because you can deform one into the other without tearing; a sphere is not a donut because no smooth deformation converts it. When physicists say a material is topological, they mean its electronic band structure belongs to a class that cannot be smoothly deformed into that of an ordinary insulator without closing the energy gap, a process that requires a phase transition. The surface states that result are protected by the same mathematical inevitability that makes a donut impossible to deform into a sphere. That protection is why Axiom believes it can build qubits that the environment cannot disrupt. That is what this book is about.

The Engineering Provocation

Silicon has powered the computing revolution for six decades. Gordon Moore's 1965 observation that transistor counts doubled roughly every two years became a planning assumption for the entire semiconductor industry, and it held for fifty years. It no longer holds. Gate oxide layers are now only a handful of atomic layers thick, and quantum tunneling through them creates leakage currents that conventional scaling cannot correct. Transistor channel lengths in leading-edge nodes are measured in single-digit nanometers, and fabrication variability at that scale drives performance spreads that statistical process control cannot contain. Heat dissipation in densely packed chip stacks has become the binding constraint on processor performance in data centers, not logic speed. The engineers at TSMC, Intel, and Samsung are not running out of ideas; they are running into physics. The question is no longer whether silicon will reach its limits, but what will replace it.

The answer emerging from a decade of research is a family of materials united by a common principle: they exploit quantum mechanics not as a nuisance to be managed but as a design principle to be engineered. Topological insulators conduct electricity on their surfaces while insulating in their bulk, and that surface conductance is protected against scattering by the topology of the electronic band structure. Topological superconductors support Majorana fermions, quasiparticles that are their own antiparticles, whose non-Abelian exchange statistics make them the proposed physical basis for fault-tolerant quantum computing. Spintronic materials couple the spin degree of freedom of electrons to current flow in ways that could replace conventional transistor logic with switching elements consuming a fraction of the power. These are not theoretical predictions: they are observed, characterized, and in several cases integrated into device prototypes.

The hardware stakes are concrete. Microsoft's topological qubit program, developed over more than a decade at Microsoft Station Q and partner universities, is premised on the argument that qubits built from topological superconductors will achieve fault tolerance at lower overhead than conventional superconducting circuits, because the topological protection encodes the qubit's logical state in a way that local noise cannot disrupt. In 2023, Microsoft announced experimental signatures consistent with the topological gap required by that architecture. Quantum sensors based on nitrogen-vacancy centers in diamond already achieve magnetic-field sensitivities relevant to medical imaging and navigation. Next-generation spintronic memory is being extended into logic applications using topological material interfaces that reduce switching energy by orders of magnitude. The next wave of hardware is being built right now, from these materials.

Diagram I.1 - Silicon Scaling Wall and the Topological Materials Frontier

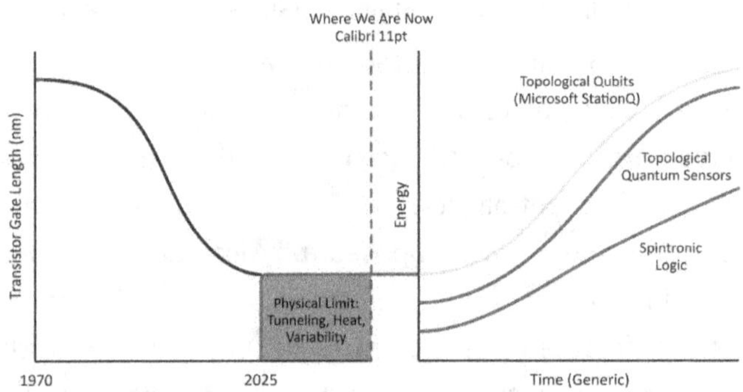

The diagram above maps the transition this book is about: sixty years of gate-length reduction compressing into a hard floor set by quantum tunneling and thermal physics, and the three emerging hardware programs that topological and quantum materials make possible. They are active engineering programs, and the materials enabling them are the subject of this book.

Who This Book Is For

This book is written for five reader personas who share a single defining characteristic: they are technically sophisticated professionals or advanced students who need rigorous, non-trivial explanations of topological and quantum materials, but who do not have a condensed matter physics graduate education and should not require one. The book never talks down to any of them. It assumes comfort with differential equations, circuit theory, and undergraduate quantum mechanics. It does not assume prior exposure to Berry phases, Chern numbers, band topology, or the quasiparticle physics that populated condensed matter over the last thirty years.

The first reader is an electrical engineer who has joined a quantum computing hardware team and needs to understand why topological qubits require a fundamentally different class of materials from superconducting transmon qubits or trapped-ion systems. This reader is Marcus Webb. The second is a hardware engineer at a semiconductor company who encountered the phrase 'topological insulator' in a roadmap document and wants the actual physics: what the band inversion is, why the surface state cannot be removed by disorder, and what protected conductance implies for a device stack. The third is a quantum computing software practitioner who wants to understand the hardware layer: what physical substrate the qubits are built on, why topological protection is architecturally distinct from active error-correcting codes like the surface code, and what hardware constraints propagate upward to the software stack.

The fourth reader is a materials science student who understands band theory and wants the precise bridge from conventional semiconductor physics to topological phases, including the Berry phase, Chern number, and Z2 invariant that makes that distinction rigorous. The fifth followed the 2016 Nobel Prize coverage, which recognized David Thouless, F. Duncan Haldane, and J. Michael Kosterlitz for theoretical discoveries of topological phase transitions, and wanted the full technical explanation rather than the press release. What all five share is a willingness to engage with serious ideas and an impatience with texts that either over-explain or under-explain.

What You Will Be Able To Do

By the last page, you will understand what makes a material topological and why topological protection is physically meaningful rather than merely metaphorical. You will be able to explain what band inversion is, what a topological invariant measures, and why the surface states of a topological insulator are immune to the scattering that limits conventional conductors. You will understand what Cooper pairs are, why some superconductors are topologically non-trivial, and why that distinction matters for quantum computing. You will be able to explain what a Majorana fermion is, why its non-Abelian braiding statistics could support intrinsically fault-tolerant qubits, and what experimental signatures distinguish a genuine Majorana mode from a trivial Andreev bound state.

You will know what angle-resolved photoemission spectroscopy, called ARPES, reveals about a band structure, what molecular beam epitaxy requires in terms of interface control, and what the difference between a Type I and Type II superconductor means for device operating constraints. Most importantly, you will be able to read a quantum materials paper, evaluate a hardware claim, and engage as a peer rather than a tourist in the field that is building the next generation of computing and sensing hardware. The promise is not the full graduate curriculum: it is the precise subset that a working engineer needs to make real hardware decisions in a field where the materials are already leaving the laboratory.

How To Read This Book

The book moves from framing and history through quantum foundations, topological physics, and device applications. Each chapter opens with a scene at Axiom Quantum. Below is a brief guide to each.

What We Are Building opens the book with the engineering map: what topological and quantum materials are, what hardware they enable, and why working engineers need to understand them now, in accessible terms, before formal physics begins.

A Brief, Wild History of Topological Physics traces the field from the Kosterlitz-Thouless phase transition in 1972 through Klaus von Klitzing's 1980 discovery of the quantum Hall effect, the 2005 prediction of topological insulators by Kane and Mele, and the 2016 Nobel Prize in Physics. The goal is risk calibration: knowing which ideas have high experimental confidence, which are active programs, and which remain theoretical matters for anyone making engineering decisions based on the field's trajectory.

The Quantum Foundation covers wavefunctions, energy quantization, and the measurement postulate: the precise subset of undergraduate quantum mechanics that topological materials physics actually uses. Electrons in Solids builds from Bloch's theorem through band structure, connecting conventional semiconductor band theory to the topological extension that follows.

What Is Topology? is the conceptual pivot. It builds geometric intuition for topological classification, from coffee cups and donuts to the Berry phase, the Chern number, and the Z2 invariant that classifies time-reversal-invariant topological insulators, presenting them as measurements that can be extracted from a band structure rather than as abstract objects.

Topological Insulators makes the physics concrete: band inversion at the crystal orbital level, why surface states are protected, how bismuth selenide (Bi2Se3) and Hg1-xCdxTe are grown and characterized, and what device architectures exploit the protected surface conductance. Beyond Insulators extends the framework to Weyl semimetals, Fermi arc surface states, and the chiral anomaly unique to Weyl systems.

Superconductivity covers Cooper pairs, BCS theory, and the transition to topological superconductors, with particular attention to proximity-coupled heterostructures that engineer effective topological superconductivity in non-intrinsic materials. Topological Quantum Computing is where the entire physics apparatus converges on hardware: Majorana fermions, non-Abelian braiding, and the engineering tradeoffs of topological qubit architectures compared to superconducting and trapped-ion approaches.

Quantum Sensors examines topological materials for precision measurement applications: navigation-grade gyroscopes, medical-grade magnetometers, and timing references. Topological Materials for Real Devices applies the full physics to near-term commercial applications in spintronics and magnetoresistive devices, with explicit attention to fabrication constraints and yield challenges.

The Quantum Materials Laboratory covers the experimental toolkit: ARPES, scanning tunneling microscopy, molecular beam epitaxy, and millikelvin transport measurements, from the perspective of what each reveals about topological character and what it requires from a materials development program. The Road Ahead closes the book with an honest map of open problems, emerging material classes, unconventional superconductors, axion insulators, higher-order topological phases, and the engineering opportunities the field's current state creates.

Meet Axiom Quantum

Diagram I.2 - The Axiom Quantum Team

A strong central metaphor underpin esent the convergence of theory and experiment.

Axiom Quantum was founded in Boston in 2021 with a single engineering mandate: build fault-tolerant quantum computers from topological materials. The company occupies a converted research building near the MIT campus, where condensed matter physicists, hardware engineers, quantum theorists, and sensing specialists work in the same facility. The organizational structure mirrors the book's core argument that topological materials cannot be understood or built with if those four disciplines are kept siloed from one another. Each chapter opens with a scene from Axiom Quantum that grounds the physics in a precise engineering context.

Dr. Priya Nair, 48, Chief Science Officer, spent fifteen years at MIT studying topological insulators and Weyl semimetals before joining Axiom to translate that research into manufacturable hardware. She sets the scientific direction: which materials are worth growing, which fabrication approaches are feasible, and which engineering shortcuts will destroy the topological protection the architecture depends on. Her recurring role is to explain precisely why the physics constrains the engineering in ways that cannot be negotiated around.

Marcus Webb, 36, Head of Hardware Engineering, came to Axiom from a semiconductor company where he designed cryogenic control systems and dilution refrigerator infrastructure. He understands systems design, device physics, and manufacturing constraints from twelve years of hands-on work, but is approaching topological materials from the outside. His questions are always engineering questions: what does this mean for the process flow, what fabrication tolerance does the physics actually require, and what breaks first when the device leaves the lab? His moments of recognition drive the book's most important engineering moves, and he is the reader's primary avatar.

Dr. Sasha Korolev, 41, Head of Quantum Theory, earned his doctorate in topological phases of matter and conducted postdoctoral work on Berry phases and Majorana fermion physics at the Perimeter Institute. At Axiom, he translates condensed matter theory into hardware engineering constraints, turning 'topological invariant' into 'this is what happens to the device when you apply a magnetic field.' He is the book's most technically precise voice.

Dr. Yuki Tanaka, 32, Director of Quantum Sensing Applications, completed her doctorate at Caltech on topological material-based magnetometers and postdoctoral research at NIST before joining Axiom to build its quantum sensing division. Her mandate is to find the places where topological materials create engineering value that can reach the market before topological qubits do: navigation-grade gyroscopes, medical-grade magnetometers, and timing references whose stability derives from topological protection. She provides the book's clearest answers to the question every hardware reader eventually asks: Can you actually build something with this?

Takeaway

Marcus Webb's first question, asked in a basement laboratory on his first week at Axiom Quantum, is the right question to begin with. Answering it requires the full arc of the chapters that follow: quantum foundations, band physics, topological classification, and the device architectures that topological protection makes possible. This book argues that topological and quantum materials represent the most consequential materials transition in computing and sensing since the transistor, and that the engineers who understand them first will define the hardware architectures of the next two decades. The materials exist. The devices are being designed. The engineering programs are running. The first chapter starts where Marcus starts: with the engineering map of what is being built and why.

1 What We Are Building

Marcus Webb arrived at Axiom Quantum on a Monday in February, three weeks after signing an offer letter that had surprised him more than it had surprised anyone else. He had spent nine years designing cryogenic control systems at a semiconductor equipment company, and he understood dilution refrigerators, microwave coaxial lines, low-noise amplifiers, and the particular set of engineering headaches that come with keeping a device operating at temperatures colder than deep space. What he did not know, and what had been quietly obvious to him during the final round of interviews, was anything meaningful about topological physics. He had assumed that was fine. He assumed he would learn.

His first real day on the technical floor quickly corrected that assumption. Priya Nair had scheduled an hour with him to walk through what she called the materials roadmap. The whiteboard in her office was already covered: a timeline on one axis, engineering readiness on the other, with clusters of material names at different coordinates. Bismuth selenide. Indium arsenide nanowires. Hybrid semiconductor-superconductor heterostructures. He recognized the last one and felt briefly on solid ground. Then she pointed to the word written large at the top of the board, connected to every cluster by lines: TOPOLOGICAL.

Marcus looked at the board, then at her. "Why can't we just use better superconducting qubits?" Priya set down her marker. She did not look impatient. She looked like someone who had been waiting for exactly this question. "Because the material itself can be the error correction," she said. "Let me show you what that means." She pulled up a chair and began at the beginning.

What Marcus learned in the next two hours became the foundation of everything this book will teach you. The engineering case for topological materials is not subtle. It is architectural.

Why It Matters

The quantum computing field has a coherence problem, and everyone working in hardware knows it. A qubit is useful only for as long as it maintains its quantum state, and the quantum states of every qubit platform available today are fragile in ways that demand massive engineering overhead. Superconducting transmon qubits, the hardware substrate of machines from IBM, Google, and Rigetti, have coherence times in the hundreds of microseconds. That sounds short because it is short. A quantum processor, to be useful, must maintain coherence across thousands of gate operations. The numbers today are tight, and the engineering solutions to tight numbers are expensive.

The standard response is quantum error correction: encode one logical qubit across many physical qubits, continuously monitor the physical qubits, detect errors, and apply corrective operations before errors propagate. This works. It is also costly at a scale that grows badly. IBM's most credible near-term roadmap to fault-tolerant quantum computing requires on the order of 1,000 physical qubits per high-quality logical qubit. A system with enough logical qubits to solve commercially relevant problems would require millions of physical qubits, millions of microwave control lines, a cryostat of building-scale complexity, and a classical control system unlike anything currently in use. Marcus had seen the back-of-the-envelope calculations. He had done some of them himself. The engineering was daunting.

The topological approach starts from a different premise. Instead of accepting fragile qubits and engineering elaborate correction systems around them, it asks whether a qubit's physical substrate can be designed so that local perturbations cannot destroy the quantum state. The answer is yes, under specific conditions, for specific material classes, by using a property of those materials that has nothing to do with atomic composition and everything to do with the global geometry of their electronic quantum states. That property is topology. Understanding it at an engineer's level is the first and most important thing this book will teach you.

Hardware Limits: Silicon and Conventional Superconductors

The silicon transistor has been the dominant computing element for sixty years, and its trajectory is one of the most impressive engineering achievements in human history. Moore's Law worked because geometric scaling cooperated with classical electrostatics: making transistors smaller yields more of them per area, faster switching, and lower power. That cooperation is ending. At sub-5-nanometer node dimensions, the gate oxide separating a transistor's control electrode from its channel is only a handful of atoms thick, and quantum-mechanical tunneling allows electrons to leak through it regardless of the applied voltage. Gate leakage at these scales is not a manufacturing defect. It is a fundamental consequence of quantum mechanics. Heat dissipation already limits clock speeds, which is why modern processors scale horizontally in core count rather than vertically in clock frequency. The International Roadmap for Devices and Systems now acknowledges that conventional geometric scaling has effectively ended and that the path forward requires new device architectures, new materials, or both.

The superconducting qubit story is structurally parallel. Progress on transmon qubits over the past fifteen years has been genuine and impressive: coherence times improved from nanoseconds to hundreds of microseconds, two-qubit gate fidelities crossed 99.9 percent in research settings, and IBM demonstrated 1,000-plus qubit processors. The problem is not that superconducting qubits have failed to improve. The problem is that each improvement revealed the depth of the error correction overhead required to make them useful for general computation. A single high-quality logical qubit requires on the order of 1,000 to 10,000 physical transmon qubits, depending on the code and physical error rates. A 100-logical-qubit system, enough to begin addressing commercially relevant problems, would require between 100,000 and 1,000,000 physical qubits. The cryogenic engineering of such a system, independent of the qubit physics, is a major unsolved problem. Marcus had been the person trying to solve parts of it at his previous company.

Diagram 1.1 - The Silicon Scaling Wall

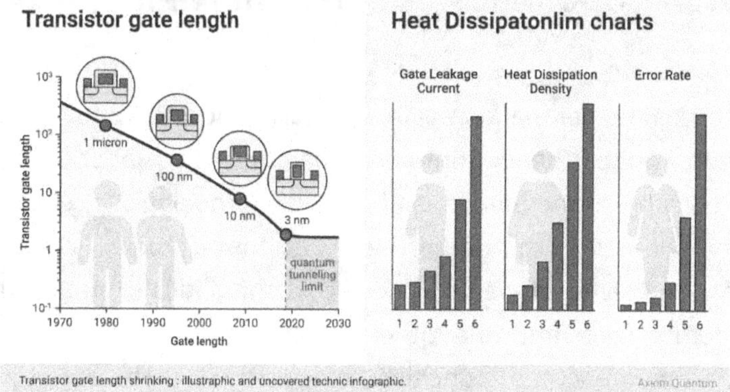

The trapped-ion alternative achieves higher single-qubit fidelities and operates at room temperature. Still, it incurs its own speed and qubit-count overhead, and its laser and optical control systems pose engineering challenges of comparable magnitude. None of the conventional approaches is obviously wrong. They are all legitimate engineering bets. But they all share one fundamental assumption: qubits are fragile, and fragility must be managed through external correction overhead. The topological approach challenges that assumption at its root.

Diagram 1.2 - Physical vs. Logical Qubit Overhead

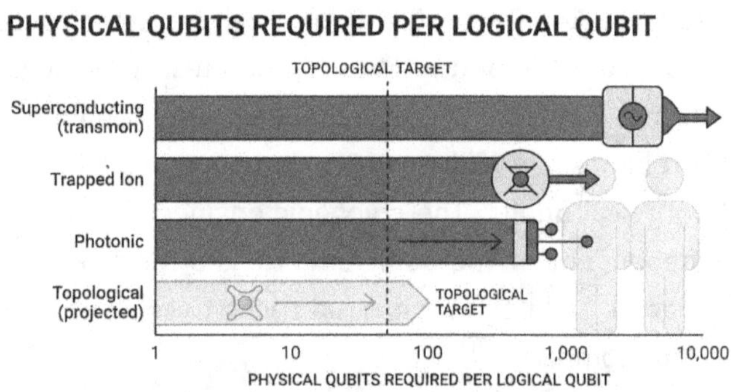

Physical qubits required per logical qubit for four major quantum computing architectures.

What Topological Means: An Engineer's First Contact

Priya picked up her marker again and started not with equations but with a rubber band. Consider three objects: a rubber band, a coffee cup with no handle, and a donut. A topologist's central observation is that the rubber band and the handleless coffee cup are the same shape in a specific mathematical sense: you can deform one into the other by any smooth continuous transformation without punching holes or tearing. The donut is different. You cannot turn a donut into a sphere without punching through it, because the donut has a hole and the sphere does not. The number of holes is a topological invariant, a property that does not change under any continuous deformation, however drastic, as long as you do not cut or glue. A mathematician would say the donut and the sphere have different topological genus.

Now translate this into solid-state physics. A material's electrons occupy quantum states that extend throughout the material, and those states have a structure in momentum space, the mathematical space in which each point represents a possible electron momentum. The collection of occupied electron states in momentum space has a geometry. Geometry can have topological properties that are preserved under continuous deformations of the material's parameters, provided that the deformation does not close the electronic energy gap. A topologically trivial material has electron states that are topologically equivalent to those of a sphere. A topologically non-trivial material has electron states equivalent to a donut. You cannot deform one into the other without closing the gap and passing through a phase transition. The topological character is therefore robust to impurities, defects, small applied fields, and other local perturbations that do not close the gap globally.

The engineering consequence follows directly. At the boundary between a topologically non-trivial material and a topologically trivial one, the topological invariant must change. Mathematics guarantees the energy gap must close at that boundary, which means conducting surface states must exist there. Those surface states are a topological necessity, not an accident of surface chemistry, and they cannot be removed by any perturbation that does not break the underlying symmetry of the bulk material. They are, in the vocabulary Marcus would come to use, topologically protected.

Diagram 1.3 - Topology: From Rubber Bands to Electron States

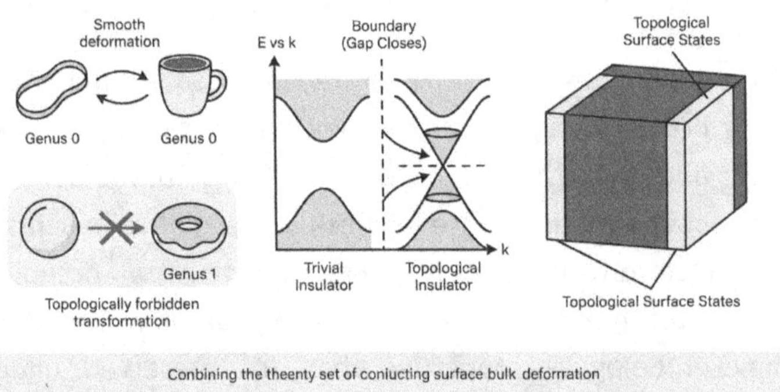

Marcus stopped Priya to confirm he understood. "So the protection isn't because the material is perfect," he said. "It's because the protection comes from a property that doesn't depend on perfection." Priya nodded. "That's exactly right. Error correction works by monitoring imperfect qubits and correcting their errors. Topological protection works by building qubits from a material where the relevant quantum state is immune to the class of local perturbations that would destroy it. The qubit doesn't need fixing because the physics doesn't allow those errors in the first place." Marcus picked up his notebook for the first time that morning.

Topological Protection vs Error Correction

The distinction Priya drew is worth dwelling on, because it is not only a physics distinction. It is an architectural distinction with direct engineering consequences for every downstream design decision: the physical qubit count, the cryogenic control complexity, the classical processing overhead, the required gate fidelity, and the thermal footprint of a system scaled to useful logical qubit counts.

Conventional quantum error correction, in its most widely implemented forms, including the surface code and concatenated stabilizer codes, works by encoding a logical qubit across a two-dimensional array of physical qubits. Ancilla qubits within the array are repeatedly measured to obtain syndrome measurements that reveal whether an error has occurred without collapsing the logical state. When a syndrome indicates an error, a classical control system decodes the pattern and applies a corrective operation. The system is constantly measuring, decoding, and correcting. The logical qubit is coherent not because any individual physical qubit is protected, but because the correction machinery keeps up with the error rate. This places stringent requirements on every component. Physical error rates must be below the threshold (typically around 1% per operation). Measurements must be fast relative to coherence time. Classical decoding must match the quantum error rate in real time. When Marcus designed cryogenic control systems, the phrase he heard most from quantum hardware customers was "threshold," almost always in the context of how close they were to it.

A topological qubit architecture reverses the engineering logic. Quantum information is not stored in the state of a single physical two-level system, which requires active protection. It is a non-local property of a many-body quantum state, specifically, the non-local correlations of a topological phase. The canonical example, covered in Chapters 8 and 9, is a Majorana fermion pair created at the ends of a topological superconducting wire. The qubit information is stored in the total fermion parity of the pair, delocalized along the wire. No local perturbation at either end can access the quantum information, since it is not localized there. It is in the non-local correlation between them.

Diagram 1.4 - Error Correction versus Topological Protection: Architecture Comparison

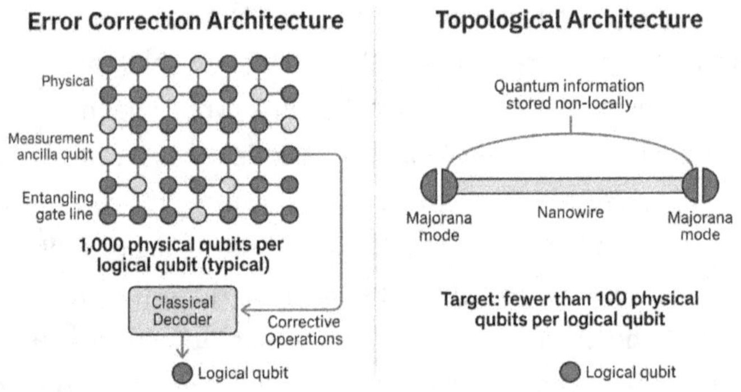

The error mechanisms that dominate conventional qubit architectures, local electromagnetic noise, thermal photons, surface charge fluctuations, and substrate phonons, do not couple to the topological logical qubit state because that state is non-local. They couple to the local physical system, but the local physical system does not contain the quantum information. The information is in the topology. This does not mean topological qubits are immune to all errors: quasiparticle poisoning and symmetry-breaking perturbations remain real concerns. But the error budget is dramatically different, and the required overhead for fault tolerance is dramatically lower. The reduction in physical qubit count propagates through the entire engineering stack: fewer control lines, lower cryogenic thermal load, a smaller refrigerator footprint, simpler classical electronics. The topological architecture does not merely promise better qubits. It promises a qualitatively simpler system architecture.

The Microsoft StationQ Bet: An Engineering Case Study

No discussion of the engineering case for topological qubits is complete without examining the defining industrial commitment in the field: Microsoft's two-decade investment in topological quantum computing, organized since 2006 under the StationQ program. For the engineering reader, the StationQ story is not primarily about physics. It is a story about how a major technology company made a long-duration, high-risk architectural bet on an approach not yet experimentally verified, maintained that bet through twenty years of incremental progress and periodic public skepticism, and arrived at a stage where the underlying physics is confirmed, and the engineering is the remaining challenge.

Microsoft's decision to pursue topological qubits was made in the early 2000s, motivated primarily by a 2001 paper by Alexei Kitaev, which showed that a one-dimensional superconducting chain would support localized zero-energy modes at its ends with the mathematical character of Majorana fermions, particles that are their own antiparticles. These modes would store quantum information non-locally in a way inherently protected from local decoherence. Kitaev subsequently joined Microsoft Research, and StationQ was built around the goal of physically realizing this proposal. The path from Kitaev's model to a physical system took nearly a decade. A 2010 theoretical breakthrough by Roman Lutchyn and Jay Alicea showed that a semiconductor nanowire with strong spin-orbit coupling, placed in proximity to a conventional superconductor and subjected to a magnetic field, would enter a topological superconducting phase with Majorana modes at its ends. The required materials, indium arsenide nanowires and aluminum superconductors, were already well-characterized. The prediction was specific, the materials were available, and the experiments were designable.

Diagram 1.5 - The StationQ Timeline: From Theory to Engineering

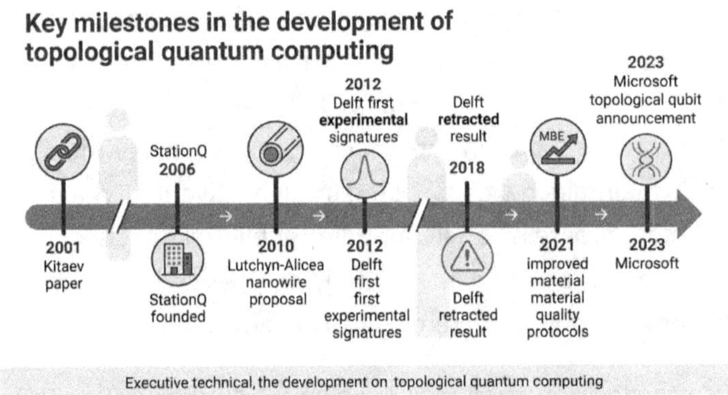

The first experimental signatures of Majorana modes in InAs/Al nanowire devices were reported by a group at Delft University in 2012. The subsequent decade was intense and not smooth: a landmark 2018 paper from the Delft group reporting signatures consistent with Majorana physics was later retracted following careful reanalysis of the data. This episode is worth understanding not as a failure of topological physics, but as an illustration of how difficult it is to unambiguously distinguish Majorana signatures from other phenomena that produce similar-looking experimental signals. Microsoft's 2023 topological qubit announcement, built on an InAs/Al platform with refined materials growth and measurement protocols, represented the most significant milestone yet. The announcement claimed demonstration of a topological gap, Majorana modes at the wire ends, and the ability to perform qubit operations. Independent verification is ongoing. But the physics underpinning the result is well understood, and the remaining challenges are engineering challenges of a kind that the semiconductor and superconductor communities know how to attack.

For Marcus, and for the engineering reader of this book, the StationQ story teaches something more valuable than a specific experimental result. The architectural bet on topological protection was made because, if realizable, the physics of topological protection would change the engineering mathematics of fault-tolerant quantum computing in a way that no amount of incremental improvement on conventional architectures can replicate. The overhead difference is not a factor of two or five. It is potentially a factor of 100 or more. That factor changes the economics, the system architecture, and the path to commercially relevant computation. That is the reason for the bet. Understanding why the bet makes sense is the first step toward evaluating it honestly.

The Materials Zoo: A First Look at What This Book Covers

Priya's whiteboard contained a taxonomy of material classes, each linked to a distinct set of applications and a corresponding chapter in the physics curriculum Marcus was about to begin. This section provides the first look at that taxonomy: not to explain any of it in depth, but to give you the map of the terrain the book covers and to explain why each class earns a chapter.

The first and most extensively studied class is that of topological insulators. A topological insulator is electrically insulating in its bulk because there is a full energy gap between occupied and empty electronic states. Still, it supports conducting states on its surface that are topologically protected. Those surface states have a helical character: the electron spin is locked to their motion and is protected by time-reversal symmetry. Spin-momentum locking means the surface electrons cannot be backscattered because backscattering would require simultaneously reversing both momentum and spin, which spin-orbit coupling prohibits. The first well-characterized topological insulators were bismuth selenide (Bi2Se3) and bismuth telluride (Bi2Te3). These are real materials, grown by molecular beam epitaxy or chemical vapor deposition, with measurable topological surface states that have been directly imaged using angle-resolved photoemission spectroscopy, abbreviated ARPES. Chapter 6 covers topological insulators in full.

The second class is the topological superconductor. A topological superconductor is a superconductor with a non-trivial topological invariant in its electronic structure, supporting boundary states that are not ordinary conducting electrons but Majorana modes: zero-energy states whose quantum character makes them potentially ideal as qubit building blocks. The most studied candidate system is the InAs/Al hybrid nanowire: a semiconductor nanowire with strong spin-orbit coupling, coated with a thin aluminum shell that becomes superconducting at low temperature, placed in an external magnetic field. The topological superconducting phase appears above a critical field value, and Majorana modes emerge at the wire ends within that phase. Topological superconductors are the heart of Chapters 7 and 8.

Diagram 1.6 - Materials Zoo: The Four Topological Classes

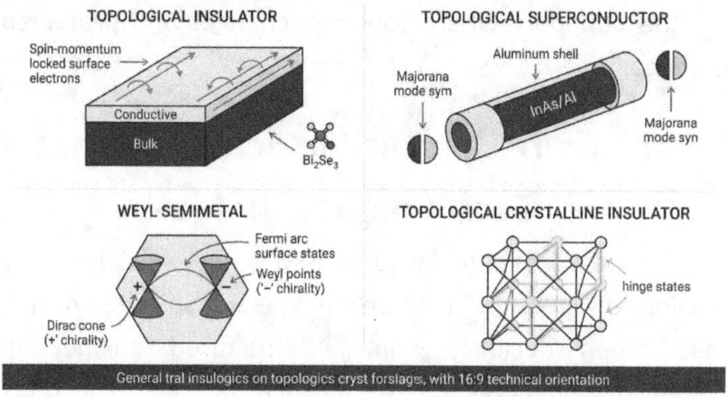

The third class is the Weyl semimetal. Where a topological insulator has a bulk energy gap that closes at the surface, a Weyl semimetal has a bulk spectrum that crosses zero at isolated Weyl points in momentum space. At each Weyl point, the dispersion forms a cone whose chirality acts like a topological charge, always appearing in pairs of opposite sign. Weyl semimetals support Fermi-arc surface states connecting opposite-chirality Weyl points and exhibit exotic transport, including very high carrier mobilities and negative longitudinal magnetoresistance, as signatures of the chiral anomaly. The first confirmed Weyl semimetal was tantalum arsenide, TaAs, in 2015. Chapter 7 covers Weyl semimetals and the fourth major class, topological crystalline insulators and higher-order topological phases, which support boundary states on crystal hinges or corners.

Across all these classes, a unifying theme emerges: topological properties are bulk properties, but they manifest at boundaries because, at any interface where the topological invariant changes, there must be states that span the gap. This bulk-boundary correspondence is one of the most important ideas in the field. The engineering implication is that, in a topological architecture, the device is often the interface between material classes, the boundary where topology changes and protected states appear.

The Thirteen-Chapter Curriculum: What Each Chapter Builds

Priya's whiteboard eventually turned to a second diagram: a progression of chapters that Axiom's leadership team had sketched when deciding what a structured engineering curriculum in topological materials would look like. The book you are holding is the public version of that curriculum. Each chapter is a prerequisite for the next, and the sequence is designed so that every abstract concept appears only after the engineering motivation for understanding it has been established.

This first chapter provides the framing. Chapter 2, "The Physics That Changed Everything," covers the sequence of discoveries from Klaus von Klitzing's 1980 quantum Hall experiment, through the 1986 high-temperature superconductor discovery by Georg Bednorz and K. Alex Muller, through Charles Kane and Eugene Mele's 2005 theoretical prediction of the quantum spin Hall insulator, through the 2016 Nobel Prize awarded to David Thouless, F. Duncan Haldane, and J. Michael Kosterlitz for their work on topological phases. The history chapter is a map of the engineering risks and opportunities the field has already navigated, presented as case studies that illustrate how topological physics moves from theoretical prediction to experimental verification to device relevance. Chapters 3 and 4 build the physics foundation: quantum mechanics for engineers, wavefunctions, Bloch theorem, band theory, band gaps, and band inversion, the key mechanism behind topological insulators. These chapters will feel familiar to readers with a solid-state physics background, but are structured to establish specifically the concepts required for topological physics, particularly the Berry phase and the topological invariant.

Diagram 1.7 - The Thirteen-Chapter Learning Ladder

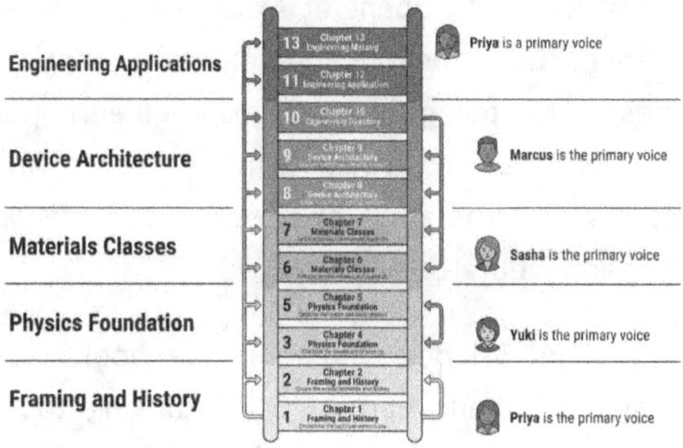

Possible caption

Chapter 5, "The Mathematics of Topology," introduces the Berry phase, Berry curvature, and Chern numbers through physical intuition rather than mathematical formalism. Sasha Korolev is the primary voice here. Chapters 6 and 7 cover the materials classes in engineering detail. Chapter 8 covers the InAs/Al nanowire topological superconductor platform: how the topological phase is induced, which experimental signatures confirm it, and what material-quality requirements enable Majorana modes to be well localized. Chapter 9 covers the qubit architecture: how Majorana modes store and process quantum information through braiding, what non-Abelian anyon statistics mean for gate operations, and the roadmap from current experimental capabilities to a fault-tolerant topological qubit. Chapter 10 is Yuki Tanaka's primary chapter on quantum sensing: how topological surface states can be exploited for sensing applications exceeding conventional device precision. Chapters 11 through 13 cover topological electronics, materials characterization, and the engineering outlook, closing the curriculum with tools for reading the research literature and assessing the decade ahead.

The Four Voices at Axiom Quantum

Every chapter of this book opens at Axiom Quantum, and the scenes there are anchored by four characters who represent the four disciplines that topological materials engineering actually requires. They are not illustrative simplifications. They are composite portraits of the kinds of people doing this work at real companies and laboratories.

Priya Nair, 48, Chief Science Officer, is the book's scientific anchor. She spent fifteen years at MIT studying topological insulators and Weyl semimetals before joining Axiom to translate research into manufacturable hardware. She is the person who knows exactly what physics requires and exactly where engineering compromises will break topological protection. Her voice is rigorous and never hand-waving, and her willingness to say "the physics does not allow that" keeps Axiom's engineering decisions grounded in reality. Marcus Webb, 36, Head of Hardware Engineering, is the reader's primary avatar. He came to Axiom from cryogenic control systems at a semiconductor equipment company, where he was genuinely expert in device physics, dilution refrigerators, microwave engineering, and fabrication process management. What he does not know is topological physics, and the book is organized around his process of learning it. His moments of recognition, when a topological concept snaps into place against something he already knows deeply, are the book's most powerful teaching moments. Marcus is not a dilettante approaching quantum hardware from outside. He is a serious engineer who knows everything about conventional superconducting device stacks and is encountering the things those stacks cannot do.

Sasha Korolev, 41, Head of Quantum Theory, is the book's most technically precise voice. A theoretical physicist specializing in topological phases, Berry phases, Chern numbers, and Majorana fermion physics, Marcus translates abstract mathematical structure into engineering constraints that Axiom can act on. When Sasha explains Berry curvature, he describes it as the thing that makes a specific class of measurements asymmetric, affecting how you design the measurement circuit. Yuki Tanaka, 32, Director of Quantum Sensing Applications, completed her doctorate on topological material magnetometers at Caltech and postdoctoral research at the National Institute of Standards and Technology before joining Axiom to build the sensing division. Her chapters argue that the path to commercial revenue from topological materials may run through quantum sensing rather than quantum computing, because sensors built from topological materials are closer to device readiness and address large, commercially mature markets.

Diagram 1.8 - The Axiom Quantum Cast

Character Card

What Can We Build With This?

The engineering case for topological materials is not abstract. It has hardware consequences that can be described in terms of components, system architectures, and device specifications. Three hardware targets frame the engineering opportunity that the rest of this book teaches you to evaluate.

The first and most discussed target is the topological qubit. The architecture that Microsoft and Axiom are pursuing involves Majorana modes created at the ends of topological superconducting nanowires. A minimal logical qubit requires two nanowires and four Majorana modes, with quantum information stored in the total fermion parity of the Majorana pair. Qubit operations are performed by braiding: physically exchanging Majorana modes along paths whose topology, rather than timing or amplitude, determines the gate outcome. This inherent protection from timing and amplitude errors is the source of the topological qubit's advantage. IBM's current surface code architecture requires approximately 1,000 physical qubits to realize a high-quality logical qubit. Theoretical estimates for a topological architecture achieving similar logical quality suggest tens rather than thousands of physical components. The cryogenic engineering challenge of a 10,000-component topological system is qualitatively different from housing 1,000,000 transmon qubits. It fits in a laboratory and its thermal load falls within the range of a conventional dilution refrigerator.

Diagram 1.9 - Topological Qubit Hardware Target

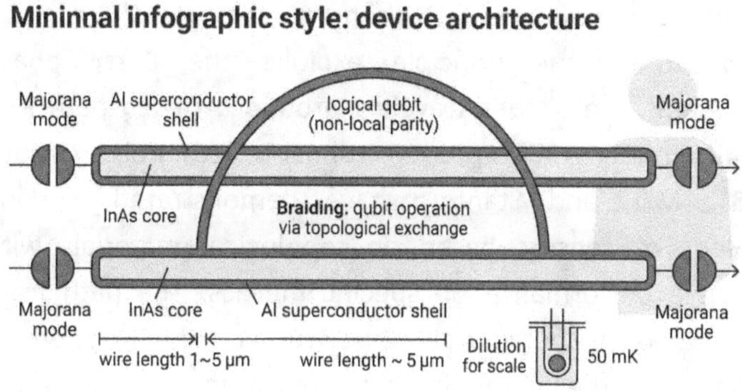

The second hardware target is the topologically protected interconnect. Moving quantum information between distant qubits requires quantum communication channels that preserve coherence over macroscopic distances, one of the most challenging unsolved engineering problems in quantum hardware. Topological surface states in certain material systems are immune to backscattering, meaning they propagate without the energy dissipation that would destroy quantum coherence in a conventional conductor. A quantum interconnect built from a topological insulator surface channel would transport quantum states with fidelity limited by thermal noise and quasiparticle poisoning rather than by scattering. This is a longer-horizon engineering target, but it represents a qualitatively different scaling strategy from the optical interconnects and transducers being developed for conventional qubit architectures.

The third hardware target is the quantum sensor built from topological materials. A magnetometer built from a topological insulator surface state can, in principle, detect magnetic fields near the quantum noise limit, because surface electrons travel without backscattering and without the Johnson-Nyquist noise that limits conventional resistive sensing elements. A gyroscope built on the same principle exploits the Berry phase accumulated by electrons traveling around a closed path in a topological material. This phase is robust to local noise. Groups at NIST, MIT, and Stanford have demonstrated working prototypes of sensors based on topological materials with competitive performance on specific metrics. The path from prototype to manufacturable device is the engineering challenge, and the materials characterization and fabrication chapters of this book directly address it. Marcus ran through the logic of each application as he walked home that evening. The numbers Priya had sketched were not promises. They were engineering targets derived from verified physics in existing materials. The gap between target and reality was the gap between a well-defined engineering challenge and its solution.

The Book's Engineering Promise: What You Will Be Able to Do

By the last page of this book, you will have a specific, practical capability that you did not have when you opened it. Not an impression of topological materials, or a general familiarity with the terminology. A capability.

You will be able to read a paper in a journal on topological materials and evaluate its central claim. When a paper reports evidence for Majorana modes in a nanowire device, you will know what experimental signature is being reported, what alternative explanations must be ruled out, and whether the stated controls are adequate. When a paper reports a new topological insulator candidate with high-mobility surface states, you will know what the ARPES data should look like, what the Hall effect measurement should show, and what the fabrication challenges are for turning that material into a device. You will not be a condensed matter PhD. But you will be someone who reads the primary literature without a translator, evaluates claims rather than relays them, and engages with a topological materials researcher as a peer engineer rather than an interested outsider.

You will be able to make hardware architecture decisions informed by knowledge of topological materials. If you are evaluating a quantum computing architecture, you will understand the engineering tradeoffs between surface code error correction on transmon qubits and topological protection on Majorana-based qubits, at a level of specificity that allows you to assess vendor claims and evaluate research roadmaps. If you are working on quantum sensing hardware, you will understand what topological insulator surface states offer compared with conventional metallic sensing elements, and where material-quality constraints lie.

Diagram 1.10 - Engineering Capability Map: Before and After This Book

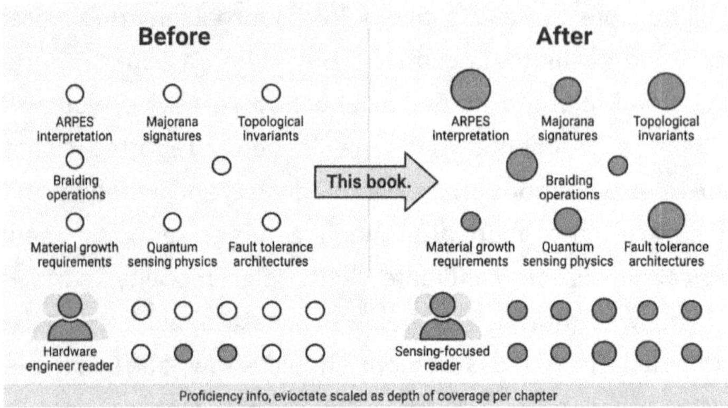

You will understand why topological protection is physically meaningful rather than metaphorical. The popular science accounts of topological materials repeat the rubber-band analogy and then treat the protection as a magic property, without explaining what it protects against, why local perturbations cannot destroy it, or what physical conditions must be maintained for the protection to hold. After Chapters 3 through 7, you will understand all of these things at a level that satisfies both the intuition and the engineering judgment. That knowledge is the difference between someone who has heard of topological protection and someone who can build with it.

Where the Field Stands in 2025

It would be intellectually dishonest to frame this curriculum without acknowledging the field's current state. Topological quantum computing has not been demonstrated at a scale or fidelity sufficient for general fault-tolerant computation. The topological qubit that Axiom and Microsoft are building is still in engineering development, and the experimental challenges are real, acknowledged by the researchers working on them, and not likely to be resolved quickly. A curriculum that glosses over these challenges in the service of enthusiasm would be doing the engineering reader a disservice.

What has been demonstrated and can be treated as established is extensive in scope. The topological surface states of bismuth selenide and dozens of other topological insulators have been directly imaged by ARPES and confirmed by transport measurements. The bulk topological invariant of these materials has been calculated using first-principles methods and experimentally confirmed. The topological superconducting phase in InAs/Al nanowires has been entered and characterized across multiple research groups. Signatures consistent with Majorana modes have been observed in these devices, though the standards for definitive proof continue to be refined as the field learns from its earlier over-interpretation of ambiguous data. Weyl semimetals have been confirmed across multiple material platforms, and their exotic transport signatures have been measured. The 2016 Nobel Prize in Physics was awarded for the theoretical framework that underlies all of these results.

The honest engineering assessment places the field at a stage Marcus would recognize from semiconductor experience as early device engineering. The physics is understood. The materials exist. The first devices are being characterized. The gap between first-device demonstrations and manufacturable, scalable, commercially viable systems is the engineering challenge of the next decade. The engineers who understand topological materials well enough to work on that challenge are in short supply. The demand for them is growing rapidly as quantum hardware programs scale up.

Diagram 1.11 - Technology Readiness: Topological Materials Applications

Technological Readiness Level Chart

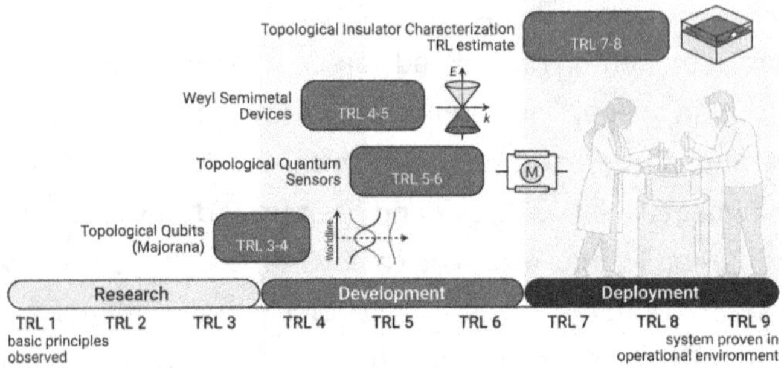

Takeaway

Topological materials are not a new class of superconductors or a variant of existing semiconductor platforms. They are materials whose most important engineering properties arise from the global geometry of their quantum state space, a geometry described by topology rather than local chemistry or atomic composition. That global geometric character gives certain quantum states in these materials a protection from local perturbations that any amount of material perfection or active error correction engineering cannot achieve. It is a protection that, in the precise language of topology, is robust to any deformation that does not close the energy gap and change the topological invariant.

The engineering case for building with these materials comes down to one architectural insight: the overhead required for fault-tolerant quantum computation is dominated by the cost of error correction for fragile physical qubits, and topological protection offers an alternative architecture in which dominant local error mechanisms are suppressed by the physics of the material rather than managed by classical control systems. A reduction in the physical-to-logical qubit ratio, if achieved with sufficient fidelity, would make fault-tolerant quantum computation feasible at system scales that are tractable using existing cryogenic and electronic technologies. That is not an incremental improvement on the conventional approach. It is an architectural discontinuity.

Marcus left Priya's office that evening with a list of topics he had never studied: Berry phase, Chern numbers, band inversion, Majorana fermions, spin-orbit coupling in semiconductor heterostructures, topological invariants, and non-Abelian braiding. The list was long. But Priya had shown him that every item on that list answered a specific engineering question he already cared about. Marcus was not intimidated by physics he had not yet learned. He was motivated by engineering problems he already understood. That is the orientation this book aims to give every reader: not the obligation to learn condensed matter theory, but the engineering motivation to understand exactly which parts of it matter for building the next generation of hardware.

Chapter 2 takes a step back before moving forward. Before building a physics curriculum, it is worth understanding where physics came from: the sequence of experiments, theoretical predictions, and Nobel Prize-winning discoveries that gave rise to the field of topological materials. The history is a map of how physics transitions from theoretical prediction to experimental confirmation to engineering relevance. That map is directly useful for a reader who wants to assess where topological quantum computing currently sits on that path. Begin there.

Diagram 1.12 - Bridge to Chapter 2: History as Engineering Map

Conceptual map diagram

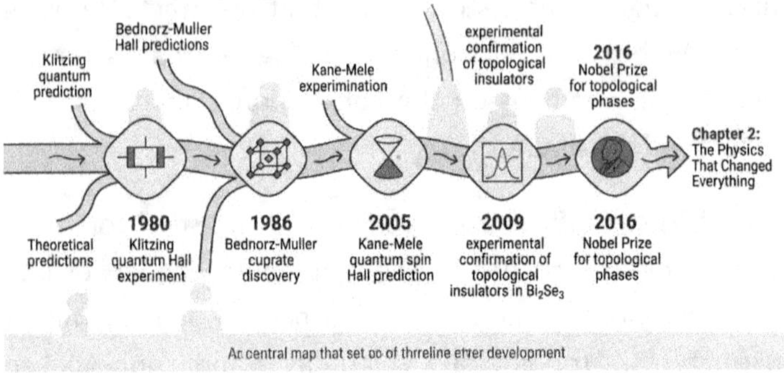

2 A Brief, Wild History of Topological Physics

The whiteboard in Axiom Quantum's theory room was already half-covered when Marcus arrived. Sasha Korolev had gotten there early, as he often did on mornings he decided something needed explaining from first principles. A horizontal line ran the length of the board with years written at intervals in handwriting that looked like a physician's: 1972, 1980, 1982, 1984, 1988, 2005, 2006, 2007, 2009, 2015, 2016, 2023. Below each year, a phrase. Some Marcus recognized. Mostly, he did not.

"Every material choice we make traces back to something on this line," Sasha said without turning around. "The reason we use bismuth selenide. The reason we believe Majorana modes are possible in our device stack. The reason the surface states won't scatter at a crystal defect." He turned. "If you understand how each moment happened, you'll understand why I'm confident about some things and aggressively uncertain about others. That calibration is the most useful thing I can give you before we go into the materials."

Marcus pulled a stool up to the board. He had come in expecting a materials briefing. He was getting a history lecture, and found, to his mild surprise, that he did not mind. "Start at the beginning," he said. Sasha uncapped his marker. "Nineteen seventy-two. Birmingham, England."

Why It Matters

Most engineering fields have histories that are interesting but not load-bearing. Knowing who invented the transistor does not change how you design a CMOS circuit. Topological physics is different. Its history is the fastest route to its logic, and its logic is what an engineer needs to evaluate claims about topological qubits, topological insulators, and topological protection. The field is fifty years old, and in that time, every major theoretical prediction has been experimentally confirmed. That record is not just a point of pride. It is a material fact about the risk profile of the underlying physics, and the engineer who knows that record can distinguish a claim standing on fifty years of theoretical and experimental foundation from one that is three experimental cycles away from a retraction.

This chapter is the map. By the end, you will know the key conceptual milestones, why each one mattered for hardware, and how to place any new topological materials claim against the established pattern. You will also know where the field has been wrong, where it has been overconfident, and where it is genuinely uncertain today. The field spans an unusual range: at one end, Kosterlitz and Thouless in 1972 were working on pure mathematics of phase transitions with no application in sight; at the other end, Microsoft in 2023 was announcing device measurements from a specific heterostructure grown by molecular beam epitaxy in a specific laboratory. The line between those points is not straight. It bends through a dozen moments when a theoretical idea found an unexpected physical home, when an experiment confirmed something that had seemed untestable, or when the community had to revise a claim it had confidently made. An engineer reading that line carefully comes away knowing how to read the field.

Kosterlitz-Thouless: First Topological Transition

In 1972, John Kosterlitz and David Thouless published a paper about a two-dimensional superfluid and what happens when you raise its temperature. The conventional wisdom, based on the Mermin-Wagner theorem, held that two-dimensional systems cannot undergo a phase transition to an ordered state at nonzero temperature. Yet two-dimensional superconductors have been experimentally observed and clearly exhibit a transition. Kosterlitz and Thouless found the resolution. The relevant objects were not atoms but topological defects called vortices: points around which the phase of the superfluid wavefunction winds by 360 degrees. At low temperatures, vortices appear in tightly bound pairs, causing only local disturbances. Raise the temperature past a critical value and the pairs unbind, free vortices proliferate, and the superfluid phase is destroyed. The transition leaves no signature in any conventional order parameter. The only thing that changes at the critical temperature is the topological configuration of the defects.

This was the first time topology appeared as a controlling principle in condensed matter physics, and what made it radical was its invisibility to standard tools. Order parameters detect conventional phase transitions. The Kosterlitz-Thouless transition has no order parameter. What changes is a topological property, and topology does not come in continuous values. It is either one thing or another, and the transition is a sharp topological event rather than a smooth crossover. This established the conceptual template that all subsequent topological physics would use: properties of a physical system are controlled by topology rather than symmetry, and are robust because topology is discrete while perturbations are continuous. Every topological phase discovered since fits this template.

Diagram 2.1 - Kosterlitz-Thouless Vortex Unbinding

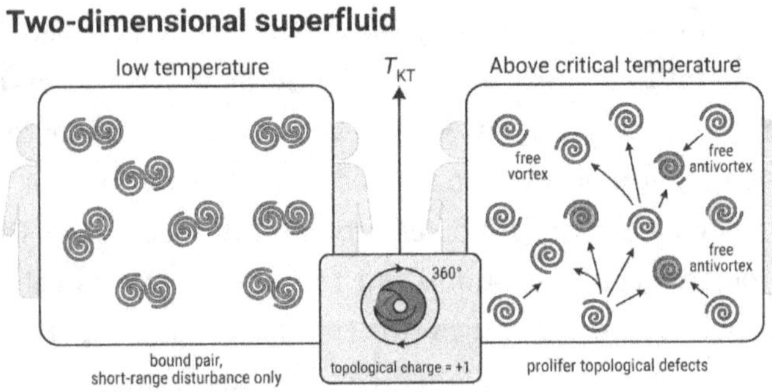

A Two-dimensional superfluid insiootced ito critical temperature

For the working engineer, the lesson is more specific than topology matters. A topological integer cannot change continuously. A vortex has a charge of plus one or minus one; there is no charge of plus 0.7. Small disturbances cannot change the topological state unless they cause a topological event, the creation or annihilation of a vortex. This same discreteness protects edge states in topological insulators, Majorana modes in topological superconductors, and quantized conductance in the quantum Hall effect. The physics differs across each case, but the protection mechanism is always the same: an integer cannot be perturbed into a non-integer.

The Integer Quantum Hall Effect: Klaus von Klitzing, 1980

In February 1980, Klaus von Klitzing was measuring the Hall conductance of a silicon MOSFET at the High Magnetic Field

Laboratory in Grenoble. He found that the Hall conductance did not vary smoothly as classical physics predicted. Instead, it took precise plateau values, staying exactly constant over ranges of field, with the plateau values exact integer multiples of e^2/h, the electron charge squared divided by Planck's constant, to a precision of one part in ten million. This precision was impossible to explain by conventional solid-state physics. Real materials have impurities and thermal fluctuations. Something was protecting the measurement from the material's disorder.

The explanation came in the 1982 TKNN paper by Thouless, Kohmoto, Nightingale, and den Nijs: the first proof that a macroscopic measurable property of a real material is a topological invariant. The invariant is the Chern number, an integer characterizing the topology of electron wavefunctions across the entire Brillouin zone. The integer quantum Hall plateaus correspond to the Chern number, which is why they are quantized and robust: the Chern number cannot change unless the system undergoes a topological phase transition that closes the band gap. The practical consequence is the edge state: a theorem called the bulk-boundary correspondence guarantees that a nonzero Chern number in the bulk forces conducting edge states that cannot be removed without changing the bulk topology. These edge states conduct in one direction only along each edge, with no backscattering. This is the first instance of topological protection in a real material, predating the topological insulator by twenty-five years.

Diagram 2.2 - Integer Quantum Hall Effect: Hall Bar and Conductance Plateaus

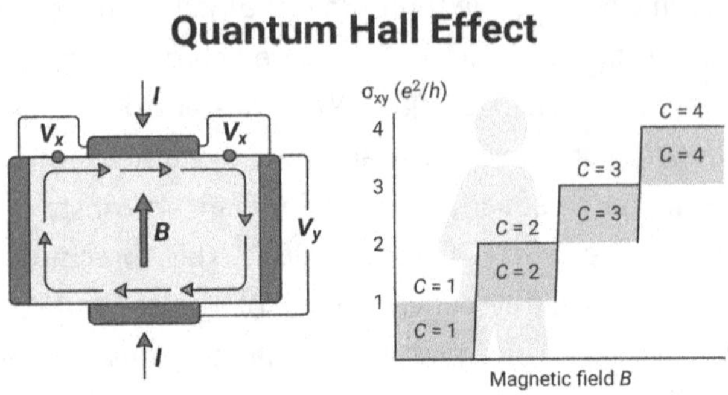

Quantum Hall Effect. Infographics 16:9 hocotic technical palette

Von Klitzing received the 1985 Nobel Prize in Physics, and the quantum Hall resistance now defines the ohm in the International System of Units. For the engineer, this demonstrates that topological quantization can be measurement-grade precise in a real, imperfect material, which is exactly the quality you want in a qubit. The question the rest of the field spent thirty years answering is: Can you get that topological robustness without the enormous magnetic fields the quantum Hall effect requires?

Berry Phase: The Geometric Heart of Topological Physics

In 1984, Michael Berry at the University of Bristol showed that when the external parameters of a quantum system trace a closed loop, the wavefunction acquires an additional phase beyond the trivial time-dependent phase. This Berry phase depends only on the geometry of the path through parameter space, not on the speed of traversal. It is purely geometric: the same loop always gives the same Berry phase because it measures something about the shape of the quantum state space itself. When a quantum particle moves in a closed loop in momentum space, its wavefunction evolves as it moves. If the quantum state space has a twist in the region traversed, the wavefunction will not return to exactly its original orientation even though the particle is back at its starting point. The mismatch expressed as a phase angle is the Berry phase. The quantity that measures how twisted the state space is at each point is the Berry curvature, and integrating it over a closed surface yields an integer: the Chern number.

The connection to the quantum Hall effect is direct: the Chern number, identified in 1982 as the topological invariant underlying the Hall conductance, is exactly the Berry phase integrated over the entire Brillouin zone, divided by 2 pi. Berry was working abstractly on the geometry of quantum state space; Thouless and colleagues were explaining a specific experiment. The Berry phase is the unifying language: quantum systems in periodic structures can have wavefunctions with nontrivial topological geometry, and that geometry controls macroscopic physical properties. This unification is not decorative. The Berry phase is the load-bearing concept behind every topological protection claim in this book. When a topological surface state is said to be protected against backscattering by time-reversal symmetry, the mechanism is a Berry phase argument: an electron scattering backward accumulates a phase of pi relative to a forward-going electron, and those two paths interfere destructively.

Diagram 2.3 - Berry Phase: Geometric Phase on a Closed Loop

Berry phase-Brillouin zorminal

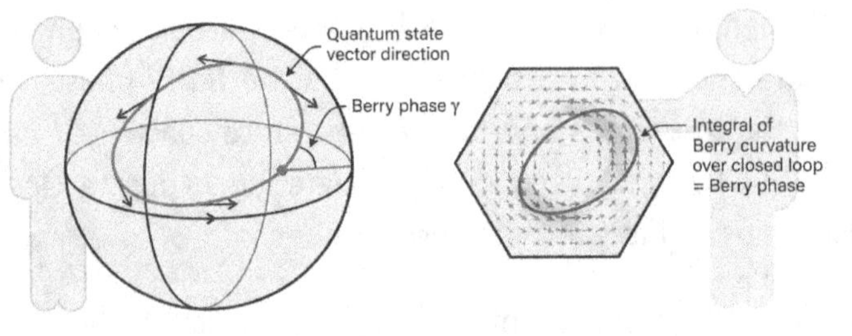

Infographic space or close the Brillouin zone presentation and lexcutive technical.

The Berry phase was experimentally verified in the years following Berry's paper through interference experiments in quantum systems ranging from spin-1/2 particles to molecular systems to solid-state devices. It is now measured routinely in topological materials to determine whether a material has a Dirac or Weyl band structure, because a Dirac electron traveling around the Dirac cone in momentum space accumulates a Berry phase of exactly pi, which can be detected as a shift in quantum oscillation patterns. This measurability is what makes the Berry phase not just a theoretical concept but also a practical tool for determining whether a material is topological.

Haldane's Model, 1988: Topology Without a Magnetic Field

Duncan Haldane's 1988 contribution is the most consequential theoretical result in the history of topological physics, because it opened the door that everything that came after walked through. The TKNN paper explained why the quantum Hall effect was topological. Haldane showed that you could have a topological phase without the quantum Hall effect's most demanding ingredient: the enormous external magnetic field. What Haldane showed was that the magnetic field in the quantum Hall effect plays two distinct roles, and only one is essential for the topology. The first role is breaking time-reversal symmetry. The second role is to create Landau levels, the specific quantum structure used in the TKNN analysis. He proved that topological phases with broken time-reversal symmetry can exist in the absence of a net magnetic flux by constructing an explicit model of a two-dimensional honeycomb lattice with complex next-nearest-neighbor hopping terms. The complex hopping breaks time-reversal symmetry in the absence of an external field, and the resulting band structure has the same Chern number as in the quantum Hall effect, with the same protected edge states.

The Haldane model remained a theoretical construction for seventeen years. A solid-state realization was achieved in 2013 with chromium-doped magnetic topological insulators, producing the quantum anomalous Hall effect: Haldane's model in a real material without an external magnetic field. But the theoretical importance of the model was felt long before its experimental realization, because it changed the conceptual question the field was asking. Before 1988: Where else can you find the quantum Hall effect? After 1988: what other topological phases exist, and what physical mechanisms generate them? That shift produced the topological insulator, the topological superconductor, and the Weyl semimetal. Haldane shared the 2016 Nobel Prize for exactly this reason: his model was the key that unlocked the rest of the field.

Diagram 2.4 - Haldane Model: Honeycomb Lattice with Complex Hopping

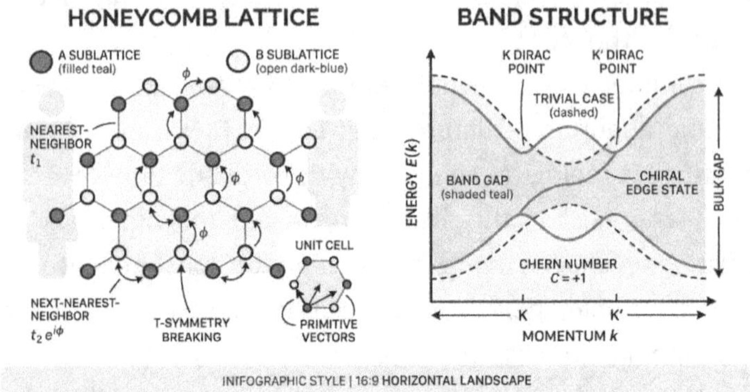

For the engineer, the Haldane result carries a direct hardware message: topological protection does not require a permanent fifteen-tesla magnetic field as an operating condition. The relevant quantity is not the field strength but whether time-reversal symmetry is broken, and time-reversal symmetry can be broken by magnetic ordering, spin-orbit coupling, or the engineered complex hopping of Haldane's model. This opens the door to topological phases in materials that can be operated in a laboratory cryostat rather than a dedicated magnet facility, and ultimately to topological phases accessible at temperatures and field conditions compatible with device integration.

Kane-Mele 2005 and the Z2 Topological Insulator

By 2005, the topological condensed matter framework was largely limited to systems with broken time-reversal symmetry. Charles Kane and Eugene Mele at the University of Pennsylvania asked whether a system with unbroken time-reversal symmetry could have a nontrivial topological phase. The naive answer is no: the Chern number is necessarily zero in such a system because time-reversal forces the Berry curvature at momentum k to cancel the Berry curvature at momentum minus k. Kane and Mele found a different story by studying spin-orbit coupling in graphene. Spin-orbit coupling opens a gap at graphene's Dirac points. What is remarkable is that the resulting gapped phase is topologically nontrivial in a way that does not require breaking time-reversal symmetry. The relevant invariant is not the Chern number but the Z2 invariant, which takes only two values: 0 for a trivial insulator and 1 for a topological insulator, namely the quantum spin Hall insulator. The Z2 invariant counts whether edge states come in pairs that cancel (trivial) or in an odd number of Kramers pairs protected by time-reversal symmetry (nontrivial).

The quantum spin Hall edge states are helical: counter-propagating pairs on each edge, one spin-up electron moving right and one spin-down electron moving left. Time-reversal symmetry protects them from backscattering by any time-reversal-symmetric perturbation, because backscattering would require the electron to reverse both its momentum and its spin simultaneously. No ordinary scatterer can do that. These edge states are therefore protected against all common sources of disorder: lattice defects, impurities, surface roughness, anything that preserves time-reversal symmetry. This protection against disorder is the property that drives interest in devices based on quantum spin Hall systems.

Diagram 2.5 - Kane-Mele Model: Z2 Topological Insulator and Helical Edge States

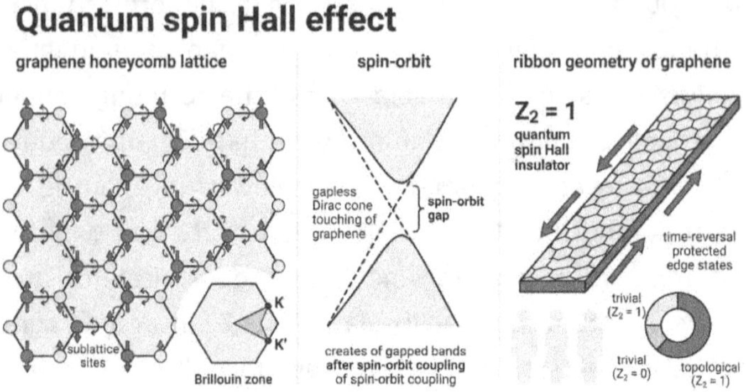

Kane and Mele's paper was published in 2005, and the field responded quickly. Within months, Bernevig, Hughes, and Zhang at Stanford translated the theoretical prediction into a specific materials prescription: mercury telluride and cadmium telluride quantum wells should exhibit the quantum spin Hall effect. The timeline from theoretical prediction to experimental confirmation was two years, a cycle that reflects how precisely the theory targets real materials.

Bernevig-Hughes-Zhang 2006 and the HgTe Confirmation

In 2006, Bernevig, Hughes, and Zhang published a specific quantitative prediction: a mercury telluride (HgTe) quantum well sandwiched between cadmium telluride (CdTe) barriers would exhibit the quantum spin Hall effect when the HgTe layer exceeded a critical thickness of approximately 6.3 nanometers. The prediction rested on band inversion, the central concept linking materials design to the topological phase. In a conventional semiconductor, the conduction band derives from s-orbitals and the valence band from p-orbitals. In HgTe, the relativistic effects of the heavy mercury nucleus invert this ordering: the p-orbital-derived band ends up above the s-orbital-derived band. This inversion changes the topology of the wavefunction. The topological invariant can distinguish between normal-order and inverted systems, even though both appear insulating in the bulk. In the quantum well geometry, increasing the HgTe layer thickness tunes the system continuously from normal ordering (CdTe-like, thin well, Z2 = 0) to inverted ordering (HgTe-like, thick well, Z2 = 1), with a topological phase transition at the critical thickness where the gap closes and reopens with new topology.

Diagram 2.6 - Band Inversion in HgTe/CdTe Quantum Wells

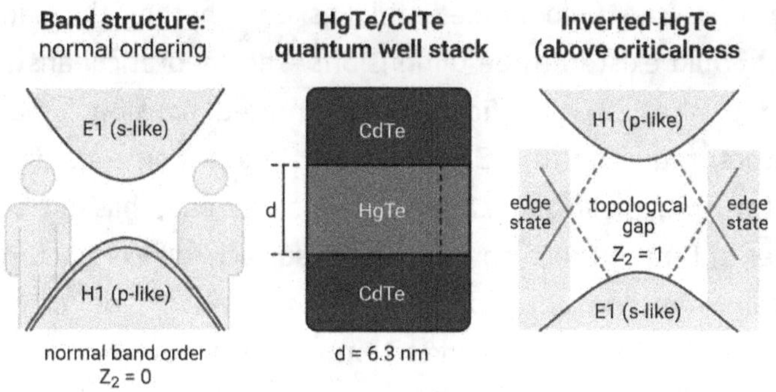

The experimental confirmation came from Laurens Molenkamp's group at the University of Wurzburg, published in Science in 2007. Their experiment measured resistance as a function of well thickness and found exactly what theory predicted: wells thinner than 6.3 nanometers behaved as conventional insulators. Wells thicker than 6.3 nanometers exhibited a resistance plateau at approximately 12,900 ohms, the value expected for two helical edge-state channels conducting in parallel, regardless of sample size or the level of bulk disorder. Three years from Kane-Mele to König: the field was advancing quickly because the theory was providing precise targets to aim at. For the engineer, the HgTe story demonstrates that the topological phase transition happened at a specific layer thickness controlled by molecular beam epitaxy, a fabrication parameter the semiconductor community already knew how to control. What was new was not the fabrication technique but the understanding of what to fabricate, which is exactly the value that topological theory provides.

3D Topological Insulators: Bi2Se3 and Bi2Te3

The quantum spin Hall effect in HgTe was confined to two dimensions. The field immediately asked whether the same physics could exist in three dimensions. The theoretical answer extended the Z2 classification to three-dimensional band insulators, requiring four Z2 invariants. The strong topological insulator, with a strong Z2 index equal to one, has an odd number of Dirac surface cones on each surface, which any time-reversal-symmetric perturbation cannot remove: you cannot continuously deform an odd number into zero. The first confirmed three-dimensional topological insulator was bismuth antimony (Bi1-xSbx). Theorists predicted in 2007 that the right composition should yield a strong topological insulator, and Hasan's group at Princeton confirmed this in 2008 using angle-resolved photoemission spectroscopy (ARPES). ARPES works by shining intense ultraviolet light on the material's surface, ejecting photoelectrons from the surface states. Measuring the energy and momentum of those electrons maps out the surface state band structure. In bismuth antimony, it revealed the fivefold Dirac surface cone structure predicted by theory—from prediction to confirmation: one year.

Diagram 2.7 - ARPES Measurement of Topological Surface States

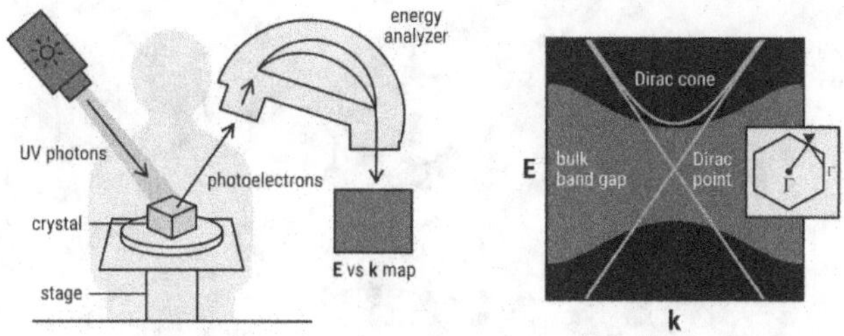

That material was bismuth selenide (Bi2Se3). Zhang et al. predicted its topological properties in 2009, and experimental confirmation by groups at Princeton, Stanford, and Beijing followed almost immediately. Bismuth selenide has a band gap of approximately 0.3 electronvolts, large enough for room-temperature operation, a single Dirac cone at the Gamma point, and a layered crystal structure that cleaves easily. Its cousin, bismuth telluride (Bi2Te3), shares similar properties and has long been known as an excellent thermoelectric material. The ARPES images of the single Dirac cone in Bi2Se3's band gap became the iconic image of the topological insulator era. For the engineer, the significance extends beyond validation: these are materials already used in thermoelectric production, known quantities in crystal growth, phase purity, and processing. The topological surface states are a new property of a material platform that engineers already knew how to handle.

Diagram 2.8 - Dirac Cone Surface State on Bismuth Selenide

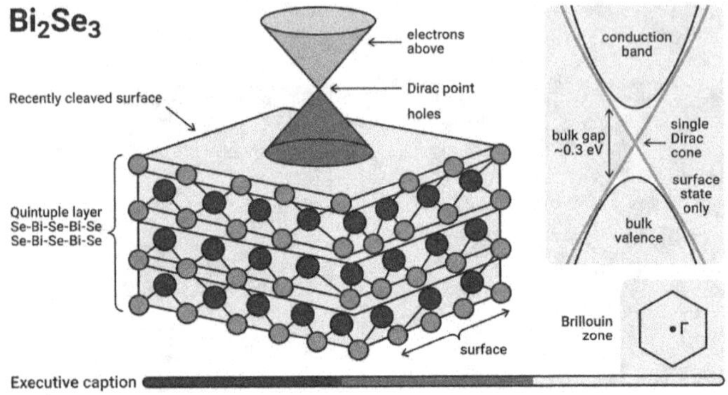

Weyl Semimetals, 2015: Topology Without a Gap

In 2015, two independent experimental groups confirmed the existence of a Weyl semimetal, a new class of topological material in which the topological physics is associated with specific points in the Brillouin zone where two bands touch, not with a gap. The theoretical foundation reaches back to 1929, when Hermann Weyl showed that the Dirac equation for relativistic electrons could be split into two equations describing massless particles of definite handedness, now called Weyl fermions. These particles were predicted to be elementary but have never been observed in particle physics. In 2015, they appeared as quasiparticles in crystals of tantalum arsenide (TaAs) and related compounds, marking the first time a long-predicted particle was discovered in a solid-state material rather than in a particle accelerator. A Weyl semimetal has pairs of band-touching points called Weyl nodes, each with a topological charge of ±1, which is the Berry phase flux through a surface enclosing the node. These charges cannot be destroyed by any small perturbation, only by bringing a plus-one and a minus-one node together to annihilate. The surface of a Weyl semimetal carries Fermi arcs: open-curve surface states terminating at the projections of Weyl nodes with opposite charges, a topological feature with no analog in any other material class.

Diagram 2.9 - Weyl Semimetal: Bulk Weyl Nodes and Surface Fermi Arcs

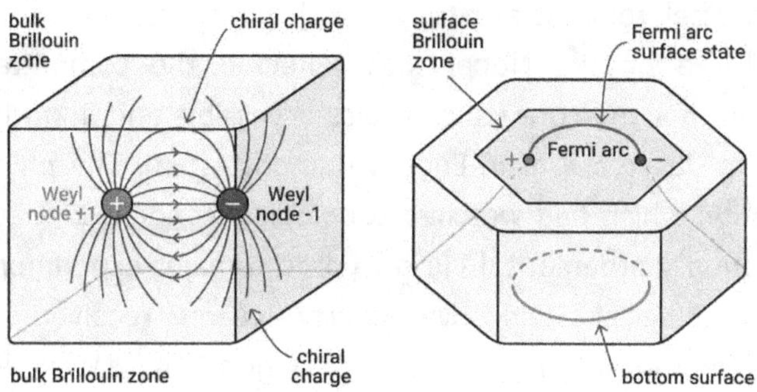

The discovery of Weyl semimetals demonstrated that topological physics extended beyond insulators to metals and semimetals. Weyl semimetals also exhibit the chiral anomaly: parallel electric and magnetic fields generate a current of opposite chirality that violates the naive conservation law for individual Weyl fermion species, yielding a characteristic negative magnetoresistance signature now used to identify the material class. For the engineer, Weyl semimetals are relevant primarily as a demonstration that the same Berry phase and Chern number concepts that explain the quantum Hall effect also explain transport in this qualitatively different class of semimetals. Applications, including ultralow-dissipation transistors and high-frequency electronic devices that exploit Fermi-arc scattering, are still in the research stage, not the engineering stage.

The 2016 Nobel Prize: A Field-Defining Validation

On October 4, 2016, the Royal Swedish Academy of Sciences awarded the Nobel Prize in Physics to David Thouless, Duncan Haldane, and John Michael Kosterlitz for their theoretical discoveries of topological phase transitions and topological phases of matter. The announcement used a bagel, a doughnut, and a pretzel to illustrate topological invariants, an unusual choice for a physics Nobel that reflected the committee's conviction that the core concept was accessible and important enough to deserve a plain-English demonstration. The physics community, which had watched topological condensed matter grow from a mathematical curiosity into a major experimental and technological field over thirty years, received the announcement with measured satisfaction. The Nobel was awarded for work done in 1972 and 1988. The field had not waited for the prize.

For the hardware engineer, the 2016 Nobel carries a specific message beyond the usual significance of validating scientific quality. The prize was awarded for theoretical work: the discovery and classification of topological phases as a conceptual framework. The experimental confirmations followed the theoretical foundation laid. What the prize says is: the theoretical framework is not speculative. It is a mature, rigorous theory validated by experiment in every instance where it made a testable prediction. The engineering challenges in topological devices include implementation, materials quality, interface control, fabrication precision, and operating temperature. They are not physics challenges. The physics is settled. As of 2016, every major theoretical prediction of topological condensed matter physics made in a testable form had been confirmed: Kosterlitz-Thouless in superfluid helium films, quantum Hall effect to ten significant figures, Haldane model in optical lattice cold atoms, Z2 topological insulator in HgTe, three-dimensional topological insulators in Bi1-xSbx and Bi2Se3, Weyl semimetals in TaAs. The theory had a perfect predictive record, which is not the norm in materials physics.

Diagram 2.10 - Timeline: Key Milestones in Topological Physics 1972-2023

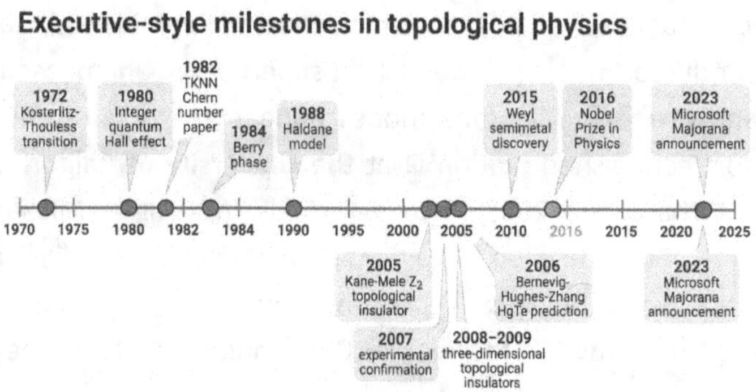

Microsoft's Majorana Program: The Current Hardware Frontier

The current most ambitious application of topological physics in hardware is Microsoft's topological qubit program. The theoretical foundation was established by Alexei Kitaev in 2001. Kitaev showed that a one-dimensional p-wave superconductor would host Majorana fermions at its ends. A Majorana fermion is a quantum particle that is its own antiparticle: it carries no charge and no spin, and two Majorana fermions can encode a qubit whose state is shared nonlocally across the pair. The non-locality is the source of topological protection: no local perturbation can measure or disturb a quantity distributed between two spatially separated Majorana modes, making the qubit immune to local noise at a fundamental level. This is the topological qubit proposal: protection is built into the material's physics rather than into an active error-correcting code.

A real p-wave superconductor does not exist in nature. What does exist, as Lutchyn, Sau, and Das Sarma showed in 2010, is a recipe for engineering a synthetic topological superconductor: a semiconductor nanowire with strong spin-orbit coupling, a conventional s-wave superconductor on the wire, and an applied magnetic field. When properly combined, the superconductor induces a topological superconducting phase in the nanowire, and Majorana modes appear at the wire ends. Microsoft established Station Q at the University of California, Santa Barbara, in 2005, led by Fields Medallist Michael Freedman, to develop the mathematical and physical foundations of topological quantum computing. The program expanded to hardware facilities in Copenhagen, Delft, Sydney, and Redmond.

Diagram 2.11 - Topological Qubit Architecture: Majorana Nanowire

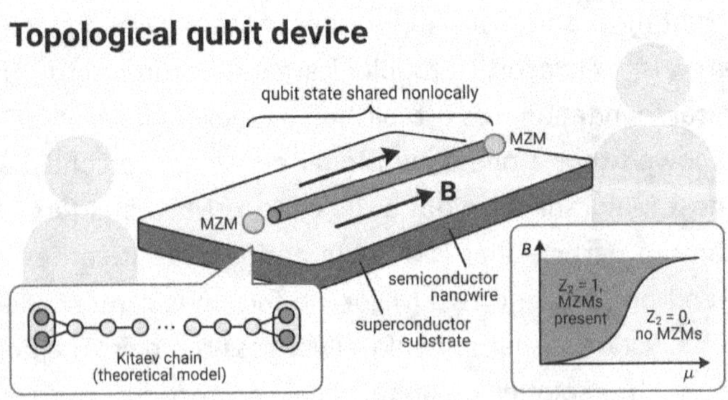

In 2021, Nature published a paper from a Microsoft-affiliated collaboration reporting Majorana mode signatures in an indium arsenide/aluminum nanowire device. The paper was retracted in 2023 after Nature's editors found the data did not meet the evidentiary standard for the claim. The retraction was the most prominent in the history of topological physics and significantly undermined the program's public credibility. In 2023, Microsoft announced a new result in a revised device architecture using indium arsenide quantum wells, with measurements described as consistent with the topological phase required for Majorana modes. The scientific community's reception was cautious, reflecting the scars from the 2021 retraction and the genuine difficulty of distinguishing a Majorana signature from alternative explanations for similar measurements. The question of what constitutes adequate evidence for a topological phase in a heterostructure device was actively debated at the time this chapter was written.

For the engineer, the Microsoft story is a reminder that the topological physics that is settled, the Z2 invariants, the surface states, the bulk-boundary correspondence, is settled because the confirming experiments are clean and unambiguous. Frontier physics, such as Majorana modes in engineered heterostructures, requires measurements at the edge of what is currently possible. The history tells you which kind of claim you are evaluating: settled or frontier. The 2016 Nobel Prize has been settled. The topological qubit is the frontier. Both are worth understanding, but they require different levels of engineering confidence before you build a product around them.

What Can We Build With This?

The answer to the question "What can you build from a history chapter?" is: a calibration instrument. An engineer who has absorbed the pattern of topological physics has something no amount of technical detail alone can provide: a framework for evaluating claims about topological materials and devices against the established record of how predictions in this field are made, tested, and confirmed or revised. This framework applies directly to investment, hiring, partnership, and architectural decisions in quantum computing hardware.

Here is the pattern, stated as precisely as possible. In the fifty-year history of topological condensed matter physics, every theoretical prediction made within the framework of band topology and the Z2 or Chern number classification has been experimentally confirmed. Kosterlitz-Thouless vortex unbinding: confirmed. Integer quantum Hall effect topological origin: confirmed. Berry phase: confirmed and now used in precision measurement. Haldane model: confirmed in cold atoms and solid-state materials. Kane-Mele Z2 topological insulator: confirmed in HgTe. Three-dimensional topological insulators: confirmed in Bi1-xSbx and Bi2Se3. Weyl semimetals with Fermi arcs: confirmed in TaAs. The theory's predictive record is, by the standards of condensed matter physics, exceptional.

The risk assessment framework has three tiers. The first tier is confirmed physics with manufacturing-ready materials: quantum Hall conductance quantization used to define the ohm, topological surface states in Bi2Se3 and Bi2Te3, measurable by ARPES in any well-equipped laboratory, and the quantum anomalous Hall effect demonstrated in magnetic topological insulator films. A claim in this tier carries a physics risk close to zero. The engineering risk is materials quality, interface control, and fabrication precision, risks you can engineer around. The second tier is confirmed physics with materials that require specialized growth not yet in production at scale: HgTe/CdTe quantum wells, topological crystalline insulators, and Weyl semimetal devices. The physics is confirmed; the challenge is bringing the materials platform to engineering maturity. A claim in this tier is a real but addressable engineering bet. The third tier is frontier physics with contested experimental signatures: Majorana modes in semiconductor heterostructures, non-Abelian braiding operations, and topological qubit gate fidelity. The theoretical framework is rigorous, but experimental signatures are subtle, and alternative explanations have not been fully ruled out. Any major architecture decision based on third-tier physics requires explicit hedging.

The time between theoretical prediction and experimental confirmation in this field has been shrinking. Kosterlitz-Thouless to experimental confirmation: roughly eight years. Kane-Mele 2005 to HgTe confirmation 2007: two years. Theoretical prediction of three-dimensional topological insulators to Bi2Se3 confirmation: less than one year. This acceleration reflects the maturation of ARPES and molecular beam epitaxy as experimental tools, and the growth of the community. For the engineer planning a hardware roadmap, theoretical predictions made today within the established framework can be expected to be experimentally tested within a three- to five-year window. If a new topological material class is predicted now, you can plan for experimental validation on that timescale.

The history also reveals what the retraction record looks like. The topological condensed matter community has a strong record of prediction and confirmation, but also cases where initial reports were more ambiguous than initially presented and where eagerness to confirm predictions led to premature consensus. The Microsoft 2021 retraction is the largest of its kind. Smaller examples include candidate topological insulator materials that turned out to be trivial insulators with surface resonances, and Majorana candidates in nanowires that later showed trivial Andreev bound states rather than genuine topological zero modes. An engineer who knows this pattern asks of any new claim: what is the measurement, how specific is the signature, and how many alternative explanations have been ruled out? That question is more useful than asking whether this is topological, and history teaches you to ask it.

Diagram 2.12 - Risk Assessment Map: Topological Claims from Settled to Frontier

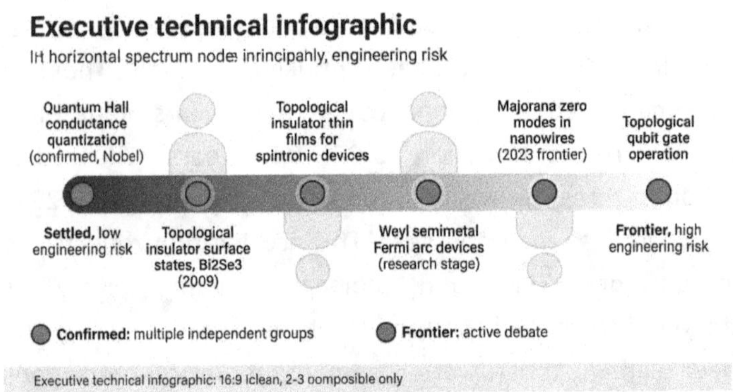

Takeaway

The history of topological physics covers fifty years, five Nobel Prize laureates, and a progression from pure mathematics to manufacturable materials that is unusually direct and well-documented. The key stations in that history, the Kosterlitz-Thouless vortex transition, the von Klitzing quantum Hall discovery, the TKNN Chern number, the Berry phase, the Haldane model, the Kane-Mele Z2 insulator, the HgTe confirmation, the Bi2Se3 surface state, the Weyl semimetal, and the ongoing Majorana program, are not historical footnotes. They are the load-bearing intellectual structure that explains why the materials in the chapters ahead behave as they do: why surface states cannot be removed, why conductance is quantized, and why the topological qubit is a coherent engineering bet rather than speculation.

The engineering lesson from this chapter is the risk assessment framework: the history gives you a clear map of what is settled and what is frontier, and that map is your most valuable tool for evaluating claims, proposals, and partnerships in topological quantum computing and sensing. Settled physics is a foundation you can build on. Frontier physics is a bet you make with calibrated confidence. The distinction between the two is the most important judgment call this chapter equips you to make.

The next chapter takes a necessary step back before going deeper into the materials. To understand why band inversion produces a topological phase, why the Z2 invariant is defined as it is, and why the Berry phase unifies all the phenomena above, you need a working command of the quantum mechanical foundations: wavefunctions, the Bloch theorem, the band structure of solids, and the role of symmetry in constraining electronic states. Chapter 3 provides that foundation at the engineer level, with the same hardware framing established in this chapter. The payoff is that every concept from Chapter 4 onward, from topological invariants to Majorana modes to non-Abelian braiding, becomes something you can derive rather than something you have to take on faith.

3 The Quantum Foundation

The conference room on the third floor of Axiom Quantum's Cambridge building was called the Faraday Room, where the theory and hardware teams had most of their heated arguments. Sasha Korolev was at the whiteboard when Marcus Webb came in, still wearing the cleanroom overshoes he had forgotten to remove after his morning session in the fab. Sasha had drawn a grid of dots meant to represent a crystal lattice, but Marcus interrupted before he could explain what it was for.

"I want to be direct," Marcus said, dropping into a chair. "I've designed cryogenic control systems. I know what a wavefunction is in principle: a probability amplitude that evolves according to the Schrodinger equation. What I don't know is what it means for our chip. When Priya says the topological surface state is protected by time-reversal symmetry, or when you tell me spin-orbit coupling determines whether we're in a topological phase, I can follow the words, but I can't feel the physics. Tell me what it means for the device stack. Not the textbook version. The version I need to build something with."

Sasha set down the marker and pulled up a stool. "Start with the wavefunction," he said. "Not as a mathematical object. As an engineering specification. Everything else we need, every concept between here and the final chapter, follows from understanding that one thing correctly." Marcus opened his notebook. The following chapter is what Sasha said.

Why It Matters

Every decision you will make as an engineer working with topological or quantum materials rests on a quantum mechanics foundation that differs in a few specific, important ways from what is taught in a standard device physics course. Those courses teach the wavefunction as a formalism for predicting measurements. Still, they rarely emphasize that the wavefunction has a property, its complex phase, that carries physical consequences beyond the probability distribution. For conventional semiconductors, that phase is largely irrelevant: silicon transistors do not care about the quantum-mechanical phase of the electron wavefunctions in the channel because the devices operate in regimes where quantum coherence is thermally scrambled. Topological materials are fundamentally different. Their most important properties, the ones that make them useful for qubits, quantum sensors, and spintronic devices, arise from the behavior of the phase of the wavefunction as electrons move through the crystal. Without a working understanding of what a phase means physically, you cannot understand why a topological surface state is protected, why a Majorana fermion is its own antiparticle, or why a topological qubit is more robust than a conventional superconducting one.

This chapter covers exactly the concepts that the rest of this book depends on, in the order that makes the engineering logic clearest, with every abstraction connected to a device consequence. An engineer who has finished it can read a quantum materials paper without a translator, evaluate whether a band structure diagram supports a topological claim, and follow a conversation about spin-orbit coupling, time-reversal symmetry, and band inversion without losing the thread. It introduces several concepts that will appear in every subsequent chapter without re-derivation: the Bloch theorem and Bloch waves, the Brillouin zone as the crystal's natural momentum space, spin-orbit coupling as a material parameter rather than a perturbative correction, and the distinction between symmetry-protected phases and symmetry-broken phases.

The Wavefunction as an Engineering Specification

A specification tells you everything a component does and everything it is allowed to do under defined operating conditions. The wavefunction is the quantum mechanical analog of that specification. It is the complete description of a quantum particle's state, containing within it every prediction that can be made about any measurement. Position, momentum, energy, spin orientation, and any derived quantity are all encoded in the wavefunction. Given a wavefunction, you can compute the probability distribution for any measurement outcome, and those predictions are the most accurately tested in the history of physics.

What makes the wavefunction unusual compared to anything in classical device physics is that it is complex-valued. It has two components at every point in space and time: an amplitude and a phase. The amplitude determines the probability: the squared magnitude of the wavefunction at a given position gives the probability of finding the particle there. The phase encodes how the quantum state will interfere with other quantum states. Two electron wavefunctions arriving at the same point in space with the same amplitude but opposite phases cancel: the probability of finding an electron there goes to zero. Two arriving with the same phase reinforce each other. This is quantum interference, the mechanism behind every topological effect in this book. The physical reality of the phase is confirmed by the Aharonov-Bohm effect, experimentally verified in 1986:

an electron traveling around a magnetic field region, without entering the field, acquires a measurable phase shift. The field exerts no classical force on the electron; it modifies the phase of the wavefunction, and that modification changes observable quantities. This is the conceptual prototype for everything that happens in topological materials.

Diagram 3.1 - The Wavefunction: Amplitude and Phase

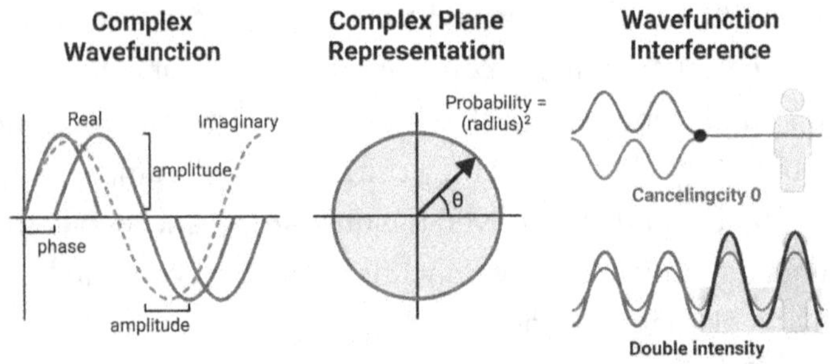

The wavefunction encodes both probability amplitude and phase.
Phase differences determine constructive or destructive interference.

For a hardware engineer, the most important consequence of this picture is that any interaction with the environment that randomizes the phase of a quantum state, a process called decoherence, destroys the quantum information encoded in that state. This is why quantum computing hardware operates at millikelvin temperatures in carefully shielded cryostats: thermal fluctuations and electromagnetic noise introduce random phase shifts that must be kept far below the energy scale of the quantum states to maintain coherence. Topological protection is a strategy for making the phase of the quantum state insensitive to local perturbations via global geometric constraints. Understanding why that strategy works requires understanding the Bloch theorem and its implications for wavefunctions in a periodic crystal lattice.

The wavefunction lives in Hilbert space, the space of all possible quantum states for a given system, with the key property that any linear combination of valid quantum states is also valid. This linearity makes quantum superposition possible. An electron in a superposition of two states with a definite phase relationship has both amplitudes physically present to participate in future interference events. Between measurements, the wavefunction evolves smoothly and deterministically according to the Schrodinger equation.

Eigenvalues, Eigenstates, and Observables

Every physical measurement in quantum mechanics corresponds to an operator, and the states in which a system gives a definite, reproducible answer to that measurement are called eigenstates of the operator. The value returned by the measurement is the eigenvalue. The energy eigenstates of a quantum system are its natural basis: they evolve in time by accumulating phase at a rate proportional to their energy, and they are the relevant states for questions about what the system does over time. When the band structure diagram in a quantum materials paper shows energy levels as a function of crystal momentum, it is showing a set of energy eigenvalues and their corresponding eigenstates. When a topological surface state is described as existing inside the gap, it means there is a family of energy eigenstates localized at the surface with energies in the bulk gap, whose existence is guaranteed not by a local chemical feature but by a global topological property of the bulk band structure.

One observable deserves special attention: spin. Quantum spin is an intrinsic angular momentum carried by electrons with no classical analog. An electron has a spin quantum number of one-half, meaning measurements of its spin along any axis return exactly one of two values, spin-up or spin-down. The spin eigenstates along a given axis are orthogonal quantum states. However, spin measurements along different axes are not independent: an electron in the spin-up eigenstate along z is in a superposition of spin-up and spin-down along x. The Pauli matrices describe this interdependence and obey commutation relations that have no classical counterpart. The reason spin matters so acutely for topological materials is spin-orbit coupling: spin is not just a label, it is a physical degree of freedom that couples to the electron's orbital motion through a relativistic mechanism, and that coupling is what allows the crystal's symmetries to impose structure on the band topology.

Diagram 3.2 - Spin Eigenstates on the Bloch Sphere

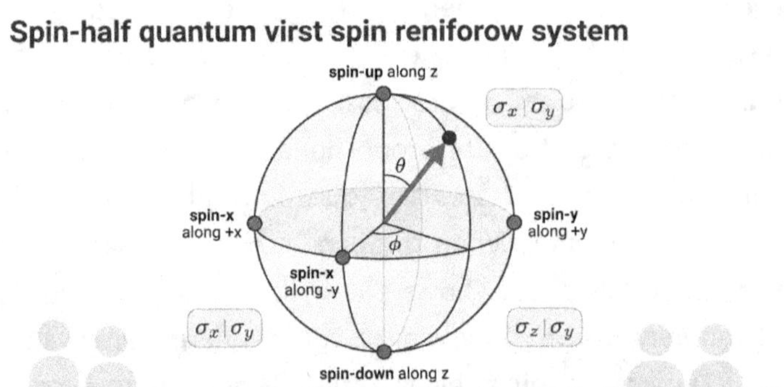

Any pure spin state corresponds to a point on the Bloch sphere. The poles are the energy eigenstates; equatorial states are equal superpositions. Spin-orbit coupling causes the quantization axis to depend on the electron momentum vector.

There is also the crystal momentum operator, labeled k. In a periodic crystal, k is the analog of classical momentum but defined relative to the crystal's reciprocal lattice. The crystal momentum of an electron in a band structure gives a vector in the Brillouin zone, the fundamental unit cell of momentum space. Every filled energy band in a crystal corresponds to a continuous family of energy eigenstates parameterized by k, and the relationship between energy eigenvalue and k value is the band dispersion E(k), which is exactly what a band structure diagram plots. Reading that diagram is the primary skill this chapter builds.

The Bloch Theorem and Bloch Waves in Periodic Potentials

A crystal is a periodic arrangement of atoms, and the electrons experience a potential energy landscape with the same periodicity as the atomic lattice. In silicon, the lattice constant is about 5.4 angstroms; in bismuth selenide (Bi2Se3), the repeating unit is a quintuple layer about 1 nanometer thick. The Bloch theorem states that in a perfectly periodic crystal potential, each energy eigenstate is a product of a plane wave with a wavevector k and a function that has the same periodicity as the crystal lattice. The plane wave component carries the crystal momentum k and determines the electron's long-range phase behavior. The periodic function, called the Bloch function or cell-periodic part, modulates the amplitude and phase within each unit cell, reflecting the local atomic chemistry. The two together are called a Bloch wave or Bloch state. Each Bloch wave with a given k and energy E(k) is an energy eigenstate, and the collection of all these eigenstates as k is varied across the Brillouin zone traces out one energy band.

The physical picture of a Bloch wave is a plane wave rolling through the crystal with a well-defined wavevector k, sculpted within each unit cell by the local atomic potential, with its amplitude concentrated near the atomic cores, where the potential is attractive. The overall wave remains coherent throughout the crystal because the periodic modulation is exactly in phase with the lattice periodicity. The Brillouin zone is the unit cell of the crystal's reciprocal lattice: every point inside it is closer to the reciprocal lattice origin than to any other reciprocal lattice point. The high-symmetry points of the Brillouin zone, labeled by capital Greek letters, are the k-space locations where crystal symmetry operations fix k: the Gamma point at zone center represents zero crystal momentum, while X, M, K, and H points represent special symmetry positions. The band dispersion at and near these points determines the most physically important material properties, including whether band inversion, the signature of topological non-triviality, occurs.

Diagram 3.3 - Bloch Wave in a Periodic Crystal Potential

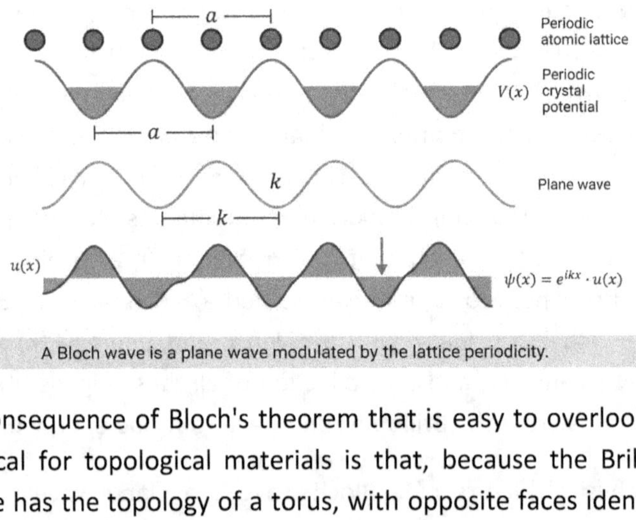

A Bloch wave is a plane wave modulated by the lattice periodicity.

A consequence of Bloch's theorem that is easy to overlook but critical for topological materials is that, because the Brillouin zone has the topology of a torus, with opposite faces identified by reciprocal lattice vectors, the Bloch functions, as functions of k, trace out paths on a torus rather than in open space. This compactness is what makes winding numbers and topological invariants meaningful. A function defined on a torus can wind around the torus's holes a nonzero integer number of times, and that winding number cannot change continuously without tearing. It is an integer-valued topological property, and it is the definition of the Chern number, the Z2 invariant, and the other topological invariants that will appear in Chapter 5. The Bloch theorem is not just the foundation of band theory: it is the geometric stage on which the topology of quantum materials plays out.

The Brillouin zone is most useful when you know which high-symmetry points to focus on. For a hexagonal crystal like bismuth selenide, the Gamma point at zone center and the M points at the zone boundary midpoints are time-reversal invariant momenta, pinning the Kramers pairs that form the Dirac cone of the topological surface state. For a cubic crystal like the half-Heusler alloys, band inversions occur at the Gamma point. Identifying which high-symmetry point is relevant for a given material system is one of the first things an engineer infers from the crystal symmetry, before any detailed band-structure calculation is needed.

Diagram 3.4 - Brillouin Zone of a Hexagonal Crystal with High-Symmetry Points

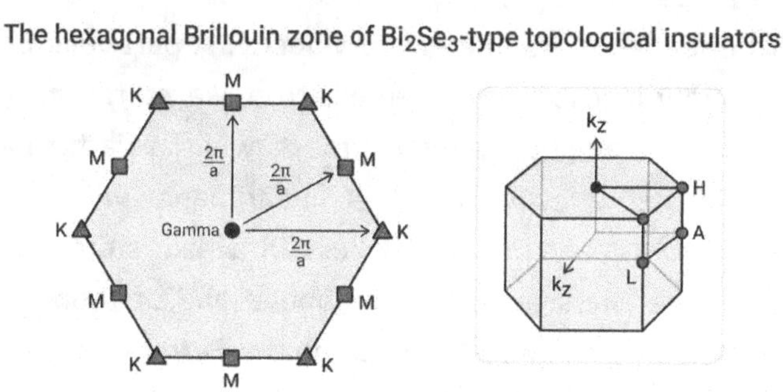

The hexagonal Brillouin zone of Bi2Se3-type topological insulators. High-symmetry points Gamma, M, and K are where crystal symmetry fixes the band structure. Band inversion in topological insulators occurs at the Gamma point.

Band Structure: What E(k) Means & How to Read a Band Diag

A band structure diagram plots the energy E of electronic states as a function of crystal momentum k. It is the single most informative compressed representation of a material's electronic structure, and reading one correctly is the primary technical skill this chapter is designed to teach. Every quantum materials paper includes band-structure data, either from density functional theory calculations or from angle-resolved photoemission spectroscopy (ARPES), in which UV light ejects electrons from a material's surface, and a detector array maps their energies and emission angles to reconstruct the momentum-resolved electronic structure. The horizontal axis is a path through the Brillouin zone connecting high-symmetry points. The energy scale is set so that the Fermi energy is zero. Bands plotted below this energy are occupied; bands above are empty at zero temperature.

Each curve in the band diagram represents a band, a family of Bloch states parameterized by k, and its shape encodes the electron's effective mass and group velocity. A parabolic band near a minimum describes a free-electron-like state: sharper curvature implies a lighter effective mass, while a flatter band implies a heavier effective mass. A linear band, where E is proportional to k, describes a massless Dirac-like state. Dirac-linear bands are the signature of graphene and of topological surface states, and their appearance at the Fermi energy in a surface-sensitive measurement is one of the clearest signatures of topological behavior.

Diagram 3.5 - Band Structure Diagram: Metal, Semiconductor, and Topological Insulator

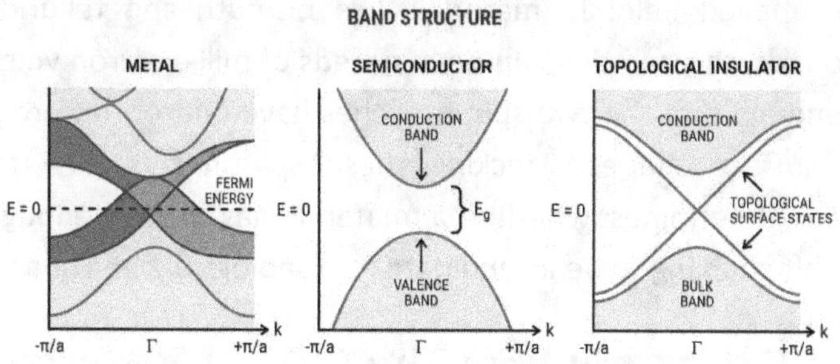

Schematic comparison of metal, semiconductor, and topological insulator band structures. In a topological insulator a bulk gap hosts linearly dispersing surface states whose Dirac crossing is protected by time-reversal symmetry.

The band gap is the energy range between the top of the highest fully occupied band and the bottom of the lowest empty band. In silicon, the band gap is about 1.1 electronvolts. In bismuth selenide (Bi2Se3), the bulk band gap is about 0.3 eV. But the gap in a topological insulator is fundamentally different from the gap in silicon in one respect that size alone does not reveal: its topological character determines whether the surface of the material is forced to host metallic states. A trivial insulator with the same gap size as Bi2Se3 would be insulating all the way to its surface. The topological insulator has metallic surface states that cannot be removed without closing and reopening the bulk gap. The topological distinction requires examining the band structure globally, tracking how the wavefunction character evolves as k traverses the Brillouin zone. Local measurements of the gap size cannot reveal it.

In a crystal with both time reversal and spatial inversion symmetry, every band is doubly degenerate at every k point because each state at k is paired with its time-reversed partner. Breaking one of these symmetries, by applying a magnetic field or choosing a crystal structure without inversion symmetry, can lift this degeneracy and split the bands. The size of the resulting spin splitting is proportional to the spin-orbit coupling strength or the applied field. In materials like bismuth and telluride compounds, this splitting can be hundreds of millielectron volts, large enough that the two spin branches have entirely different Fermi surface shapes. Tracking these splittings is how an engineer determines whether a material has strong enough spin-orbit coupling to be a candidate for topological behavior.

Spin-Orbit Coupling: The Critical Material Parameter

Spin-orbit coupling (SOC) is the interaction between an electron's intrinsic spin angular momentum and the angular momentum of its orbital motion around an atomic nucleus. An electron orbiting a nucleus at speed v experiences, in its own rest frame, a magnetic field proportional to v cross E. That magnetic field couples to the electron's magnetic dipole moment, and the resulting energy depends on the relative orientation of spin and orbital angular momentum. Quantum-mechanically, this appears as a Hamiltonian term that mixes spin and orbital degrees of freedom, locking the electron's spin direction to its crystal momentum, with profound consequences for band structure.

The engineering consequence of SOC is that the spin of an electron in a SOC material is not a free label independent of the electron's momentum. Each k-state has a preferred spin orientation determined by the crystal symmetry and coupling strength. In materials with broken inversion symmetry, this leads to Rashba splitting: instead of a single band with two degenerate spin states, two bands spiral around each other in k-space. In topological insulators, the spin-momentum locking is complete on the surface: electrons moving in the positive x-direction must have their spins pointing in the y-direction, and electrons moving in the negative x-direction must have their spins pointing in the minus y-direction. This is why topological surface-state electrons cannot backscatter: reversing a surface electron's momentum requires flipping its spin. In the absence of a time-reversal-breaking perturbation, that channel is unavailable.

Diagram 3.6 - Spin-Orbit Coupling and Rashba Splitting

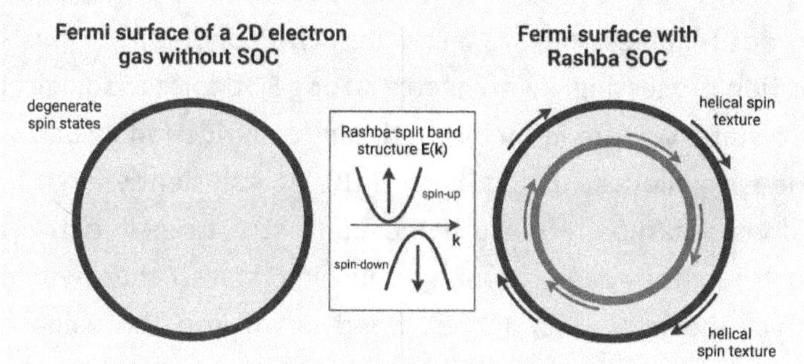

Rashba spin-orbit coupling splits a doubly degenerate band into two bands with helical spin textures. At each point on the Fermi surface, spin is locked perpendicular to momentum, the precursor to topological surface state spin-momentum locking.

The strength of spin-orbit coupling scales roughly as the fourth power of the atomic number Z of the heaviest element in the crystal. This follows from the relativistic correction to wavefunctions near the atomic nucleus: a heavier nucleus produces a stronger Coulomb field, inner-shell electrons accelerate to relativistic velocities in that field, and the relativistic correction, which appears naturally as the spin-orbit term in the nonrelativistic limit of the Dirac equation, scales as Z to the fourth power over the cube of the principal quantum number. This is why light elements such as carbon and silicon have negligible SOC, whereas heavy elements such as bismuth ($Z = 83$), mercury ($Z = 80$), and tellurium ($Z = 52$) exhibit extremely strong SOC. It is not a coincidence that all experimentally confirmed topological insulators include at least one of these heavy elements: bismuth selenide Bi2Se3, bismuth telluride Bi2Te3, antimony telluride Sb2Te3, and mercury telluride HgTe. All rely on the large SOC of their heavy constituent elements to drive the band inversion that gives rise to topological behavior.

For a hardware engineer selecting materials for a topological device, this Z-to-the-fourth scaling has immediate practical implications. Your choice of material locks in the SOC strength and is not tunable after the fact via growth conditions or post-deposition processing. If you need a strong SOC for a topological surface state, you are in the bismuth- and telluride-family or the half-Heusler alloys like LuPtSb or YPtBi. At sufficiently large Z, SOC does not merely perturb the band structure; it entirely restructures the band ordering, pushing states that would otherwise be in the conduction band down into the valence band and vice versa. This exchange of character between valence- and conduction-band states near a high-symmetry point is called band inversion, and it is the defining signature of a topological insulator.

Diagram 3.7 - Relativistic Origin of Spin-Orbit Coupling: Z-Scaling

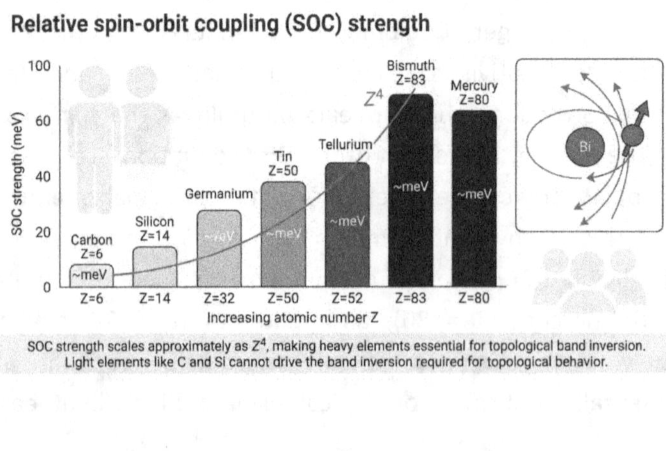

SOC strength scales approximately as Z^4, making heavy elements essential for topological band inversion. Light elements like C and Si cannot drive the band inversion required for topological behavior.

Relativistic Effects: Why Heavy Elements Matter

The connection between relativistic physics and topological materials is quantitative and direct. The Dirac equation, Paul Dirac's 1928 relativistic quantum-mechanical wave equation for the electron, contains two corrections relative to the nonrelativistic Schrödinger equation that are negligible for light elements but dominate for heavy ones. The first is the mass-velocity correction: as an electron near a heavy nucleus accelerates to relativistic speeds in the strong Coulomb field, its effective mass increases and its inner-shell orbitals contract toward the nucleus. The second is the spin-orbit term itself, which arises naturally in the nonrelativistic limit of the Dirac equation for an electron in an external potential, with a magnitude proportional to the potential's gradient.

For bismuth selenide Bi2Se3, the large SOC is directly responsible for the band inversion that makes it a topological insulator. Without SOC, the lowest conduction band of Bi2Se3 would consist of bismuth p-orbital states and the highest valence band of selenium p-orbital states, with normal semiconductor ordering. The large SOC inverts this ordering near the Gamma point, pushing the bismuth-character states below the Fermi level and the selenium-character states above it. The resulting band inversion covers an energy window of about 300 meV, far too large to be closed by reasonable electric fields, temperature perturbations, or disorder: it is a robust topological feature, not a fragile crossing. The HgTe quantum well system, in which the Molenkamp group in Wurzburg first experimentally confirmed a two-dimensional topological insulator in 2007, following theoretical predictions by Kane and Mele in 2005 and a specific quantum-well proposal by Bernevig,

Hughes, and Zhang in 2006, operates via the same mechanism. The quantized conductance plateau in edge transport, which appeared and disappeared as the well thickness crossed the critical value, was direct evidence of the topological phase transition driven by relativistic band inversion in mercury.

Diagram 3.8 - Band Inversion in HgTe: Relativistic Mechanism

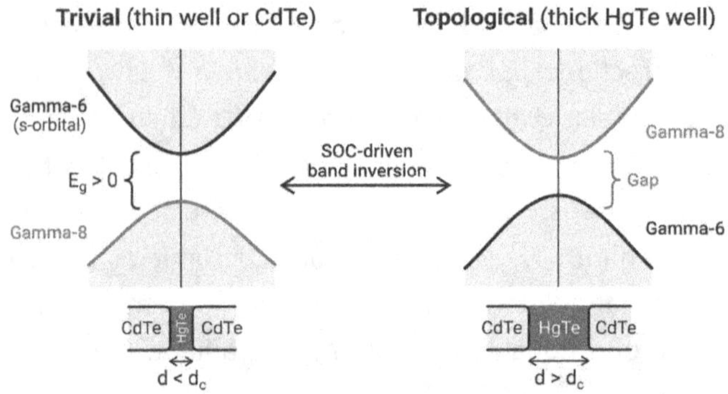

The practical lesson for materials selection is that topological band inversion requires either a material composed of heavy elements with Z generally above about 50, or an interface structure in which a light-element material borrows the SOC of an adjacent heavy-element one through quantum mechanical hybridization across the interface. The latter strategy is relevant to superconducting topological phases, in which a conventional s-wave superconductor, such as niobium, is brought into contact with a topological insulator or a semiconductor with strong Rashba SOC, thereby inducing pairing in the topological material via the proximity effect. Microsoft's topological qubit program, as described in their 2023 and 2025 publications, is built on InAs semiconductor nanowires with an aluminum superconducting shell. The choice of InAs over GaAs or silicon is driven directly by the need for a large enough SOC to open a topological gap. Understanding the relativistic origin of that SOC requirement converts a rule of thumb into a principled engineering constraint.

Time-Reversal Symmetry and Kramers Degeneracy

Time-reversal symmetry is the invariance of the laws of physics under reversing the direction of time. For a quantum system, time reversal is represented by an operator T that acts on wavefunctions by taking the complex conjugate and flipping the spin. Taking the complex conjugate reverses the direction of phase evolution, which is exactly what time reversal requires. For a particle with spin zero, T-squared equals plus one. For an electron with spin one-half, T squared equals minus one. This sign difference is the key to everything that follows.

Kramers' degeneracy follows from T-squared equals minus one. The theorem states that if a quantum system with half-integer spin is time-reversal symmetric, every energy eigenstate is at least doubly degenerate. The proof: Suppose psi is an energy eigenstate. Then T times psi is also an energy eigenstate with the same energy. If psi and T times psi were in the same state, they would be proportional. But for spin one-half, T squared equals minus one, and working through the algebra shows that psi and T times psi are orthogonal: two distinct states with the same energy, the Kramers pair. In any material that preserves time-reversal symmetry, Bloch states at k and minus k are degenerate. More powerfully, at the time-reversal invariant momenta (TRIM), specifically the Gamma point and zone boundary points at half a reciprocal lattice vector, the Kramers pairs are pinned together by a constraint that any time-reversal-symmetric perturbation cannot lift. This pinning mechanism protects the topological surface state. On the surface of a topological insulator, the Dirac cone vertex sits precisely at a TRIM point, and its two spin-polarized branches are a Kramers pair. Breaking time-reversal symmetry by applying a magnetic field or adding magnetic impurities lifts the Kramers degeneracy, opens a gap at the Dirac point, and destroys the topological protection.

Diagram 3.9 - Kramers Degeneracy at Time-Reversal Invariant Momenta

Kramers degeneracy in a topological insulator band structure

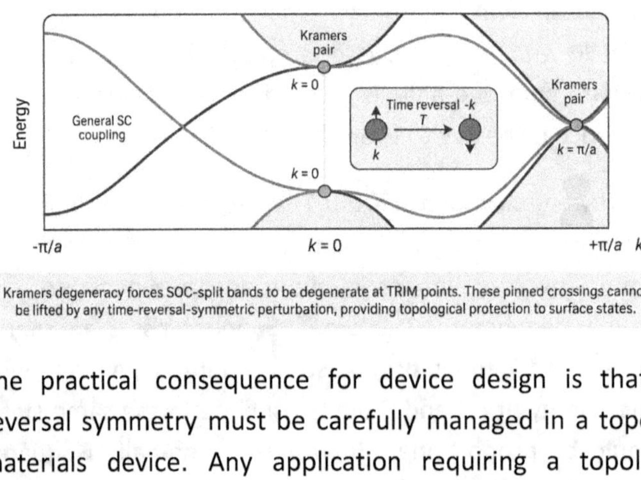

Kramers degeneracy forces SOC-split bands to be degenerate at TRIM points. These pinned crossings cannot be lifted by any time-reversal-symmetric perturbation, providing topological protection to surface states.

The practical consequence for device design is that time-reversal symmetry must be carefully managed in a topological materials device. Any application requiring a topologically protected surface state must avoid magnetic impurities, stray magnetic fields, and magnetic proximity effects from adjacent layers. This imposes constraints on cryogenic magnetic shielding, electrode metal selection, and acceptable levels of magnetic contamination in deposition chambers. At Axiom, the aluminum superconducting contacts are nonmagnetic by design, but contamination with iron or nickel during handling immediately suppresses surface-state transport. The absence of magnetic impurity contamination is not just a fabrication cleanliness goal; it is a requirement for topological symmetry protection, and the tolerance is set by the size of the bulk SOC gap, not by conventional leakage-current specifications.

Symmetry-Protected and Symmetry-Broken Phases

The concept of a phase of matter in condensed matter physics has two distinct meanings. The first, older meaning is the Landau classification: a phase is defined by an order parameter, a physical quantity that is zero in a symmetric phase and nonzero in a less symmetric ordered phase. In a ferromagnet, the order parameter is the net magnetization. In a conventional superconductor, it is the Cooper pair amplitude. Landau's framework classifies most phase transitions by identifying the broken symmetry and the order parameter. The second meaning, which became central after the theoretical work of Kosterlitz, Thouless, and Haldane in the 1970s and 1980s and was recognized by the 2016 Nobel Prize in Physics, is the topological classification. Two phases are distinct not because one has broken a symmetry that the other preserves, but because the wavefunctions of their electrons cannot be continuously deformed into each other without closing the energy gap. A trivial insulator and a topological insulator can have identical symmetry groups. Yet, they are distinct phases because the topological invariant computed from the phase structure of the Bloch wavefunctions across the Brillouin zone differs between them.

A symmetry-protected topological phase is a topological phase whose non-triviality depends on the presence of a specific symmetry. Time-reversal symmetric topological insulators are the canonical example: their topological invariant is only well-defined if time-reversal symmetry is preserved. If time reversal is broken, the gap can close and reopen in a topologically trivial way, and the surface state disappears. The symmetry is not optional: it is the structural scaffold that makes the topological classification meaningful. A list of symmetry requirements is therefore always part of the device specification for a topological material. The operating temperature and field must keep the material in its topological phase, which requires that the relevant protecting symmetries remain intact.

Diagram 3.10 - Topological Phase Diagram: Trivial vs. Topological Insulator

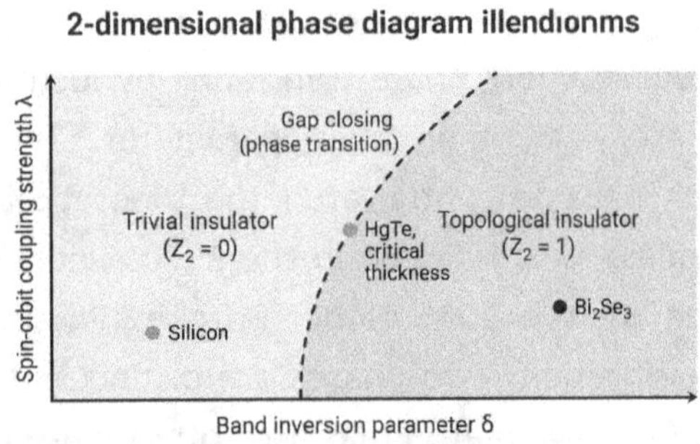

The topological phase diagram separates trivial (Z_2=0) from topological insulators (Z_2=1). The boundary is a gap-closing transition. Representative materials are positioned by SOC strength and degree of band inversion.

The distinction between symmetry-protected topological phases and symmetry-broken phases matters in device engineering because the two types of protection degrade differently. A symmetry-broken order parameter is fragile in that disorder can create local regions where the order parameter is suppressed, thereby forming domain walls that scatter charge carriers. In a conventional superconductor, disorder can locally suppress the pair amplitude and weaken the gap. Symmetry-protected topological phases are robust against local disorder as long as the protecting symmetry is preserved globally and the bulk gap is nonzero: the topological invariant is immune to any perturbation that does not close the gap. This robustness sets the tolerance budget for disorder in topological device fabrication and distinguishes topological protection from mere energetic suppression. There is also a gapless topological category: Weyl semimetals have topologically protected band crossing points connected on the surface by Fermi arcs, protected by the topology of the Weyl nodes rather than by time-reversal symmetry, and they will be covered in Chapter 7.

The engineering implication is concrete. When an engineer reads a paper claiming that a magnetic topological insulator preserves topological surface states despite broken time reversal, they should ask: Which symmetry now protects the state? Magnetic topological insulators rely on crystalline mirror or rotational symmetries, shifting the classification from a Z2 topological insulator to a crystalline topological insulator. The protection is real but depends on different symmetries, which impose different constraints on what perturbations will or will not destroy the surface state. The taxonomy directly determines the device fabrication tolerance specification.

Diagram 3.11 - Taxonomy of Quantum Phases: Symmetry-Protected and Symmetry-Broken

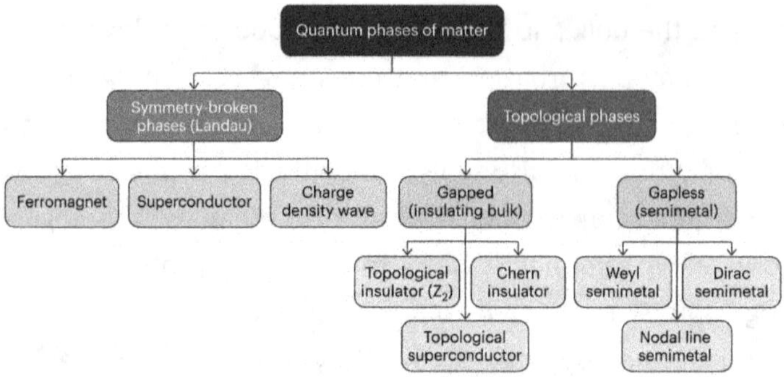

Two classification frameworks for quantum phases: Landau symmetry-breaking (left) and topological (right). Topological phases subdivide into gapped phases with topological surface states and gapless phases such as Weyl semimetals with Fermi arcs.

The Pauli Exclusion Principle and How Electrons Fill Bands

The Pauli exclusion principle states that no two electrons can occupy the same quantum state, specified in a crystal by crystal momentum k, band index n, and spin quantum number. Electrons therefore fill energy states from the bottom up as temperature approaches zero, with the total number fixed by charge neutrality. When all electrons are accommodated, the result is either a fully filled set of bands separated from the empty bands by a gap, making the material an insulator or a semiconductor, or a set of partially filled bands in which the Fermi level cuts through one or more bands, making the material a metal.

For topological insulators, the Pauli filling picture has a subtlety that distinguishes them from trivial insulators. A trivial insulator has a full valence band with the same orbital and spin character throughout the Brillouin zone. A topological insulator with band inversion has a full valence band. Still, the orbital character of the top of the valence band at the Gamma point has been swapped with the character of the conduction band bottom. The valence band near the Gamma point contains states that, without SOC, would belong to the conduction band. The band remains filled, so the material is insulating in the bulk. But the pattern of wavefunction phases across the Brillouin zone is different, and that difference is what the topological invariant measures. The invariant is a global integral over the Brillouin zone, not a local property, which is why topological properties are robust against local disorder and why detecting them requires transport measurements that probe the boundary states or spectroscopic measurements that map the full Brillouin zone.

What Can We Build With This?

The concepts in this chapter are the working vocabulary of quantum materials device engineering, and using them correctly is the difference between being able to read the primary literature and being unable to evaluate its claims. Consider a practical example: Marcus's team at Axiom is evaluating three candidate materials for the semiconductor nanowire layer in a topological qubit stack. The three candidates are indium arsenide (InAs), indium antimonide (InSb), and germanium with silicon cladding (Ge/Si). To evaluate which is most suitable, Marcus reads three recent band-structure papers and extracts the following:

From the InAs paper: the bulk bandgap at the Gamma point is about 360 meV, the effective electron mass is 0.023 times the free electron mass, very light, meaning high electron mobility, and the Rashba spin-orbit parameter from quantum well splitting is about 40 meV-angstroms. The light effective mass is favorable for qubit applications because it implies high mobility and a long mean free path. Still, it also implies a highly delocalized wavefunction and sensitivity to interface roughness. The Rashba SOC is strong enough to open a topological gap in a proximity-coupled geometry, which is why InAs is Axiom's current baseline material.

From the InSb paper: the bulk bandgap is only 235 meV, the effective mass is lighter still at 0.014, and the Rashba parameter can reach 200 meV-angstroms in the right heterostructure, much larger than InAs. A larger SOC allows a larger topological gap, translating into higher operating temperatures and greater robustness against disorder. But the smaller bandgap means greater susceptibility to electrostatic gating through the gap, and the very light effective mass increases coupling to charge noise. From the Ge/Si paper: the bulk Ge gap is about 740 meV (indirect); the effective hole mass in strained Ge quantum wells is about 0.05 times the free mass; and the Rashba SOC for holes can reach 50 to 100 meV-angstroms in optimized structures. Germanium is compatible with silicon manufacturing infrastructure, but its indirect bandgap and hole-based conduction require a rethink of junction design.

Diagram 3.12 - Band Structure Literacy as a Materials Selection Tool

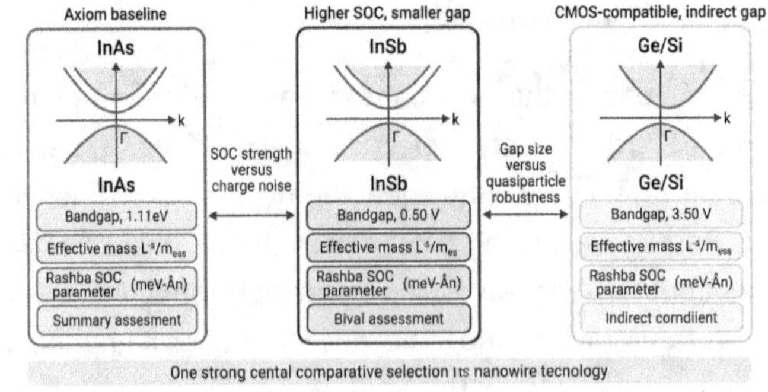

This kind of side-by-side evaluation of materials is exactly the competence that makes an engineer effective on a quantum hardware team. It requires knowing what the bandgap at the Gamma point implies for operating temperature tolerance, what the effective mass implies for mean free path and interface sensitivity, what the Rashba SOC parameter controls in terms of topological gap size and quasiparticle robustness, and that Kramers degeneracy at the TRIM points sets the tolerance to magnetic disorder. None of these judgments requires deriving the topological invariant from scratch: they require using the vocabulary fluently. Band structure literacy also allows a hardware engineer to flag implausible claims: a paper claiming a 300 meV topological gap in a light-element material with Z below 20 contradicts the Z-to-the-fourth scaling immediately, and a paper reporting quantized edge conductance at room temperature in a material with a 30 meV bulk gap contradicts the basic condition that the gap must be much larger than the thermal energy. These filters protect an engineer from wasting fabrication resources on claims that do not survive basic physics scrutiny.

Takeaway

This chapter has laid the quantum-mechanical foundation on which every subsequent chapter depends. The wavefunction is a complex-valued engineering specification with both amplitude, which gives the probability, and phase, which determines interference and topological character. The phase is physically real and measurable via interference experiments, and it distinguishes a topological insulator from a trivial one even when the bulk gap is the same. Bloch waves and the Bloch theorem establish that in a periodic crystal, the natural quantum states are plane waves modulated by the lattice periodicity, parameterized by a crystal momentum k in the Brillouin zone, and that the toroidal topology of the Brillouin zone is what makes topological winding numbers meaningful. Band structure diagrams encode the energy of these states as a function of k, and reading them correctly, identifying gaps, crossings, effective masses, band character, and spin splittings, is the primary technical skill for evaluating quantum materials literature.

Spin-orbit coupling is the material parameter that controls topological behavior in real crystals. It scales as Z^4, making heavy elements such as bismuth, tellurium, and mercury essential constituents of topological materials. Strong SOC can invert the energy ordering of the valence and conduction bands near a high-symmetry point, producing band inversion, the band-structure signature of a topological phase. Time-reversal symmetry protects the Kramers degeneracy at time-reversal invariant momenta, pins the Dirac cone of a topological surface state, and forbids backscattering of the helically spin-polarized surface electrons. Breaking time-reversal symmetry destroys this protection. The distinction between symmetry-protected topological phases and symmetry-broken phases maps onto two fundamentally different protection mechanisms, with distinct implications for device tolerance to disorder and perturbations.

Marcus put his notebook down when Sasha finished. "So when you talk about the topological invariant," Marcus said, "you are not talking about something we measure directly. You are talking about something we compute from the band structure, from these phase relationships we have been discussing." Sasha nodded. "And the next chapter will show you exactly what happens when the electrons in that band structure are not independent of each other, which they are not in any real material. Band theory, as we have described it today, treats each electron as moving through an average potential from all the others. The corrections matter, especially for topological superconductors, and that is where the physics gets interesting in a new way." Marcus opened his notebook again. The next chapter was already waiting.

4 Electrons in Solids

The ingot is the size of a thumb, jet black, with a faint metallic sheen that catches the light at an angle and then disappears. Priya Nair holds it between two fingers, suspended over the conference table like a jeweler presenting a stone, and waits for the room to settle. Across the table, a chief engineer from the fabrication partner has just asked the question she was expecting: why bismuth selenide? His company has made superconducting junction stacks for three different quantum hardware programs. His process nodes are stable and characterized. Why, he wants to know, should he care about a material his team has never touched?

Marcus Webb is sitting two seats down, and Priya notices him lean forward. He came from a semiconductor background, and six months ago, he would have asked the same question, probably with the same polite skepticism. Now he is watching the exchange with the focused attention of someone who recognizes the pivot point and knows that the answer to that question is why the company exists.

Priya sets the ingot on the table and pulls up a band structure diagram on the screen. Two sets of curves, energy on the vertical axis, crystal momentum on the horizontal axis, and in the center of the diagram, a gap that is clearly visible but clearly wrong in a way that takes a moment to register. The valence band curves belong where the conduction band curves are. The conduction band curves belong where the valence band curves are. The labels are reversed from everything the fabrication engineer has ever seen. Priya taps the screen. "This is bismuth selenide," she says. "That inversion is not a drawing error. That inversion is the device. Let me show you exactly what band inversion means, and why it is the only physical mechanism that gives you conducting surface states that disorder, defects, or interface roughness cannot destroy. Once you see it, you will understand why no conventional superconductor can do what this material does." The fabrication engineer puts down his pen. Marcus opens his notebook.

Why It Matters

Every device decision in topological quantum hardware starts with a band structure. Not a crystal structure, not a composition specification, not a fabrication process window, though all of those matter. The band structure is the upstream constraint that everything else flows from, because the band structure is the physical record of what the material's electrons are doing, where they are allowed to go, and what quantum states they are forced to occupy. If the band structure has the right topology, the material's surface will conduct in a way that cannot be switched off. If it does not, no amount of refinement in fabrication will produce that property.

For engineers who trained on conventional semiconductor device physics, band theory is familiar territory. Valence bands, conduction bands, band gaps, Fermi levels, effective mass: these are the conceptual tools of transistor design, and engineers who have worked with silicon, gallium arsenide, or indium phosphide already have a working vocabulary. The challenge is that topological band theory uses the same vocabulary but assigns it a different and more fundamental meaning. The band gap in silicon is the energy gap that determines whether the material conducts electricity. The band gap in bismuth selenide is a topological gap whose character, not just its size, determines whether the surface conducts.

Understanding the difference between these two kinds of band gaps is the central conceptual work of this chapter.

The payoff is direct. Engineers who understand band inversion can read a band structure diagram and determine, from the band structure and the location of the inversion, whether a material is a topological insulator, a trivial insulator, or something in between. That is a practical, decision-relevant skill: it means being able to evaluate a material's claim in a journal paper, a conference presentation, or a vendor datasheet and determine whether the physics supports the engineering application. Every material specification in a topological device design is ultimately a band structure specification. This chapter gives the engineer the framework to write those specifications with precision.

The chapter begins with the simplest possible picture of electrons in a solid. It builds systematically through the nearly-free-electron model, tight-binding intuition, effective mass, density of states, and the classification of materials by their band gap, culminating in band inversion as the topological modification that changes everything. Along the way, the Brillouin zone is introduced as the engineer's primary navigational tool in momentum space, and the specific physics of heavy elements such as bismuth, lead, mercury, and tellurium is explained in terms of the strength of spin-orbit coupling that enables band inversion. The chapter closes with the HgTe/CdTe quantum well system, the two-dimensional electron gas formed at heterointerfaces, and the practical question of how an engineer reads a band diagram to identify whether band inversion has occurred.

The Free Electron Gas: A Useful Wrong Model

The simplest model of electrons in a metal is also, in some ways, the most instructive. Imagine removing every atom from a metal except the atomic cores, keeping only the free electrons that can move through the crystal. Then imagine that these electrons do not interact with one another at all, and that the atomic cores exert no potential on them. What you have is the free electron gas: a quantum mechanical system of non-interacting electrons confined to a box.

The free electron gas is wrong as a description of any real material. Electrons interact strongly with atoms and with each other. The lattice potential is not zero. But the free electron gas gets several things right that prove foundational. First, electrons fill energy states from the bottom up, following the Pauli exclusion principle: no two electrons can occupy the same quantum state. The energy of the highest occupied state at zero temperature is the Fermi energy. This quantity ranges from a few electron-volts in simple metals to values that depend on carrier concentration in semiconductors. The density of states at the Fermi energy, the number of available quantum states per unit energy per unit volume at the Fermi level, is the primary determinant of how a material responds to applied fields, phonon scattering, and external perturbations.

Second, the free electron gas predicts that all materials should be metals, because without a lattice potential, there are no forbidden energy regions, no band gaps, and electrons at the Fermi surface are always available to carry current. The fact that real materials include insulators and semiconductors is therefore a direct consequence of the lattice, and understanding why the lattice opens energy gaps is the first major step toward understanding band topology. The free electron gas is the baseline against which band structure effects are measured: it is what you would have if the crystal were not there, and band theory is the story of what the crystal does to that baseline.

Marcus, who spent a decade designing cryogenic control systems for silicon-based quantum hardware, knows the Fermi level as a device engineering parameter: it is the quantity you shift with doping to control transistor threshold voltages and carrier concentrations. What he is about to encounter is a deeper version of that same concept, one where the character of the states at and near the Fermi level, not just their density, determines whether a material is topologically trivial or non-trivial.

Diagram 4.1 - Free Electron Gas Energy vs. Momentum

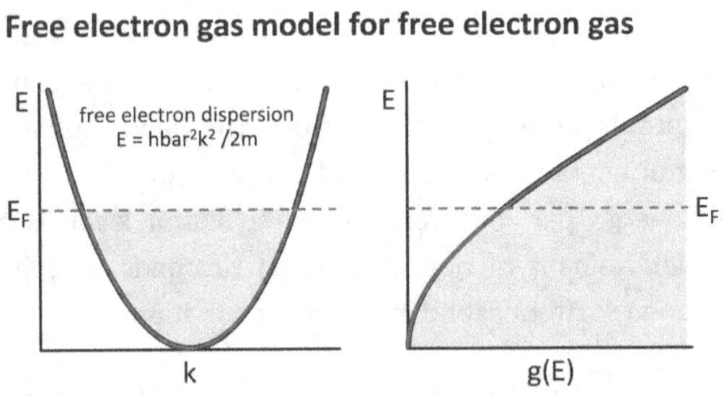

The Fermi energy sets an important engineering scale. In copper, one of the canonical free-electron-like metals, the Fermi energy is approximately 7 electron-volts, meaning that the highest occupied electronic states carry kinetic energies far larger than room temperature thermal energy (approximately 0.025 electron-volts). This is why metals conduct even at room temperature: the thermal smearing of the Fermi surface is small compared to the Fermi energy, and there are always plenty of electrons available at the band crossing energy to carry current. In a semiconductor like silicon, the situation is different: the Fermi level sits in a gap, and conduction requires thermal activation of electrons across that gap or deliberate introduction of dopant atoms to shift the Fermi level into the conduction band.

Understanding where the Fermi level sits relative to a material's band structure is the most basic diagnostic an engineer can perform on that material, and it determines everything from conductivity to optical absorption to the superconducting transition temperature. For topological materials, Fermi-level placement takes on an additional dimension: it determines whether the topological surface states, which exist at specific energies within the band gap of the topological insulator, are accessible to external probes and whether they contribute to transport in a device geometry. An engineer who wants to exploit the surface states of bismuth selenide must ensure that the bulk Fermi level lies within the bulk gap; otherwise, bulk conduction drowns the surface signal. That constraint is a band-engineering specification, and it starts with understanding the free-electron baseline and how the lattice modifies it.

The Periodic Lattice and How Band Gaps Form

The step from the free electron gas to real band structure is conceptually simple: add the periodic potential of the crystal lattice. When an electron wave travels through a periodic potential, it undergoes Bragg reflection at momenta that are commensurate with the lattice periodicity. At these special momenta, the electron wave can form two distinct standing waves with different spatial distributions relative to the lattice: one that concentrates electron probability density on the atomic cores, lowering its energy, and one that concentrates probability density between the cores, raising its energy. The energy difference between these two standing wave configurations is the band gap.

The RF engineer's intuitive version of this is a periodic waveguide: a transmission line with regularly spaced obstacles creates stop bands at frequencies where the wavelength matches twice the spacing between obstacles. Electron Bragg reflection is the exact quantum-mechanical equivalent. The periodicity of the lattice serves as the obstacle spacing, and the electron wavelength as the RF wavelength. At momenta where the de Broglie wavelength is commensurate with the lattice constant, the electron cannot propagate freely; instead, it is split into two energy branches separated by a gap, and that gap is a forbidden energy region in the electronic spectrum.

The nearly-free electron model captures this physics with a minimal perturbative treatment: start with the free electron parabola and add the smallest possible lattice potential as a perturbation. The result is a band structure that looks like the free-electron parabola almost everywhere, but with gaps opening at the Brillouin zone boundaries, at momenta that are exactly half of a reciprocal lattice vector. These gaps are the first appearance of band structure in the quantum mechanical sense: forbidden energy windows that separate allowed bands of electronic states. The size of the gap at a given zone boundary is proportional to the strength of the lattice potential at the corresponding Fourier component, which, in practical terms, means it depends on the chemistry of the atoms, their sizes, and their valences.

Diagram 4.2 - Band Gap Formation at the Brillouin Zone Boundary

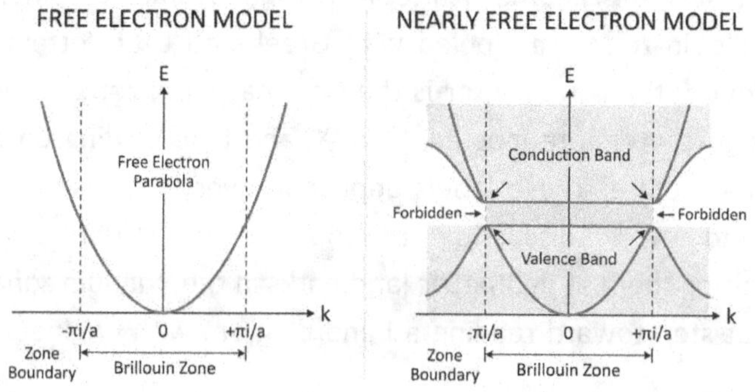

Caution: cenesss throwectuad Free-electronn-like parabola in a folded zone scheme.

Bloch's theorem is the mathematical statement that makes band theory rigorous. It states that the eigenstates of an electron in a periodic potential can always be written as a product of a plane wave and a function that has the periodicity of the lattice. The plane-wave part carries the crystal momentum, labeled k, which is a good quantum number in a periodic system, just as linear momentum is a good quantum number for a free particle. The periodic function part, the Bloch function, encodes all the information about how the electron wavefunction varies within a single unit cell. The key engineering insight is that crystal momentum k labels your position in the Brillouin zone, the fundamental navigational coordinate of the band structure.

The Brillouin zone is the unit cell of reciprocal space, the Fourier transform of the real-space crystal lattice. The crystal symmetry determines its shape: for a simple cubic lattice, it is a cube, for a face-centered cubic lattice, it is a truncated octahedron, for a hexagonal lattice, it is a hexagonal prism. The interior of the Brillouin zone contains the complete set of distinct crystal momenta, and the band structure, the set of allowed energy values as a function of k, is a map of the electronic structure plotted over this geometrical object. High-symmetry points in the Brillouin zone are labeled with Greek and Latin letters by convention: the zone center is the Gamma point; zone corners and edge centers are labeled K, M, X, and L depending on the crystal structure. These labels appear in every band structure plot and every discussion of topological invariants, and recognizing them as geometric landmarks in the Brillouin zone is the first step toward reading a band diagram with engineering fluency.

Diagram 4.3 - Brillouin Zone for FCC and Hexagonal Lattices

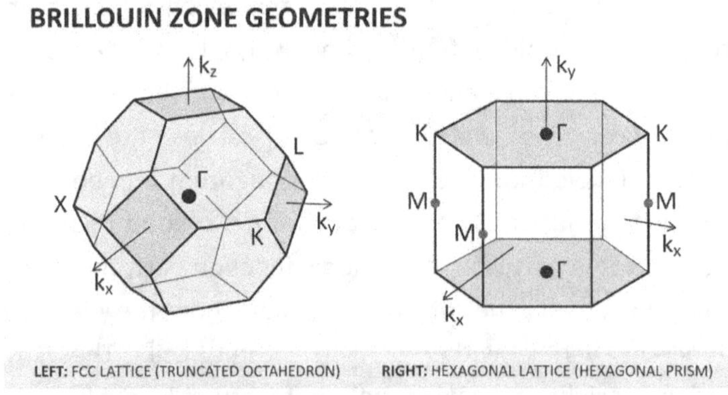

Tight-Binding: Atomic Orbitals Inside a Crystal

The nearly-free electron model starts from free electrons and adds the lattice. The tight-binding model starts from the opposite end: it begins with electrons localized on individual atoms and asks what happens when those atoms are brought close enough together that their orbitals begin to overlap. The tight-binding approach is the engineering-intuitive entry point to band theory because it maps directly onto the language of atomic orbitals that chemists and device physicists already use. It is also the framework that makes band inversion intelligible, because band inversion is explicitly a story about which atomic orbital character sits at which energy in the crystal.

The linear combination of atomic orbitals (LCAO) picture is the simplest version of the tight-binding model. Consider two hydrogen atoms brought together to form a hydrogen molecule. Each atom contributes one 1s orbital. When the atoms are adjacent, the orbitals overlap, and the two eigenstates of the combined system are the bonding combination, in which the wavefunctions add constructively between the atoms, and the antibonding combination, in which they interfere destructively. The bonding state is lower in energy than the isolated atomic orbital because the electron probability density is high between the two positive nuclear charges, providing a stabilizing electrostatic contribution. The antibonding state is higher in energy.

Extend this to a crystal with N atoms, each contributing one orbital, and the N single-atom energy levels spread into a band of N closely-spaced levels. In the limit of an infinite crystal, this band becomes a continuous energy distribution, the energy band. The overlap integral between adjacent orbitals determines the band width: a large overlap indicates a wide band, and a small overlap indicates a narrow band. A material with very narrow bands, such as the d-orbital bands of transition metal oxides, has electrons that are nearly localized on individual atoms and behaves differently from a material with wide bands, such as the s-orbital band of a simple metal, where electrons are highly delocalized.

For topological materials, the orbital character of the bands is not just a technical detail; it is the central fact. In bismuth selenide, which is the canonical three-dimensional topological insulator, the relevant bands near the Fermi level have mixed bismuth p-orbital and selenium p-orbital character. In a conventional arrangement, the selenium-derived states would sit at lower energy, closer to the valence band, and the bismuth-derived states would sit higher, closer to the conduction band. This ordering reflects the electronegativity difference between the two elements: selenium is more electronegative and pulls electron density toward itself, lowering the energy of selenium-derived states. What makes bismuth selenide topological is that strong spin-orbit coupling in the bismuth atom, which will be discussed in detail shortly, reverses this ordering. The bismuth p-orbital states are pushed below the selenium states in the vicinity of the Gamma point of the Brillouin zone. The band character has been inverted.

The tight-binding picture makes this concrete. Band inversion is not a mysterious quantum effect; it is a specific rearrangement of which atomic orbital character occupies which energy level in the crystal, driven by a physical interaction, spin-orbit coupling, that is strong enough to overcome the chemical ordering that would otherwise apply. The inverted arrangement cannot be continuously deformed back to the normal arrangement without closing the band gap and going through a phase transition, which is precisely what makes it topological. The topology is in the character of the bands, not just their positions.

Diagram 4.4 - LCAO Band Formation and Orbital Character

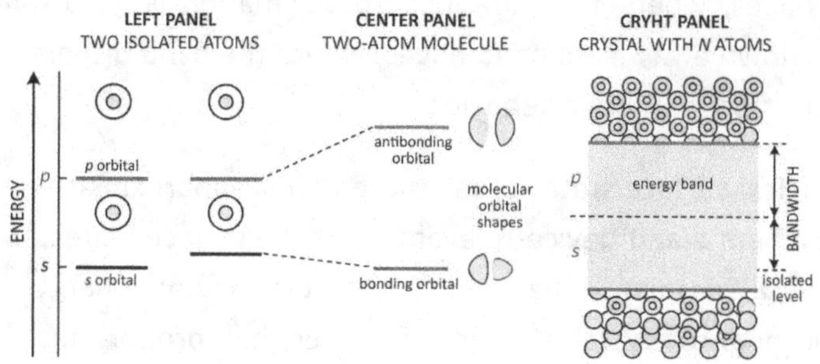

Effective Mass and What the Band Curvature Tells You

The curvature of an energy band at a given crystal momentum k is one of the most engineering-relevant quantities in solid-state physics. It determines the effective mass of carriers in that band: a high curvature implies a small effective mass, which means carriers accelerate quickly in an applied electric field, yielding high carrier mobility. A low curvature means a large effective mass and sluggish carriers. In conventional semiconductor physics, this parameter sets the speed limit for transistors, and optimizing it is a central task in semiconductor device engineering.

The formal definition of effective mass follows directly from the band dispersion: the effective mass m* is inversely proportional to the second derivative of the energy with respect to crystal momentum. For a parabolic band, the effective mass is constant. For a non-parabolic band, the effective mass varies with k, making carrier dynamics more complex. The effective mass framework allows engineers to treat electrons in quantum-mechanical bands as classical particles with a modified mass. This approximation works extremely well near band edges, where the parabolic approximation is valid, and breaks down away from band edges, where the band dispersion deviates from parabolic behavior.

Topological surface states break the parabolic approximation in a fundamental and device-relevant way. The surface states of a topological insulator have a linear dispersion: energy is proportional to crystal momentum rather than proportional to its square. This is the same dispersion as that of a photon or a massless relativistic particle, and it is described by the Dirac equation rather than the Schrödinger equation for a parabolic band. A linear dispersion corresponds to zero effective mass in the conventional sense, or more precisely, to an effective mass that is velocity-divided-by-carrier-energy. This quantity vanishes as the carrier energy approaches the Dirac point.

The practical consequence is extreme carrier mobility. In bismuth selenide, the surface-state carriers have mobilities exceeding 10,000 square centimeters per volt-second at low temperatures, compared to approximately 1,500 square centimeters per volt-second for electrons in silicon at room temperature. This is not primarily a temperature effect; it reflects the linear dispersion and the spin-momentum locking of the surface-state carriers, which suppresses backscattering that limits mobility in conventional semiconductors. An electron in the topological surface state of bismuth selenide moving in the positive k direction has its spin locked perpendicular to its momentum; reversing its momentum direction requires reversing its spin, which requires a magnetic perturbation. Non-magnetic disorder cannot accomplish this reversal, so the topological surface carriers are immune to the primary scattering mechanism that limits conventional transistor performance.

Diagram 4.5 - Parabolic vs. Linear Band Dispersion

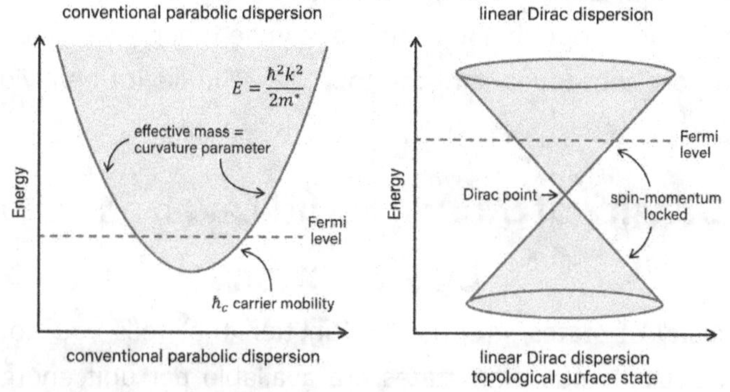

The effective mass concept also explains why band engineering, the deliberate modification of a material's band structure through alloying, strain, confinement, or heterostructure geometry, is such a powerful tool for topological device design. In the HgTe/CdTe quantum well system, which will be examined in detail later in this chapter, the effective mass of the HgTe carriers is negative in the conventional band ordering. When the quantum well thickness crosses a critical threshold, the band ordering inverts, the effective mass changes sign, and the material transitions from a trivial insulator to a two-dimensional topological insulator with conducting edge states. The engineering control parameter is the quantum well thickness, a fabrication specification that can be controlled to within a single atomic monolayer using molecular beam epitaxy.

Marcus, thinking through the device implications, recognizes the pattern immediately: it is the same logic as controlling threshold voltage in a conventional transistor by adjusting gate oxide thickness and channel doping, but the underlying physics is qualitatively different. In the transistor case, you are shifting the Fermi level relative to a fixed band structure. In the HgTe quantum well case, you are changing the topology of the band structure itself. Once the band inversion occurs, the edge states appear not as an optional feature that can be tuned away but as a mandatory consequence of the topology. The device behavior is protected.

Density of States, Fermi Level, and Classification

The density of states, g(E), is the function that tells you how many electronic quantum states are available per unit energy per unit volume at a given energy E. It is the most direct connection between band structure and the measurable properties of a material, because it determines how many carriers are available to participate in electrical conduction, optical transitions, superconducting pairing, and every other physical process that involves electrons near the Fermi level.

In a three-dimensional free electron gas, the density of states grows as the square root of energy, reflecting the increasing number of k-space states on the surface of a sphere of radius proportional to the square root of E. In real materials with band structure, the density of states develops van Hove singularities, sharp features at energies where the band dispersion has zero slope, and states pile up. These singularities appear at band edges, at high-symmetry k-points where bands are flat, and at saddle points in the dispersion where the band has positive curvature along one k direction and negative curvature along another. Van Hove singularities are not mathematical artifacts; they are observable features in optical spectra, tunneling measurements, and angle-resolved photoemission data, and they mark the energies where a material's electronic response is strongest.

The classification of materials by their band structure reduces to a simple question: where is the Fermi level relative to the density of states? For a metal, the Fermi level sits in a region of non-zero density of states, meaning there are always available states at infinitesimally small energies above the Fermi level into which carriers can be excited by an applied field. The material conducts in the zero-temperature limit. For a semiconductor, the Fermi level sits in a band gap, a region of zero density of states, with the valence band edge below the Fermi level and the conduction band edge above it. Conduction requires thermal activation across the gap, and conductivity is exponentially sensitive to both the gap size and temperature. For an insulator, the same physics applies, but the gap is large enough, typically more than 3 electron-volts, that room-temperature thermal activation produces negligible carrier density.

Diamond is the wide-gap extreme: a band gap of approximately 5.5 electron-volts means that diamond is essentially a perfect insulator at any temperature below its decomposition point. Silicon has a gap of 1.1 electron-volts, placing it squarely in the semiconductor range where room-temperature conductivity can be engineered over many orders of magnitude through doping. Gallium arsenide, used extensively in high-frequency electronics and photonics, has a direct band gap of approximately 1.4 electron-volts, making it an efficient light emitter. Bismuth selenide has a bulk band gap of approximately 0.3 electron-volts, is semiconductor-scale in size, but exhibits topological character, producing conducting surface states that have no analog in any conventional semiconductor.

Diagram 4.6 - Density of States for Metal, Semiconductor, and Topological Insulator

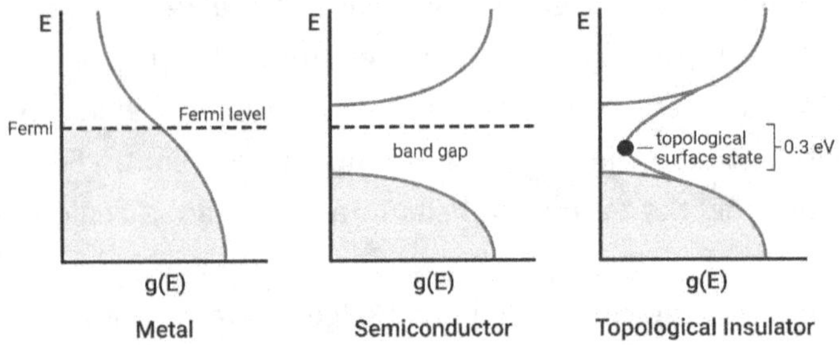

The Fermi level placement in a topological insulator is a critical device design parameter. The bulk of bismuth selenide is a semiconductor with a 0.3 electron-volt gap. Still, real bismuth selenide crystals are almost always naturally n-type because selenium vacancies and bismuth antisites introduce donor states that push the Fermi level into the conduction band. When the Fermi level is in the conduction band, bulk carriers dominate transport, and the contribution of the topological surface states to measured electrical properties is obscured. Achieving Fermi-level control, placing the bulk Fermi level cleanly within the bulk band gap so that surface transport dominates, is one of the central materials engineering challenges for bismuth selenide device applications. Strategies include compensation doping with acceptors, alloying with calcium or indium to modify the native defect chemistry, and electrostatic gating of thin films. Each of these approaches is a band-engineering intervention: a deliberate modification of the Fermi-level position within the band structure.

Band Inversion: The Key Topological Modification

Band inversion is the concept that distinguishes topological materials from all conventional material classes, and it warrants careful treatment because it is often described in terms that sound more mysterious than they are. A band inversion is simply this: in a conventional ordered band structure, the bands at a given k-point have a specific energy ordering that reflects the atomic orbital character of the states, with s-type states typically above p-type states in an anion-derived band picture, or with lighter-element-derived states above heavier-element-derived states, depending on the specific chemistry. A band inversion occurs when a physical interaction, most commonly spin-orbit coupling, is strong enough to push one of these bands past the other, reversing the expected ordering.

The map inversion analogy captures the key point. Imagine a map in which each territory is labeled as land or water. Now imagine inverting the map: every territory that was land becomes water, and every territory that was water becomes land. The territories look the same, the borders look the same, but the inside-outside relationship has been reversed at every point. A topological band inversion is precisely this kind of reversal in the character of the bands. At the Gamma point of bismuth selenide, the band that in a trivial material would have selenium s-character sits above the band that would have bismuth p-character, but in bismuth selenide, the ordering is reversed. The bismuth p-character band sits below the selenium s-character band at the zone center.

The crucial physical consequence of band inversion arises when you cross the boundary between an inverted material and a non-inverted one, specifically at the surface of the crystal where the topological insulator meets the vacuum or an interface material. The vacuum is a trivial insulator with an enormous band gap and no band inversion. Bismuth selenide is a topological insulator with a 0.3 electron-volt gap and band inversion. As you move from the bulk of the bismuth selenide to the surface and then into the vacuum, the band character must change from inverted to non-inverted. This character reversal cannot happen abruptly: it requires the band gap to close at the interface, and a closed gap means a conducting state. The surface state is the mandatory quantum mechanical consequence of the gap closing at the boundary between topologically distinct materials.

The statement that the surface state is mandatory, not optional, is the engineering headline. In a conventional semiconductor, surface states exist but are extrinsic: they arise from dangling bonds, reconstruction, or impurity chemistry, and can, in principle, be passivated or removed by surface treatment. The topological surface state of bismuth selenide is intrinsic: it is required by the topology of the bulk band structure. Any surface treatment, passivation, or non-magnetic disorder cannot remove it. It is protected by time-reversal symmetry, and the only way to destroy it is to break time-reversal symmetry by applying a magnetic field or depositing a magnetic overlayer, or to close the bulk band gap by driving a phase transition. For a qubit substrate, this protection is the primary figure of merit: it means the conducting surface states will survive the fabrication process, the interface chemistry with superconducting contacts, and the inevitable disorder in any realistic device.

Diagram 4.7 - Band Inversion Before and After: Conventional vs. Topological Insulator

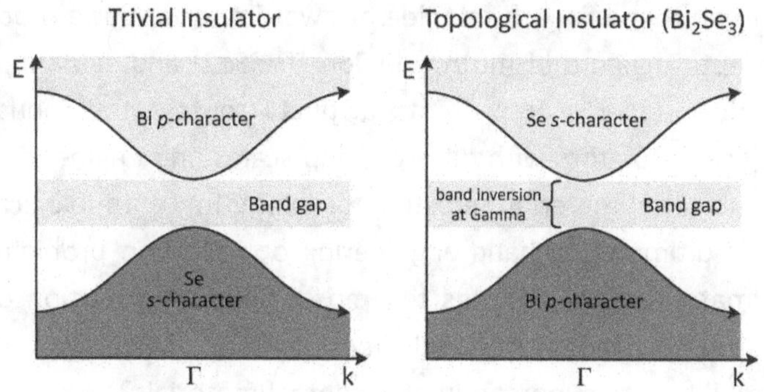

The band gap size in the inverted material matters in specific ways for device applications. A larger gap provides more robust protection of the surface states against thermal excitation of bulk carriers, which is one reason the room-temperature topological insulator is a material science goal rather than a given. Bismuth selenide's 0.3-electron-volt gap means that at room temperature (roughly 300 K), corresponding to approximately 0.025 electron-volts of thermal energy, bulk carrier excitation is not negligible, and bulk conduction competes with surface conduction. For cryogenic applications, which include every topological qubit architecture currently under development, this is not a problem. At dilution refrigerator temperatures below 100 millikelvin, thermal excitation across a 0.3-electron-volt gap is negligible, and the bulk is effectively insulating. The surface states are then the only conducting channel.

For room-temperature sensing applications, the gap size constraint motivates the search for topological insulators with larger bulk gaps. The ternary compound bismuth antimony (Bi1-

xSbx), the first experimentally confirmed three-dimensional topological insulator (as confirmed by the Princeton group in 2008 using angle-resolved photoemission spectroscopy), has a smaller gap than bismuth selenide but was important as a proof of concept. Thallium bismuth selenide (TlBiSe2) and samarium hexaboride (SmB6) represent distinct routes to robust topological insulators with different gap scales and engineering trade-offs. The material selection problem for a topological device is ultimately a band-engineering optimization problem: which material system yields the most useful combination of gap size, surface-state velocity, carrier density, and compatibility with superconducting contact materials?

Heavy Elements and Band-Inverting Spin-Orbit Coupling

Spin-orbit coupling is the physical interaction that drives band inversion in topological insulators, and understanding its origin and the factors that make it strong in certain elements is essential for determining which materials are topological and why. Spin-orbit coupling is a relativistic effect: it arises because, as seen from the electron's reference frame, an electron moving through the electric field of an atomic nucleus experiences a magnetic field. This effective magnetic field acts on the electron's spin, coupling the spin degree of freedom to the orbital motion. The energy splitting produced by this coupling scales approximately as the fourth power of the atomic number Z, which means it is negligible for light elements and becomes enormous for heavy elements like bismuth (Z = 83), lead (Z = 82), mercury (Z = 80), and tellurium (Z = 52).

In bismuth, the spin-orbit splitting of the p-orbital states is approximately 1.5 electron-volts. To put this in context, the total band gap of bismuth selenide is only 0.3 electron-volts. The spin-orbit interaction in bismuth is not a small correction to the band structure; it is the dominant energy scale that determines the band ordering. This is why topological insulators tend to be heavy-element compounds: the spin-orbit coupling must be strong enough to overcome the chemical energy differences between different orbital characters, reversing the conventional ordering and producing band inversion. Light elements have spin-orbit coupling on the scale of millielectron-volts to tens of millielectron-volts, far too small to invert bands separated by electron-volt-scale chemical energy differences.

The materials engineer's practical guide to topological insulator candidates is therefore a list of heavy-element compounds with specific structural features. Bismuth-based compounds (bismuth selenide Bi2Se3, bismuth telluride Bi2Te3, antimony telluride Sb2Te3, and their alloys) are the most extensively studied family because they combine strong bismuth spin-orbit coupling with a layered crystal structure that facilitates cleavage and surface preparation. Mercury-based compounds, particularly mercury telluride (HgTe), are topological in the bulk form, a fact first predicted theoretically by Bernevig, Hughes, and Zhang in 2006 and experimentally confirmed in the HgTe/CdTe quantum-well geometry by Koenig and collaborators in 2007. Lead-based compounds, including lead selenide (PbSe) and the alloy Pb1-xSnxSe, cross a topological phase boundary as a function of the tin fraction x, making them band-engineering-tunable topological systems.

Diagram 4.8 - Spin-Orbit Coupling Strength vs. Atomic Number

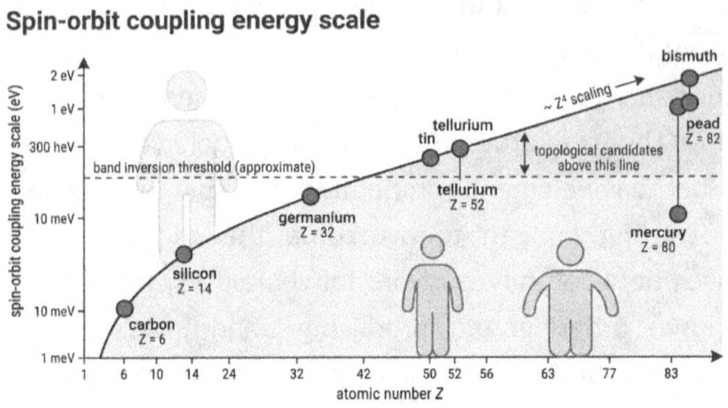

The crystal structure of bismuth selenide deserves mention because it provides the structural context that enables band inversion. Bismuth selenide adopts a layered rhombohedral crystal structure belonging to the R-3m space group, in which the basic building block is a quintuple layer: five atomic planes arranged as selenium-bismuth-selenium-bismuth-selenium, stacked along the c-axis. Adjacent quintuple layers are held together by weak van der Waals interactions, making bismuth selenide easy to cleave along the interlayer plane. This cleavage produces atomically flat surfaces with well-defined surface terminations, which are crucial for surface-sensitive measurements and for device fabrication that requires intimate contact between the surface state and an adjacent functional layer. The Bi2Se3 crystal structure is also centrosymmetric, meaning it has both time-reversal symmetry and spatial inversion symmetry. Both of these symmetries play important roles in determining the material's topological classification, as will be discussed in more detail in Chapter 5.

The engineering implication of the heavy-element requirement is that topological insulator devices will never be silicon-compatible without a deliberate heterostructure strategy. Bismuth selenide is a III-V semiconductor analog grown on substrates that are quite different from silicon: common substrates for epitaxial bismuth selenide include bismuth telluride, strontium titanate, indium arsenide, and sapphire, with lattice matching and surface chemistry as the primary constraints. Lead-based topological systems have their own substrate requirements. Mercury-based quantum wells require II-VI molecular beam epitaxy, a specialized growth capability not available in mainstream semiconductor foundries. This material incompatibility is a genuine manufacturing challenge and an engineering motivation for developing topological-insulator device architectures that minimize the number of interfaces with conventional semiconductor layers.

The HgTe/CdTe Quantum Well: The BHZ Laboratory

The HgTe/CdTe quantum well system occupies a special place in the history of topological materials because it was the first system in which a topological phase transition was predicted with specific quantitative parameters, and then experimentally confirmed with precisely the predicted signatures. The prediction was made by Bernevig, Hughes, and Zhang (BHZ) in a Science paper published in December 2006. The experimental confirmation came in 2007 from Markus Koenig and colleagues at the University of Wurzburg, based on transport data from Laurens Molenkamp's group, which showed edge-state conduction with a quantized conductance of exactly 2e^2/h at zero magnetic field in quantum wells thicker than the critical thickness. It was, in the words of the community, the first engineered topological insulator.

The BHZ model is built on a simple observation about the bulk band structures of HgTe and CdTe. Cadmium telluride is a normal semiconductor with a band gap of approximately 1.5 electron-volts: the gamma-6 band, derived from s-type orbitals, sits above the gamma-8 band, derived from p-type orbitals, at the zone center. This is the conventional ordering. Mercury telluride is a topological semimetal with an inverted band structure: the gamma-6 and gamma-8 bands are reversed at the zone center, with the p-type gamma-8 band above the s-type gamma-6 band. The inversion is driven by the enormous spin-orbit coupling of mercury (Z = 80). In bulk HgTe, this inversion makes the material a zero-gap semiconductor, a semimetal with touching bands rather than a gapped insulator, because additional symmetry considerations prevent a gap from opening without breaking some crystal symmetry.

The quantum well geometry solves this problem by breaking the bulk symmetry in a controlled way. When a thin layer of HgTe is sandwiched between layers of CdTe, quantum confinement quantizes the electronic states in the growth direction, converting the three-dimensional bulk band structure into a series of two-dimensional subbands. The critical insight of BHZ is that the relative ordering of the E1 and HH1 subbands (the lowest electron-like and heavy-hole subbands, respectively) depends on the thickness of the HgTe layer. For thin HgTe layers, below approximately 6.3 nanometers at zero temperature, the CdTe-like normal ordering is preserved: E1 is above HH1 in energy, the system is a trivial two-dimensional insulator, and no edge states exist. For thick HgTe layers, above the critical thickness, the HgTe band inversion wins out over the confinement energy, the E1 and HH1 subbands switch ordering, and the system becomes a two-dimensional topological insulator, the quantum spin Hall insulator, with conducting edge states that carry quantized conductance.

Diagram 4.9 - HgTe/CdTe Quantum Well and Subband Ordering

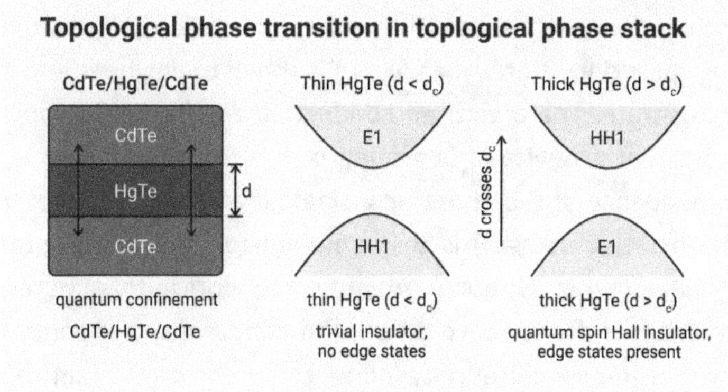

The experimental signature that Koenig's group measured was a two-terminal conductance of exactly 2e^2/h (approximately 77.5 microsiemens) in a Hall-bar geometry at millikelvin temperatures, in the absence of an external magnetic field, for quantum-well samples with HgTe thicknesses above the critical value. Below the critical thickness, the conductance dropped to zero in the insulating bulk gap. Above the critical thickness, the quantized conductance was observed, consistent with a single pair of helical edge modes, one on each edge of the sample, each carrying a conductance of e^2/h. The quantization to better than 1 percent accuracy is a direct signature of topological protection: the edge modes cannot scatter with each other, because they propagate in opposite directions on opposite edges, and any backscattering path would require traversing the bulk insulating region, and they cannot scatter with non-magnetic disorder, because the helical spin texture of the edge state blocks backscattering. The conductance is therefore perfectly quantized regardless of sample geometry, edge roughness, or impurity concentration, within the limits imposed by the bulk gap.

For Axiom's engineering team, the HgTe/CdTe result is not a historical curiosity; it is a proof of principle. The quantum spin Hall insulator edge states are the two-dimensional analog of the topological surface states that Axiom is trying to engineer into a qubit substrate. The quantized conductance is the measurable signature that a device is operating in the topological regime. The dependence of the phase on a single fabrication parameter (quantum well thickness) is the template for how topological phase engineering is done: identify the critical parameter, characterize its dependence on growth conditions, and control it to within the specification window required to maintain the topological phase. Molecular beam epitaxy, the growth technique used to fabricate HgTe/CdTe quantum wells, can control layer thickness to within one atomic monolayer, and the critical thickness window is on the order of a few tenths of a nanometer, making this a challenging yet manufacturable specification.

The 2D Electron Gas at Heterointerfaces

The two-dimensional electron gas (2DEG) is one of the most important physical systems in condensed matter physics and device engineering. It arises at the interface between two materials with different band structures. When the band alignment places a conduction-band minimum of one material below the Fermi level at the interface, electrons accumulate in a thin quantum well, forming a quasi-two-dimensional conducting layer. The electrons are free to move in the plane of the interface but are quantum-confined in the direction perpendicular to it, reducing their motion from three to two dimensions.

The canonical 2DEG systems in semiconductor technology are the AlGaAs/GaAs heterojunction and the Si/SiGe heterostructure. In the AlGaAs/GaAs system, the larger band gap of AlGaAs and the band offset between the two materials cause electrons donated by donors in the AlGaAs barrier to fall into the GaAs channel, forming a 2DEG with electron mobilities exceeding 10 million square centimeters per volt-second at cryogenic temperatures. These extraordinary mobilities arise because the ionized donors are spatially separated from the 2DEG channel by the AlGaAs spacer layer, thereby removing the primary source of Coulomb scattering. The 2DEG in GaAs is the physical substrate in which the integer and fractional quantum Hall effects were first extensively studied and in which current semiconductor qubit architectures based on quantum dots are implemented.

Topological surface states can be understood as a special type of 2DEG that forms at the surface of a topological insulator, with two crucial differences from conventional 2DEGs. First, the formation mechanism is topological rather than electrostatic: the surface 2DEG arises from an inverted bulk band structure, not from a specific band alignment or modulation-doped configuration. This means it cannot be removed by tuning gate voltages or changing interface chemistry. Second, the dispersion of the surface 2DEG is linear (Dirac) rather than parabolic, which gives it the extreme mobility and spin-momentum locking properties discussed earlier. A conventional 2DEG at a GaAs heterojunction has parabolic dispersion and no spin-momentum locking; the carriers can scatter in any direction. The topological surface state has a linear dispersion and a helical spin texture; the carriers can scatter only forward or sideways, not backward, unless they encounter a magnetic perturbation.

Diagram 4.10 - Two-Dimensional Electron Gas at a Heterointerface

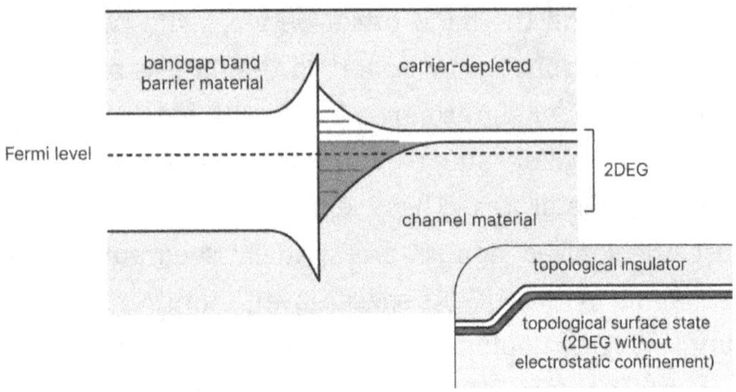

The 2DEG geometry is directly relevant to the integration of topological materials into quantum hardware. Topological qubit architectures being developed at Axiom and other organizations, including Microsoft's Station Q and Delft University, require the topological surface states to be coupled to superconducting contact layers. The coupling is achieved at an interface: either the superconductor is deposited on top of the topological insulator, forming a heterointerface where the superconducting proximity effect can convert the topological surface states into a topological superconducting state, or the topological material is grown as a quantum well within a heterostructure that includes superconducting contacts integrated into the device geometry. In either case, the quality of the 2D conducting layer at the interface, its carrier density, mobility, and freedom from disorder-induced localization, determines whether the topological quantum states survive the device integration process.

The parameter that characterizes the quality of a 2DEG, whether topological or conventional, is the mean free path: the average distance an electron travels between scattering events. A long mean free path means low disorder, high mobility, and coherent quantum transport; a short mean free path means strong disorder, carrier localization, and loss of quantum coherence. For the topological surface state 2DEG, the relevant scattering mechanism is magnetic impurities rather than structural disorder, because only magnetic perturbations can flip the electron spin and break the time-reversal symmetry protection. A bismuth selenide surface-state 2DEG with no magnetic contamination and high crystalline quality will have a mean free path of hundreds of nanometers to several micrometers at cryogenic temperatures, which is more than sufficient for the device dimensions required by current topological qubit designs.

Reading a Band Diagram: ARPES and Band Inversion

Angle-resolved photoemission spectroscopy (ARPES) is the gold standard technique for direct experimental measurement of a material's band structure. The basic physical process is the photoelectric effect: UV or soft X-ray photons illuminate the sample surface, ejecting photoelectrons, which are collected by an electron spectrometer. By measuring both the kinetic energy of the photoelectrons and the angles at which they are emitted, the spectrometer can reconstruct the binding energy and crystal momentum of the electronic states from which they came. The result is a direct image of the electronic band structure: a plot of intensity in the energy-momentum plane that shows which states are occupied, where the Fermi level lies, and the band dispersion.

ARPES is surface-sensitive because photoelectrons originate from within the top few nanometers of the sample surface. This surface sensitivity is a feature, not a limitation, when studying topological insulators: it means ARPES directly images the surface states rather than the bulk bands. For bismuth selenide, ARPES images taken at the surface show a bright V-shaped feature in the gap region, the famous Dirac cone of the topological surface states. The Dirac cone is the ARPES signature of band inversion: it represents the linear dispersion of surface-state carriers, the crossing at the Dirac-point energy, and the helical spin texture that distinguishes topological surface states from conventional surface bands. The cone sits within the bulk band gap, confirming that it is not a bulk feature but a genuine surface phenomenon, and it connects, without a gap, to both the valence and conduction bands above and below the gap, reflecting the boundary-state character of the surface mode.

The 2008 ARPES measurement of bismuth selenide by the Hasan group at Princeton University was the first clear experimental demonstration of a topological surface state Dirac cone in a three-dimensional material. The measurement showed the predicted conical dispersion, confirmed the location of the Dirac point within the bulk band gap, and established that the cone was present on all measured crystal surfaces, consistent with the topological prediction that the surface state must appear on every surface of a topological insulator. Subsequent ARPES measurements with spin resolution confirmed the spin-momentum locking: electrons on the left side of the Dirac cone have spin pointing up, electrons on the right side have spin pointing down, and the spin rotates as you go around the cone, exactly as predicted for a time-reversal-symmetric topological surface state.

Diagram 4.11 - ARPES Setup and Dirac Cone Measurement

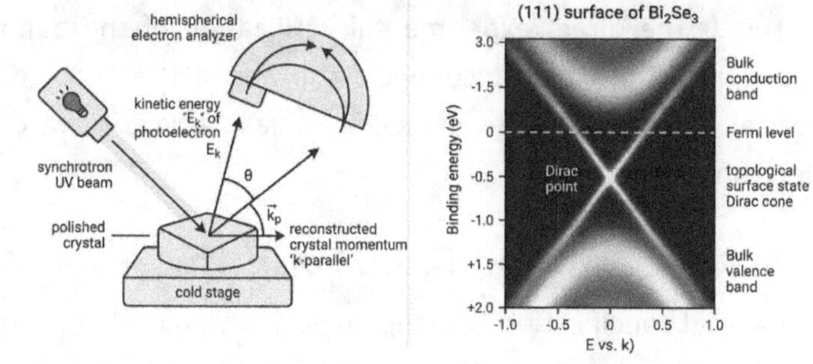

ARPES diagram (111) surface in an executive technical setup

For the engineering reader, the key skill is to look at an ARPES spectrum and determine whether band inversion has occurred. The diagnostic is the Dirac cone in the gap: if there is a cone, the material is topologically nontrivial in the gap region around it. If there is no cone, the material is trivial. The energy location of the Dirac point relative to the Fermi level tells you whether the surface states are accessible to transport (Fermi level in or near the gap, Dirac point within the accessible energy window) or buried under bulk conduction (Fermi level in the bulk conduction band). The spin resolution of the cone, confirmed by spin-ARPES measurements, tells you whether the time-reversal symmetry protection is intact, which is the prerequisite for the disorder immunity that makes topological surface states engineering-relevant.

ARPES also reveals band inversion directly through orbital-character mapping. Advanced ARPES measurements using circularly polarized light or photon-energy-dependent measurements can distinguish the orbital character of bands at different k-points, identifying which bands are s-type and which are p-type. In bismuth selenide, these measurements confirm that at the Gamma point, the band ordering is inverted: the state with bismuth p-orbital character sits below the Fermi level, where the selenium-derived state should be, and vice versa. This is the direct experimental verification of the band inversion prediction, and it connects the abstract concept of topological band ordering to a specific, measurable feature of the electronic structure.

What Can We Build With This?

Every material specification in a topological device design is, at its foundation, a band structure specification. Understanding band inversion, band gaps, effective mass, and Fermi level placement gives the engineer the vocabulary to translate between material properties and device performance. This section describes three specific engineering workflows that follow directly from the concepts developed in this chapter.

The first workflow is topological insulator screening. Given a candidate material, the engineer wants to know whether it is topologically non-trivial before investing resources in device fabrication. The screening checklist has three items: first, does the material contain heavy elements (Z> approximately 50) with strong spin-orbit coupling? Second, does the bulk band structure show band inversion at one or more high-symmetry k-points in the Brillouin zone, with an inverted number of k-points that makes the topological invariant Z2 equal to one? Third, does ARPES data show a Dirac cone in the bulk band gap on the cleaved surface? A positive answer to all three items is strong evidence for a topological insulator. The first criterion can be assessed solely from the composition. The second requires a band-structure calculation, either via density functional theory or a tight-binding model, and a relevant band-character analysis. The third requires experimentation, and it is the one that Priya Nair reaches for when a fabrication partner asks whether bismuth selenide is really doing what she says it is: the ARPES spectrum is the evidence.

The second workflow is band engineering for topological phase control. The HgTe/CdTe quantum well demonstrated that the topological phase can be turned on or off by controlling a single fabrication parameter, the quantum well thickness. This approach generalizes: in many topological material systems, the band inversion can be controlled through composition (the tin fraction in Pb1-xSnxSe), applied strain (uniaxial or biaxial strain changes the crystal symmetry and can shift the relative band energies), electric field (gating a thin topological insulator film shifts the Fermi level and can drive a topological to trivial phase transition in systems near the phase boundary), or temperature (some materials are topological at low temperature and trivial at room temperature). Engineering the topological phase means identifying which of these parameters is practically controllable in the fabrication process, characterizing the phase boundary as a function of that parameter, and targeting a point safely within the topological phase with enough margin to survive process variation.

The third workflow is Fermi-level engineering to achieve surface-transport dominance. A topological insulator whose bulk Fermi level is in the conduction band will behave like a semiconductor with a conducting surface coating; the bulk carriers will dominate transport, and the surface state contribution will be unresolvable. Achieving surface-dominated transport requires placing the Fermi level in the bulk gap through compensation doping, alloying, or gating. In bismuth selenide, the relevant compensation strategy is introducing calcium (Ca) or indium (In) dopants that act as acceptors to counterbalance the native n-type behavior from selenium vacancies. The target specification is a bulk resistivity above approximately 1 ohm-centimeter at the device operating temperature, corresponding to fewer than approximately 10^17 thermally activated carriers per cubic centimeter. This is a conventional semiconductor doping specification applied to an unconventional material. It demonstrates that topological materials are not exempt from the practical constraints of materials processing: they require the same attention to defect chemistry, doping profiles, and Fermi-level control as any other device material, with the added requirement that the bulk gap remain intact to protect the topological surface states.

Diagram 4.12 - Engineering Workflow: Reading a Band Diagram for Topological Character

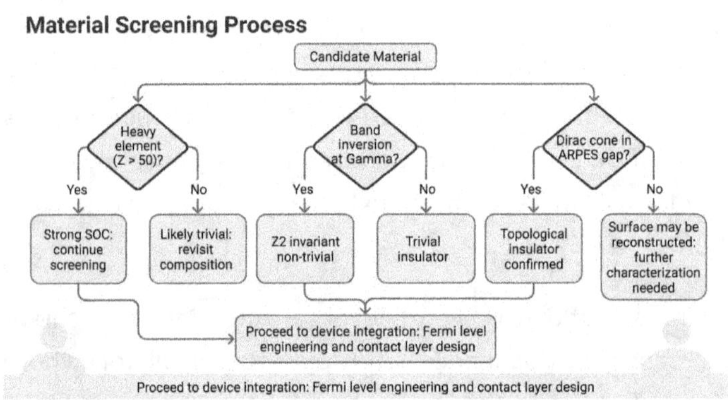

Beyond these three workflows, band structure understanding enables a fourth meta-skill: evaluating claims. The field of topological materials is fast-moving, and new material candidates are reported regularly in the literature. An engineer with a working understanding of band inversion, topological invariants, and ARPES interpretation can read a new paper, locate the band-structure figure, and independently assess whether the reported material is likely to behave as a topological insulator in a real device geometry rather than in an idealized measurement configuration. This evaluative skill, distinguishing physical reality from experimental artifacts or theoretical idealizations, is what Priya means when she says that every material specification is ultimately a band-structure specification. It is not a statement about mathematics. It is a statement about engineering judgment.

Takeaway

Band theory is the language of topological materials, and the central word in that language is band inversion. A conventional insulator has a band gap whose size determines its conductivity. A topological insulator has a band gap whose character, specifically the inversion of orbital labels across the gap, determines the existence of conducting surface states that cannot be removed. The inversion arises from spin-orbit coupling, which scales as the fourth power of the atomic number and reaches device-relevant magnitudes only in compounds containing heavy elements such as bismuth, lead, and mercury, as well as their chalcogenide partners.

The Brillouin zone is the engineer's roadmap in momentum space. Every band structure plot is a map of the Brillouin zone, and reading a band structure diagram to identify band inversion, locate the Fermi level, assess the effective mass, and find the topological surface state Dirac cone is a skill that translates directly into material selection, device specification, and experimental verification. ARPES is the technique that makes this reading experimental: it directly images the band structure, shows the Dirac cone in the gap when the material is topological, and confirms spin-momentum locking when spin resolution is applied.

The HgTe/CdTe quantum well system demonstrated that topological phases can be engineered through a single fabrication parameter, establishing the template for topological phase engineering: identify the control parameter, characterize the phase boundary, and target a robust point within the topological phase with sufficient process margin. The two-dimensional electron gas formed at topological heterointerfaces is the active medium for device transport, and its quality, characterized by carrier mobility and mean free path, sets the performance floor for any topological device architecture that relies on coherent surface transport.

The next chapter takes the concepts developed here, specifically band inversion, topological invariants, and the role of crystal symmetry, and builds the mathematical framework that makes topological protection precise. Chapter 5 introduces the Z2 topological invariant, the Berry phase as a geometric quantity in momentum space, and the formal connection between bulk topology and boundary states known as the bulk-boundary correspondence. That framework is what turns "the band character is inverted" from a descriptive observation into a quantitative, computable, and engineering-predictive statement. Sasha Korolev will take over the exposition at that point, because what comes next requires the kind of precision that only a theorist who has thought carefully about what the math actually guarantees can deliver with confidence.

5 What Is Topology?

Sasha Korolev had arrived at the Thursday morning theory session fifteen minutes early, which gave him time to raid the supply closet. By the time Marcus Webb pushed open the glass door, a glazed donut sat on one end of the long table, and a ceramic coffee mug sat on the other. Sasha stood between them with the expression of someone who has been waiting to do this for a while.

"Tell me what you see," Sasha said. Marcus set down his tablet. He was used to Sasha's preambles, but pastry as a physics demonstration was new to him. "A donut and a coffee cup," he said. "One of which I'd like to eat."

"Topologically, they are the same object," Sasha said. "And that is not a philosopher's joke. It is the most important engineering insight in this book." He picked up a marker and walked to the whiteboard. "The coffee cup has exactly one hole, through the handle. The donut has exactly one hole through its center. If you made both from clay and were allowed to stretch and squeeze without tearing, you could turn one into the other. That hole count is a topological invariant. It cannot change without tearing the surface. That fact, transplanted into the quantum mechanics of electrons in a crystal, is why some materials conduct electricity on their surfaces in ways that nothing can switch off."

Marcus wrote one word in his notebook: "invariant." Then he looked up. "Beautiful metaphor. But give me something I can measure. What is the number? Where does it come from? And what does it mean for my device if that number is one instead of zero?"

Sasha smiled. "That is exactly the right engineering question, and it has a precise answer. Let's build it from first principles."

Why It Matters

Every fabrication engineer knows that surfaces are liabilities. The moment you expose a material to the world, you invite contamination, oxidation, atomic steps, point defects, and interface roughness. In a conventional conductor, those surface imperfections scatter electrons, degrade mobility, and reduce device performance. The defect budget is always finite, always contested, and always the thing that limits how far a process can scale before yield collapses.

Topological materials offer a different contract. In a topologically non-trivial material, the conducting surface states are not properties of the surface in isolation. They are properties of the bulk band structure, mandated into existence by a quantity called the topological invariant. If that invariant is non-zero, conducting surface states must exist, and surface contamination, atomic defects, or interface roughness cannot remove them. The surface state will reshape around a defect, much like a river flows around a boulder: the channel persists because the watershed forces it to do so. To remove the surface state, you would have to drive a phase transition that closes the band gap across the entire material volume. That is not an accident you can cause with a few misplaced atoms at an interface.

The hardware implication is fundamental. It shifts the engineering specification from an impossible demand for surface perfection to a tractable demand for bulk-phase stability. Marcus's team does not need to fabricate a perfect surface. They need to fabricate a bulk material that maintains its topological phase at operating temperature under the applied fields required by their device, while accommodating the strain state imposed by their substrate. Those are hard constraints, but they are finite and characterizable. Understanding that shift requires understanding what topology means, what a topological invariant is, and why integers cannot change continuously.

The concepts here, Berry phase, Chern number, and Z2 invariant, are not mathematical decoration. They are the engineering specifications of a new class of materials. A Chern number of 1 is as concrete a specification as a band gap of 0.34 eV or a carrier mobility of 10,000 cm^2/Vs. It tells you what the material will do and, just as importantly, what it cannot stop doing, regardless of how rough your fabrication process is.

Topology: The Math of Deformation-Invariant Properties

Topology is a branch of mathematics that studies properties of geometric objects that are preserved under continuous deformation. The word 'continuous' does the essential work here. A continuous deformation is any reshaping that does not cut, tear, or punch new holes. Stretching is allowed. Squeezing is allowed. Bending and twisting are allowed. What is not allowed is any operation that changes the object's connectivity, because connectivity is precisely what topology measures.

The simplest topological classification of closed surfaces uses a number called the genus, which counts the number of holes that pass completely through the surface. A sphere has genus zero: no holes. A torus, the surface of a donut, has genus one: one hole through the center. A surface shaped like a figure-eight pretzel has genus two. These are topologically distinct objects: no continuous deformation can convert a sphere into a torus, because creating a hole requires tearing. The genus is protected against any deformation that respects the continuity rule, and that protection is absolute and mathematical, not approximate and engineering.

The genus connects to a quantity called the Euler characteristic, which counts vertices minus edges plus faces for any polyhedral representation of a surface and always equals 2 minus 2g, where g is the genus. A cube has 8 vertices, 12 edges, and 6 faces: 8 minus 12 plus 6 equals 2. A torus surface gives an Euler characteristic of zero. The key point is that you can compute a single integer that characterizes the global structure of an object in a way that is invariant under any local reshaping.

Diagram 5.1 - Genus Classification of Surfaces

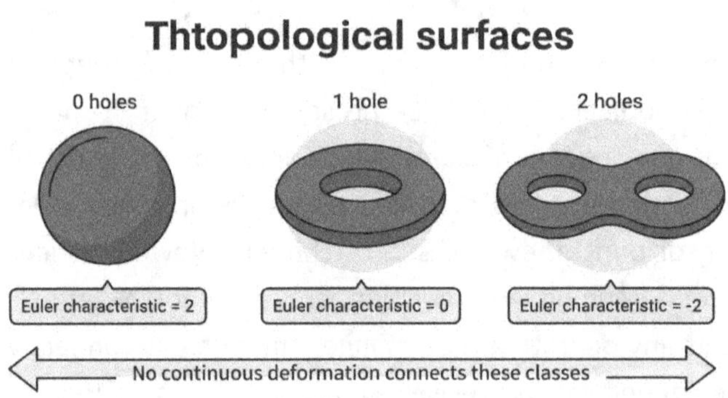

In materials physics, the relevant 'object' is not a physical shape but the space of electron quantum states in a crystal, specifically the structure of occupied energy bands as a function of crystal momentum. The 'deformation' is any perturbation of the material that does not close the energy gap between the occupied valence bands and the empty conduction bands. As long as the gap stays open, the quantum state space can be continuously deformed, and its topological invariants are preserved. Local perturbations, a contaminated surface, an interface step, or a point defect cannot close a bulk band gap. That is why the topological invariants of the bulk protect the surface states: the invariants are global properties, whereas local perturbations are, by definition, not global.

The Möbius strip exhibits a topological property that has a direct quantum analog. Take a rectangular strip of paper, give it a single half-twist, and join the ends. You now have a surface with one face and one edge. If you draw a line along the middle, you will return to your starting point having traversed both sides of the original strip without crossing an edge. This non-orientability is topologically distinct from a simple cylinder and cannot be removed without cutting and regluing.

Diagram 5.2 - The Mobius Strip and Orientability

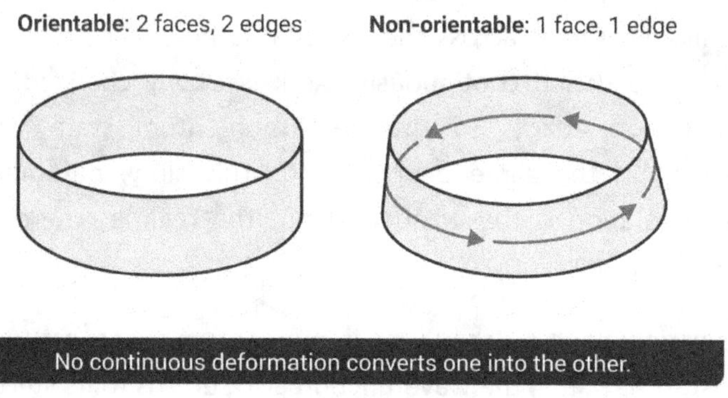

The quantum analog of non-orientability appears when electron wavefunctions are transported around loops in momentum space and return with a sign flip. This phase change cannot be gauged away. That sign flip, the Berry phase, is the quantum material's version of the Möbius strip's surprising return to start. It is the quantity that separates trivial insulators from topological ones, and the engineering consequence is the protected surface state that Axiom's device depends on.

The Berry Phase: Geometry Written Into the Quantum State

Chapter 2 of this book introduced the Berry phase in the context of the adiabatic theorem and quantum state evolution. Here, the concept is developed more carefully, because it is the cornerstone quantity on which all of topological materials physics stands. Every topological invariant used in this field, the Chern number, the Z2 invariant, the Zak phase, and the winding number, is either the Berry phase itself or derived directly from it.

Start with a quantum state, the wavefunction of an electron in a crystal, described by a vector in an abstract mathematical space. The crystal momentum k, which encodes the electron's wave-like character across the periodic lattice, is a parameter that can be varied continuously. As k is slowly changed, the wavefunction adapts to the new momentum state while remaining in the same energy band. This slow, parameter-driven evolution is the adiabatic limit, the regime where the Berry phase lives.

If k is varied along a closed loop in momentum space, returning to its starting value, the wavefunction also returns to its starting form, but with a possible additional phase factor. In ordinary quantum mechanics, phase factors are often considered unphysical: you can multiply a wavefunction by any complex number of magnitude one, and the physical predictions are unchanged. But here is the critical distinction: the phase accumulated around a closed loop is determined by the geometry of the path through the parameter space, and it cannot be removed by any redefinition of the phase convention that is smooth and consistent across the entire loop. It is a geometric invariant, not a gauge artifact.

The gyroscope analogy makes this concrete. Take a gyroscope and carry it slowly around the surface of a sphere, keeping its axis always parallel to the surface, never tilting it. When it returns to the starting point, its axis points in a different direction. The angular difference is determined entirely by the geometry of the path, specifically by the solid angle subtended by the path at the center of the sphere. This rotation of the gyroscope axis is called holonomy, and the Berry phase is the quantum analog. The electron's wavefunction plays the role of the gyroscope axis; the path through momentum space plays the role of the path on the sphere; and the accumulated Berry phase plays the role of the angular rotation on return.

Diagram 5.3 - Berry Phase as Geometric Holonomy

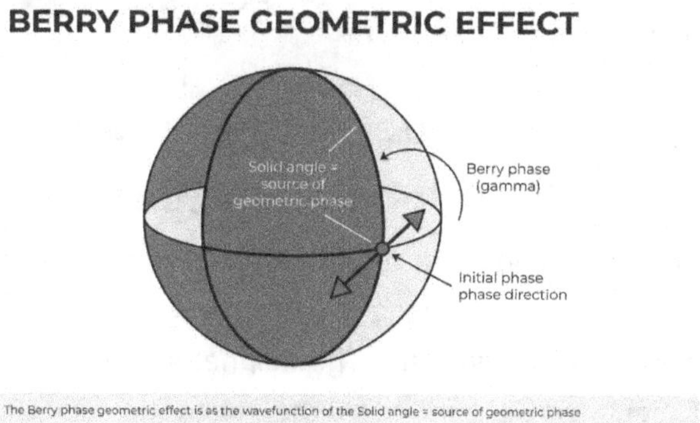

This geometric phase was identified and fully characterized by Michael Berry in 1984. The Berry phase acquired around a closed loop C in parameter space is the integral of a quantity called the Berry connection along that loop. The Berry connection at each point in parameter space measures the rate at which the wavefunction's phase changes as the parameter moves. What makes it physical is that while the Berry connection itself changes when you redefine the phase of the wavefunction, the integral around a closed loop does not. It is like the magnetic flux through a loop: the vector potential changes under a gauge transformation, but the flux, which is the integral of the vector potential around the boundary, does not.

The engineering relevance becomes concrete when the parameter space is the Brillouin zone. In a topologically trivial material, the Berry phase around any closed loop is zero: the wavefunction returns exactly as it left. In a topologically non-trivial material, the Berry phase around certain loops is quantized to a non-zero value. That quantization is not an approximation. It is enforced by the topology of the wavefunction's evolution across the Brillouin zone, and it is the quantity from which the Chern number and Z2 invariant are constructed.

Berry Curvature: A Magnetic Field in Momentum Space

The Berry connection, the vector field that encodes how fast the wavefunction's phase changes with momentum, has a natural analog in electromagnetism. The magnetic vector potential is a vector field whose curl gives the magnetic field. The Berry curvature is defined in the same way: it is the curl of the Berry connection in momentum space, and it plays the role of a magnetic field, but in momentum space rather than real space.

This analogy is not decorative. Every mathematical tool that electromagnetism uses for the magnetic vector potential applies directly to the Berry connection. The Berry phase around a closed loop in momentum space equals the flux of the Berry curvature through the surface bounded by that loop, by the same logic as Stokes' theorem applied to magnetism. The Berry curvature is peaked near points in the Brillouin zone where bands are close in energy or where band crossings are avoided, much as magnetic field lines concentrate near magnetic monopoles.

Diagram 5.4 - Berry Curvature as a Vector Field in Momentum Space

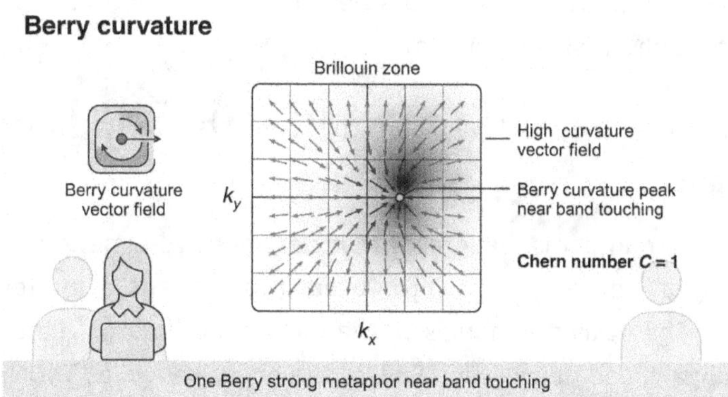

The physical consequence of Berry curvature is the anomalous Hall effect. In a magnetic material, an electric field that drives a current in one direction produces a transverse voltage. The ordinary Hall effect arises because a magnetic field deflects moving electrons. The anomalous Hall effect produces the same transverse voltage without any applied external magnetic field:

the electrons are deflected not by a real-space magnetic field but by the Berry curvature in momentum space, which acts on the electrons' semiclassical dynamics in the same way a real magnetic field would. The effect is intrinsic to the band structure, not a scattering artifact.

For Marcus at Axiom, the anomalous Hall effect is a diagnostic. Berry curvature is not directly observable, but its integral over the Brillouin zone, the Chern number, is. The Hall conductivity of a two-dimensional topological material is directly proportional to the Chern number: it is quantized in integer multiples of a fundamental constant, the quantum of conductance. Measuring the Hall conductivity with high precision gives the Chern number. The Chern number indicates whether the material is topologically nontrivial and how many protected conducting edge states it has. That chain connects an abstract geometric invariant to a bench measurement that any transport physicist can perform.

The Chern Number: Counting the Winding of Quantum States

The Chern number is the integer that classifies two-dimensional topological phases. It was introduced into condensed matter physics by David Thouless, Masaichiro Kohmoto, Peter Nightingale, and den Nijs in 1982, in the paper known as TKNN, and it is the quantity whose quantization explains why the Hall conductivity of a two-dimensional electron gas in a strong magnetic field takes precisely integer values. The 2016 Nobel Prize in Physics, awarded to Thouless, Haldane, and Kosterlitz, recognized that topological invariants such as the Chern number govern the properties of quantum phases of matter.

Geometrically, the Chern number is the total Berry curvature integrated over the entire Brillouin zone. This integral has a deep mathematical reason to be an integer. By the Gauss-Bonnet theorem of differential geometry, the integral of curvature over a closed surface always gives an integer multiple of 4 pi. The Brillouin zone of a two-dimensional crystal is effectively a closed surface, a torus, because its opposite edges are identified by crystal periodicity. The integral of the Berry curvature over this torus gives an integer, and that integer is the Chern number. It is the quantum mechanical version of the genus of the Brillouin zone torus, counting the topological winding of the electron wavefunctions rather than the topological winding of a physical surface.

The winding-number picture is the most accessible entry point for engineers. Consider a two-dimensional map that assigns a unit vector to each point in the Brillouin zone, derived from the electron wavefunction at that point. As k sweeps across the entire Brillouin zone, this vector traces out a path on the unit sphere. The Chern number counts how many times this path wraps around the sphere. You can deform the path continuously, but you cannot change the total winding number without the path jumping discontinuously across a singular point, which physically corresponds to a band touching where the energy gap closes. As long as the gap is open, the Chern number is protected.

Diagram 5.5 - Chern Number as Winding Number

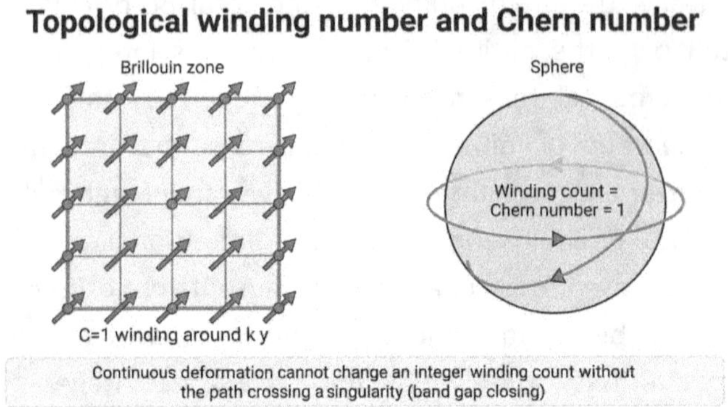

The integer protection of the Chern number is what makes it an engineering specification. To change a material with Chern number one into a material with Chern number zero, the winding number cannot change continuously. There is no smooth path from one integer to another. To change it, the vector field must pass through a configuration in which the winding is undefined, which occurs precisely when the energy bands touch and the gap closes. A band gap closing is a phase transition. No surface impurity, no interface step, no oxide layer, no temperature fluctuation small enough to leave the bulk gap open can change the Chern number.

The experimental signature of a non-zero Chern number is the quantum anomalous Hall effect: a quantized Hall conductivity of exactly one quantum of conductance per conducting channel, persisting in the absence of any external magnetic field. This is not a measurement that requires superhuman precision to distinguish from non-topological behavior. The conductance is quantized to better than one part in a billion in well-prepared samples, the same level of precision as the quantum Hall effect that Klaus von Klitzing discovered in 1980 and for which he received the Nobel Prize in 1985. When you measure a quantized Hall conductance, you are directly measuring a topological invariant of the material's band structure.

Diagram 5.6 - Quantum Anomalous Hall Effect and Chern Number

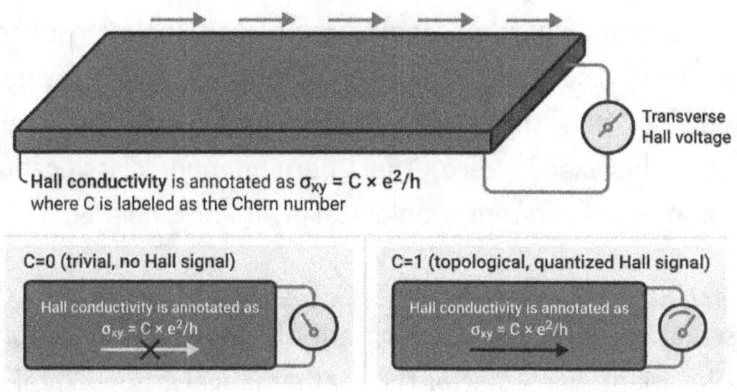

Friederich Haldane's 1988 paper proposed that the quantum anomalous Hall effect could be realized in a two-dimensional lattice model without any external magnetic field, using only a specific pattern of time-reversal symmetry breaking within the lattice itself. The Haldane model was a theoretical existence proof that the Chern number could be non-trivial in a crystalline material driven by internal magnetic flux patterns. For over two decades, it was a beautiful theoretical construct with no obvious physical realization. Then, the field of topological materials took off after the 2005 predictions by Kane and Mele, and experimentalists found Haldane-model physics in real materials, including magnetically doped Bi2Se3 and MnBi2Te4.

Z2 Invariants: Topology Under Time-Reversal Symmetry

The Chern number applies only to materials where time-reversal symmetry is broken, either by an external magnetic field or by internal magnetic order. Most materials used in electronics, including every candidate for a topological insulator built on bismuth selenide or bismuth telluride, are time-reversal symmetric. In these materials, a theorem requires the Chern number to be exactly zero. The Chern number classification does not apply. A different topological invariant is needed.

Charles Kane and Eugene Mele provided it in 2005 in two papers that triggered the modern era of topological insulators. The Z2 invariant, named after the mathematical group Z2, takes only two values: zero, meaning topologically trivial, and one, meaning topologically non-trivial. Those are the only two choices. The subscript 2 signals that flipping the invariant twice returns you to the start: zero and one are the two elements of a system where addition is done modulo 2. It is the difference between even and odd, not the difference between small and large.

The physical meaning of the Z2 invariant comes from time-reversal symmetry's special effect on electron spin. Time reversal flips spin: under time reversal, a spin-up electron becomes a spin-down electron. In a crystal with time-reversal symmetry, every electronic state at crystal momentum k has a partner state at minus k with the same energy. These are Kramers pairs, and they are protected: no perturbation that respects time-reversal symmetry can split the energy of a Kramers pair. At special points in the Brillouin zone where k and minus k are equivalent by crystal symmetry, called time-reversal-invariant momenta, the Kramers partners must be degenerate.

Diagram 5.7 - Z2 Invariant and Kramers Pair Exchange

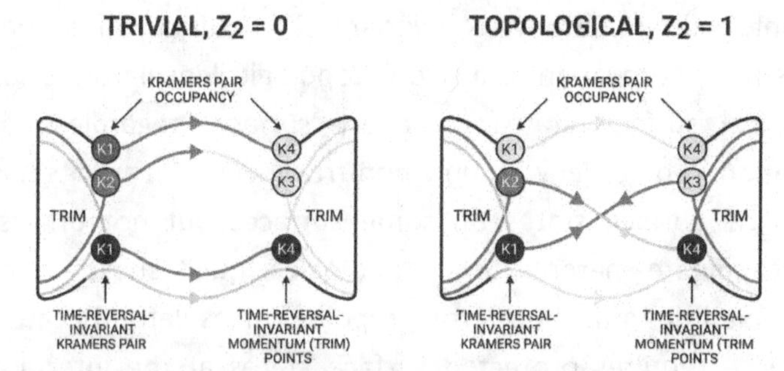

EVEN EXCHANGES = TRIVIAL (Z2=0); ODD EXCHANGES = TOPOLOGICAL (Z2=1).

The Z2 invariant counts the parity of the number of Kramers partner exchanges that occur as k is swept across the Brillouin zone. In a trivial insulator, the occupied bands can be continuously deformed so that the Kramers pairs never exchange identity. In a topological insulator, the Kramers pairs must exchange an odd number of times, and any time-reversal-preserving perturbation cannot undo odd exchange. One means odd and topological. Zero means even and trivial.

Kane and Mele's 2005 prediction concerned graphene, the single-atom-thick carbon sheet that had just been isolated in 2004. They showed that graphene should, in principle, be a topological insulator driven by spin-orbit coupling, the interaction between an electron's spin and its orbital motion in the crystal potential. The spin-orbit coupling in graphene is far too small to produce a measurable topological gap at practical temperatures. Still, the theoretical prediction was revolutionary: it showed that ordinary electronic materials could host a Z2 topological phase without magnetic fields.

In three dimensions, four Z2 invariants are needed to classify the topological phase of a bulk material fully. One is a strong invariant, and three are weak invariants. A material with a non-trivial strong Z2 invariant is a strong topological insulator: it has topological surface states on every surface, regardless of orientation. A material with only non-trivial weak invariants has topological surface states on some surfaces but not others. Every candidate material for a topological qubit substrate at Axiom Quantum must be a strong topological insulator, because the device requires protected surface states at the interface with the superconducting layer. That interface can be oriented in any direction relative to the crystal.

Diagram 5.8 - Strong vs. Weak Topological Insulator Z2 Invariants

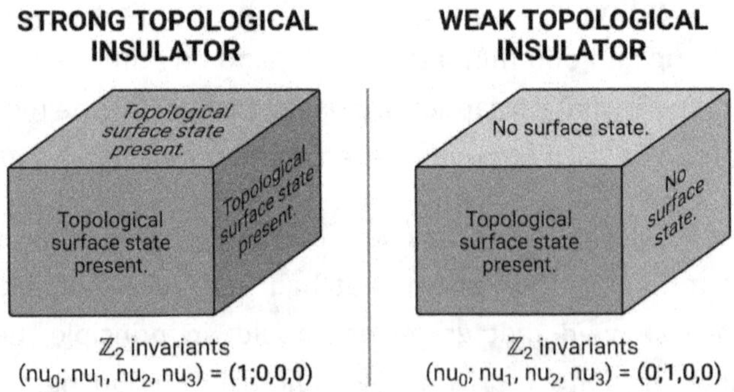

The compound Bi2Se3 is the prototype strong topological insulator, predicted by Haijun Zhang and collaborators in 2009 and confirmed by ARPES measurements within the same year. It has a bulk band gap of about 0.3 eV, which is accessible at room

temperature, and a single Dirac-cone surface state at the center of the Brillouin zone. It became the hydrogen atom of topological insulators: the simplest system in which the full physics of the Z2 topological phase can be studied experimentally without competing phases or weaker gaps.

Why Integer Values Mean Robustness

The central engineering insight of topological materials is not that they have topological invariants. It is that those invariants are integers, and integers are robust in a way that real numbers are not. Physical quantities in ordinary materials are real numbers. The band gap is 0.34 eV, with some distribution across a wafer. The carrier mobility is 9,800 cm^2/V-s, which varies with temperature and doping. Every continuous real-valued property can be nudged away from its nominal value by any perturbation, no matter how small.

An integer cannot be nudged. If a property is topologically quantized to the integer one, it is not approximately one, or one with a correction factor. It is exactly one, zero, or two. There is no 1.02 or 0.97. Any perturbation that does not close the topological gap leaves the invariant unchanged at exactly one. A perturbation large enough to change the invariant must close the gap and drive a phase transition, at which point you have fundamentally changed what the material is.

The analogy to digital logic is exact. A digital bit is either zero or one, and is robust to analog noise within the noise margin. A topological invariant is either zero or one, robust against any perturbation that keeps the system within the topological phase. The noise margin for the topological bit is the bulk band gap: as long as the perturbation energy is small compared to the gap, the invariant is protected. This is why topological materials engineers think not about eliminating defects but about maintaining the topological phase. The defects are tolerated; the gap must be preserved.

Diagram 5.9 - Integer Protection: Topological vs. Conventional Quantities

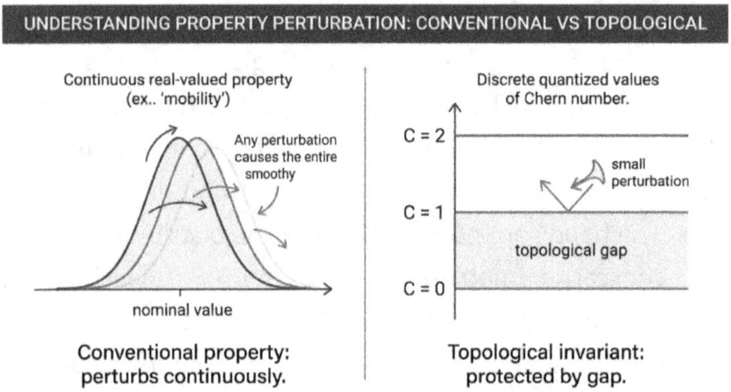

For the Hall conductivity, this means something extraordinary. In a material with Chern number 1, the Hall conductivity is exactly e^2/h, the electron charge squared divided by Planck's constant. Not approximately. Exactly, to the precision of any measurement conducted while the material remains in its topological phase. The quantum Hall effect that Klitzing discovered in 1980 was so precisely quantized that it replaced the previous definition of the ohm in the international system of units. The same precision is available in topological materials in the absence of an external magnetic field, which is the engineering payoff of the anomalous Hall effect.

A two-dimensional topological insulator with Chern number one has a single conducting edge channel that carries current without backscattering. The current cannot scatter backward into the bulk because the bulk is insulating. It cannot scatter into another forward-moving channel because there is only one forward channel. The only way to scatter backward is to find a channel moving backward, and the topology guarantees that there are none. Every scanning tunneling microscopy study of a topological surface state and every transport measurement of a quantized Hall plateau is a measurement of an integer topological invariant. The integers are not theoretical: they are what the instruments read.

Bulk-Boundary Correspondence and Surface States

The bulk-boundary correspondence is the theorem that connects the topological invariant of a material's interior to the conducting states that must appear at its surface. It is the engineering heart of topological materials physics. Without it, topological invariants would be abstract mathematical properties of band structures with no direct physical consequence. The correspondence is what makes them hardware specifications.

The logic runs as follows. Take a topological insulator with Chern number 1 and place it in contact with a topologically trivial insulator with Chern number 0. At the interface, the Chern number must change from one to zero. But the Chern number is an integer and cannot change continuously: any change requires the energy gap to close somewhere in the transition. The closing of the gap at the interface means that the interface hosts electronic states with a zero energy gap, i.e., conducting states. These conducting states are forced into existence by the requirement that the topological invariant change across the interface. They are as mandatory as the fact that a step function must have a non-trivial value at the step.

The same logic applies at the surface between a topological insulator and a vacuum. Vacuum is topologically trivial: its invariants are zero, it has no electrons and no bands to have topology. When a topological insulator meets a vacuum at its surface, the Chern number must change from non-trivial to zero, and the same argument applies. The surface must host conducting states. Those states are the topological surface states visible in every ARPES measurement of Bi2Se3, and their existence is not an artifact of surface preparation. It is a topological obligation.

Diagram 5.10 - Bulk-Boundary Correspondence Visualization

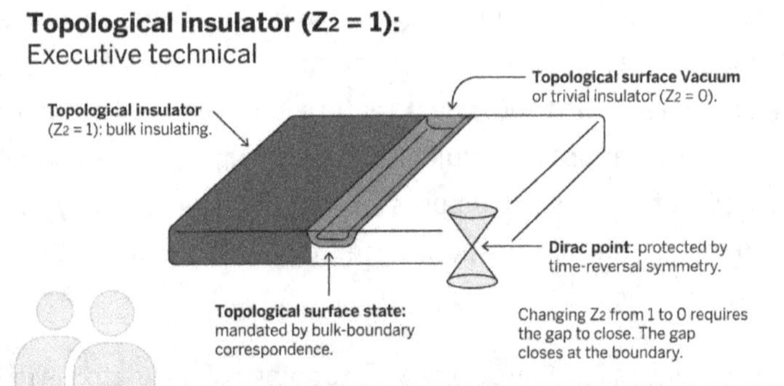

Topological insulator (Z2 = 1): bulk insulating. The gap closes at the boundary.

The topological invariant determines the precise number and character of the surface states. A material with Chern number C has exactly C conducting channels at its boundary with a trivial phase. A strong topological insulator with Z2 invariant 1 has a Dirac cone surface state on each surface. The Dirac cone, a conical dispersion relation that meets at a single point, is not a coincidence of the band structure but a symmetry-protected consequence of the Z2 topology. Time-reversal symmetry requires the surface state Hamiltonian to have a specific structure that forces the crossing point, the Dirac point, to be protected against any time-reversal-symmetric perturbation. Gap opening at the Dirac point requires time-reversal symmetry breaking.

The one perturbation that destroys the topological surface state is magnetic disorder, because magnetism breaks time-reversal symmetry. A single magnetic adatom on the surface of a Z2 topological insulator locally gapes the Dirac cone. Sufficient magnetic disorder can destroy topological surface transport even if the bulk topology remains intact. This is a genuine engineering constraint, distinct from the robustness to non-magnetic disorder that is topology's gift. Understanding the difference between magnetic and non-magnetic disorder is not optional for an engineer working with topological materials.

Diagram 5.11 - Brillouin Zone Topology: From Square to Torus

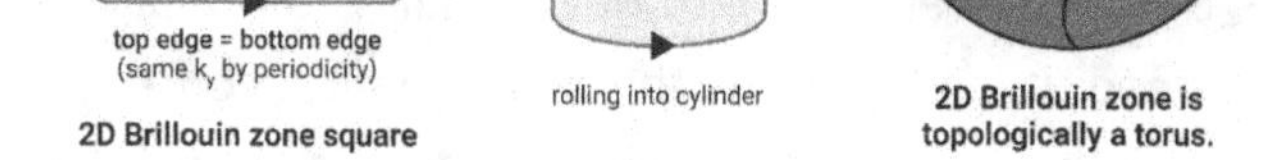

The crystal periodicity that makes the Brillouin zone a torus is what allows the Chern number to be nonzero. If the Brillouin zone were simply an open region of parameter space with a boundary, the Berry curvature integral would be constrained to zero by the topology of an open disc. It is the torus structure, enforced by crystal periodicity, that allows for non-zero Chern numbers. The engineer's takeaway is that topological invariants are band-structure properties of the occupied bands as a whole, not local properties at individual k points. You cannot determine the Chern number from a local calculation at a single k point. You need the global winding of the wavefunction across the full Brillouin zone.

The engineering consequence is that topological protection is a bulk property rather than a surface treatment. You cannot make a material topologically non-trivial by processing its surface. You make it topologically non-trivial by choosing a material whose bulk band structure has the right topology, then fabricating that bulk material with sufficient quality to maintain its topological phase. Surface engineering matters for performance, but it cannot create or destroy the topological surface state. The source of the state is the bulk.

What Can We Build With This?

The editorial note on this section is candid: the connection between topology and a buildable device is harder to make here than in later chapters, where specific materials and experiments do the work. The right move, borrowed from the Chapter 2 reframe, is not to overreach into device claims this chapter has not yet earned. It is to reframe the mathematical content as an engineering risk-management tool: what topology provides the engineer that conventional band-structure calculations cannot.

The answer is a pre-fabrication guarantee. A conventional band-structure calculation tells you the band gap, carrier density, effective mass, and mobility under ideal conditions. All of those numbers are real-valued and degrade under fabrication imperfections. The topological invariant tells you something none of those numbers can: whether the conducting surface state is protected by topology or not. If the invariant is non-trivial, the surface state must exist, must be gapless, and must be robust against non-magnetic disorder. If the invariant is trivial, any surface state that appears is a conventional surface state that can be gapped, shifted, or destroyed by the same surface processing steps that would otherwise improve device performance. This distinction cannot be learned from measuring a surface. It must be computed from the bulk band structure or inferred from a measurement of a bulk topological invariant.

This reframes the computation of topological invariants as a risk-management step in the device design workflow. Before Axiom Quantum commits to a fabrication run on a new topological heterostructure, Sasha's theory team runs the invariant calculation on the proposed material stack. Not to predict device performance, but to verify that the material is in the correct topological phase and that the surface state the device relies on is genuinely protected. If the calculation shows that the proposed heterostructure is topologically trivial under the intended strain state, or that the topological gap closes under the applied gate voltage, the fabrication run does not proceed. That computational screening step, which requires the concepts developed in this chapter, is orders of magnitude cheaper than a failed fabrication run.

Diagram 5.12 - Topological Invariant as Pre-Fabrication Risk Screen

Executive diagram workflow

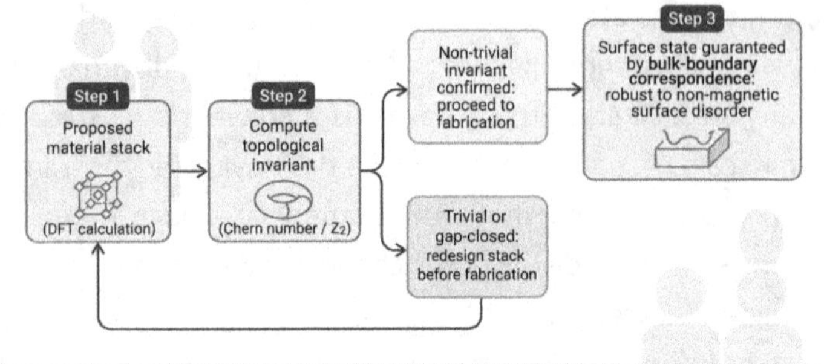

Workflow: topological mmunication foː an executive technirique

The practical consequence for Marcus's team is that topological invariant calculations reduce the defect-tolerance problem to a phase-stability problem. Instead of asking 'is our surface clean enough to support a conducting state?', they ask 'is our bulk material in the correct topological phase under operating conditions?' Phase boundaries can be mapped as a function of temperature, magnetic field, strain, and chemical composition. Once the phase diagram is known, maintaining the topological phase means operating within the phase boundary. That is a systems engineering problem, not a surface chemistry problem, and Marcus's background in cryogenic systems design is directly relevant.

The broader implication is that topological protection changes the value proposition of clean fabrication. In conventional semiconductor devices, cleanliness is everything: every defect is a potential trap, a scattering site, a reliability risk. In a topological device, cleanliness still matters, but the surface state is not among the things it protects. The fabrication overhead spent on heroic surface passivation can be redirected toward maintaining bulk-phase quality. Axiom bets that this reallocation of engineering effort is worth the difficulty of working with topological materials.

Takeaway

Topology is the mathematics of properties that persist under deformation, and its application to quantum mechanics yields material properties that survive fabrication imperfections. The coffee cup and the donut are the same topological object because both have genus one. A topological insulator and its vacuum interface are not the same topological object because the topological invariant differs, and that difference mandates a conducting surface state at the boundary. The Berry phase, the Chern number, and the Z2 invariant are the engineering specifications that quantify this topological distinction. They are integers, and local perturbations cannot nudge integers.

The bulk-boundary correspondence converts bulk topology into surface hardware. If the bulk topological invariant is non-trivial, conducting boundary states must exist. They are not a surface phenomenon. They are a boundary consequence of a bulk property, and they persist as long as the bulk maintains its topological phase. The engineering discipline required to maintain that phase is different from, and in many respects more tractable than, the engineering discipline required to maintain a perfectly clean surface.

Marcus left Sasha's Thursday session with three things in his notebook. The first was the word 'invariant.' The second was: 'integer means robust means tolerance.' The third was a question for Priya: which specific materials have been fabricated with confirmed non-trivial invariants, what are their bulk gaps, and how does the phase boundary shift under the strain conditions imposed by their substrate? That question, the translation of topological theory into a material specification and a fabrication constraint, is the subject of the next chapter.

Chapter 6 introduces topological insulators as physical materials: the bismuth chalcogenides, their crystal structures, their ARPES signatures, and what the Dirac cone looks like when an experimentalist actually measures it. The mathematics of this chapter becomes concrete experimental data in the next.

6 Topological Insulators

The sample holder is the size of a paperback. Priya Nair lifts it from its nitrogen-purged transport case with the practiced economy of someone who has handled a few hundred such samples, sets it into the ARPES stage, and locks the clamp with a quarter-turn. Bismuth selenide, she says, not to Marcus in particular but to the room. Five quintuple layers were grown by molecular beam epitaxy last Tuesday. Clean surface, no oxidation. The vacuum gauge on the analyzer reads below ten to the minus ten torr, roughly the pressure on the lunar surface, which is what you need to keep the surface you just cleaned from accumulating an atomic monolayer of oxygen in the next ninety seconds.

Marcus Webb leans against the rack of electronics that feeds the electron analyzer, arms crossed, watching the monitor. He has been at Axiom Quantum for eleven months now, long enough to understand why the room smells of turbopump oil and liquid helium, not long enough to read a band structure at a glance. Priya starts the measurement. The screen fills with color: a horizontal smear of blue where the bulk valence band lies below the Fermi level, a matching smear above it where the conduction band begins, and, between them, a gap exactly as expected for an insulator. And then, crossing through the exact center of that gap, two bright lines that meet at a single point, forming a perfect X.

Marcus stares. "That crossing in the middle of the gap," he says. "Is that a defect?" Priya shakes her head. "Surface state. It has to be there. The topology of the bulk band structure requires it." She points to the gap above and below the crossing point. "Bulk is insulating. No current. But right here, at the surface, you have a conducting state that lives inside the gap. And it cannot be removed without changing the fundamental phase of the bulk material." Marcus is quiet for a moment. "So the protection," he says slowly, "is intrinsic to the material. Without any active correction at all." Priya looks at him the way a teacher looks at a student who has just said the thing they have been building toward for an hour. "That," she says, "is exactly the point."

Why It Matters

Every chapter in this book so far has been building toward a material you can hold in your hand, put in a cryostat, and measure. Chapters 3 and 4 gave you the band structure language: the way quantum mechanics organizes electronic states into bands and gaps, and the way topology classifies those organizations into equivalence classes that cannot be continuously deformed into one another. Chapter 5 gave you the invariants: the Z2 topological index that distinguishes a topological insulator from a conventional one. This bulk-boundary correspondence predicts a conducting surface state whenever a topological material meets a topologically trivial one. This chapter is where all of that becomes concrete.

Bismuth selenide, the material on Priya's stage, is a topological insulator. Its band gap is approximately 0.3 electronvolts, which is large enough to make the bulk insulating at room temperature. Its surface state is a single Dirac cone, a pair of linearly dispersing bands that cross at a single point called the Dirac point, located inside the bulk gap. That surface state is not an accident of surface chemistry, not a consequence of dangling bonds or reconstruction, not a processing artifact. The Z2 topological invariant of the bulk mandates it. As long as the bulk stays in the topological phase and time-reversal symmetry is not broken, the surface state is there.

For a hardware engineer, the consequence is direct: the surface conductance of a topological insulator is a bulk property in disguise. You do not engineer it at the surface. You engineer it by controlling the bulk band structure. That is a completely different design space from conventional surface engineering, which means the tolerance stack for topological surface state devices looks nothing like that for a conventional heterojunction. Getting the bulk band structure right is everything. Getting the surface clean, while important for measurement quality, does not determine whether the surface state exists.

The topological surface state also carries spin information in a way conventional conducting states do not. Spin-momentum locking, the rigid coupling between the electron's spin direction and the direction of its motion, suppresses backscattering and opens the door to spintronic devices that generate spin-polarized currents without a magnetic field. And when a topological insulator is placed in contact with a conventional superconductor, the spin-momentum-locked surface state acquires superconducting correlations, producing one of the leading candidate platforms for Majorana fermion modes and topological qubits.

Quantum Spin Hall Effect: The Road to 3D

The experimental confirmation of the first topological insulator did not come from a three-dimensional bulk crystal. It was grown in 2007 from a two-dimensional quantum well composed of mercury telluride and cadmium telluride by a group led by Laurens Molenkamp at the University of Wuerzburg. To understand why that experiment was decisive, it is worth tracing the theoretical path that led to it, because the logic illuminates everything that follows in three dimensions.

In 2005, Charles Kane and Eugene Mele at the University of Pennsylvania predicted that graphene would exhibit a new quantum phase they called the quantum spin Hall insulator, abbreviated QSH insulator. A QSH insulator is the two-dimensional analog of the three-dimensional topological insulator: its bulk is gapped and insulating, but its edges carry conducting states protected by time-reversal symmetry. The edge states come in pairs: one state carries electrons moving left with spin up, and its partner carries electrons moving right with spin down. Kramers' theorem mandates this pairing, a consequence of time-reversal symmetry that requires electronic states in a time-reversal-invariant system to come in degenerate pairs.

Diagram 6.1 - Quantum Spin Hall Edge States

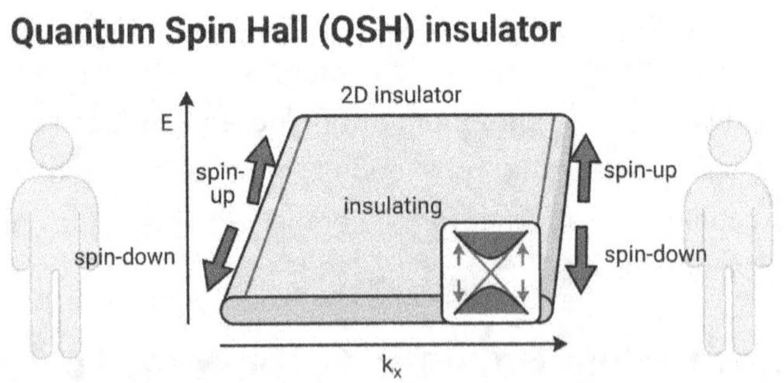

Quantum Spin Hall (QSH) insulator - indicated at a executive mistatam

The Kane-Mele prediction for graphene turned out to be correct in principle but unobservable in practice because graphene's spin-orbit coupling is extremely weak, making the predicted gap far below any achievable measurement temperature. The physical mechanism was right; graphene was simply the wrong material. The theoretical step that unlocked observation came from Bernevig, Hughes, and Zhang at Stanford, who in 2006 predicted the quantum spin Hall effect in mercury telluride cadmium telluride quantum wells at a critical thickness above which band inversion occurs. Below the critical thickness, the quantum well is a conventional insulator. Above it, quantum confinement shifts the orbital character of the bands until the s-like band drops below the p-like band, creating a Z2 nontrivial phase.

Molenkamp's group fabricated the predicted quantum wells by MBE and measured longitudinal conductance as a function of well thickness while the bulk was gated into the insulating regime. Thin wells without band inversion exhibited insulating behavior with negligible conductance. Thick wells with band inversion showed a residual conductance of twice the quantum of conductance, exactly the value expected for two edge channels, one per device edge, each carrying one conductance quantum. The conductance was quantized, robust to gate-voltage changes, and insensitive to device width, exactly as predicted by the topological protection of the edge states. The quantum spin Hall effect had been confirmed experimentally.

Diagram 6.2 - HgTe/CdTe Band Inversion

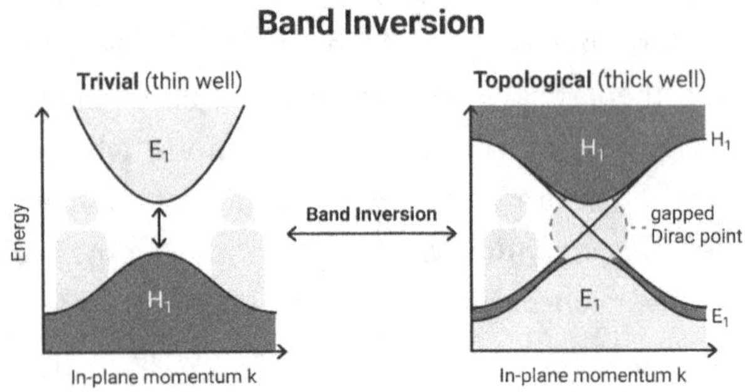

Three-dimensional topological insulators extend this logic to bulk crystals. Instead of edge states on a two-dimensional well, a three-dimensional topological insulator supports surface states on every face that interfaces with vacuum or a topologically trivial material. Instead of a single Z2 invariant, three-dimensional topological insulators are characterized by four Z2 invariants that distinguish strong topological insulators from weak ones and from trivial insulators. The strong topological insulator produces a single Dirac cone on each surface, as realized in bismuth selenide. A weak topological insulator is a stacked arrangement of quantum spin Hall layers and is more fragile to disorder.

Bi2Se3, Bi2Te3, and the 3D Topological Insulator Family

Bismuth selenide, with the formula Bi2Se3, is the material that turned the three-dimensional topological insulator from a theoretical prediction into an experimentally confirmed class. Its crystal structure belongs to the rhombohedral space group and is built from quintuple layers, each consisting of five atomic planes in the sequence selenium, bismuth, selenium, bismuth, selenium. Within a quintuple layer, the bonding is covalent and strong; between quintuple layers, the bonding is van der Waals and weak. This weak interlayer bonding means that Bi2Se3 cleaves easily along the quintuple layer planes, producing atomically flat surfaces ideal for ARPES measurements: a freshly cleaved surface is clean, unreconstructed, and representative of the bulk termination.

The band gap of Bi2Se3 is approximately 0.3 electronvolts. At room temperature, kT is about 0.026 electron volts, so the gap comfortably exceeds thermal excitation energy and the bulk should be insulating. In practice, as-grown crystals are typically n-type with a carrier concentration from ten to the seventeenth to ten to the nineteenth per cubic centimeter, because selenium vacancies act as donors. This bulk conductance is the central materials challenge: if the bulk carries current, it shunts the surface state, making it impossible to isolate the topological signal. Keeping the Fermi level within the bulk gap requires either compensation doping or electrostatic gating, and achieving this in a manufacturable thin-film geometry is one of Priya's team's primary research challenges at Axiom.

Diagram 6.3 - Bi2Se3 Crystal Structure

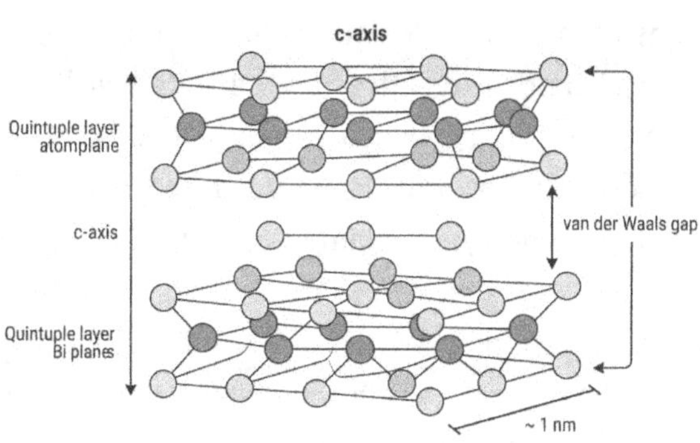

Bismuth telluride, Bi_2Te_3, is the second canonical member. Its crystal structure is isostructural to Bi_2Se_3, with the same weak van der Waals interlayer bonding and easy cleavage. Its bulk band gap is approximately 0.17 electronvolts, smaller than that of Bi_2Se_3, making it more susceptible to thermal excitation at room temperature but easier to tune to the charge neutrality point via doping control. Bi_2Te_3 also has high thermoelectric efficiency, has been exploited commercially for decades in Peltier coolers, and is among the most thoroughly characterized members of the family from a synthesis perspective, a practical advantage for growing device-quality thin films.

Antimony telluride, Sb_2Te_3, completes the canonical trio with a bulk gap of approximately 0.28 electron volts. Its Dirac point lies below the valence band maximum in as-grown crystals, requiring substantial Fermi level adjustment to access the surface state without populating bulk valence states. Sb_2Te_3 frequently appears in heterostructure contexts, particularly in magnetically doped (V, Cr)-Sb_2Te_3 systems that exhibit the quantum anomalous Hall effect, in which a quantized Hall conductance is observed at zero external magnetic field.

Beyond the canonical three, a second generation of confirmed topological insulators includes thallium bismuth selenide, $TlBiSe_2$, a ternary compound with a surface state well separated from bulk bands in energy; bismuth telluride iodide, BiTeI, a polar topological insulator with a giant Rashba splitting from broken inversion symmetry; and samarium hexaboride, SmB_6, a correlated electron topological insulator whose gap arises from many-body hybridization between localized f-electrons and itinerant d-electrons rather than from a simple band inversion. SmB_6 is significant because it demonstrates that topological surface states can arise from mechanisms beyond single-particle band theory.

Diagram 6.4 - Topological Insulator Family Band Gaps

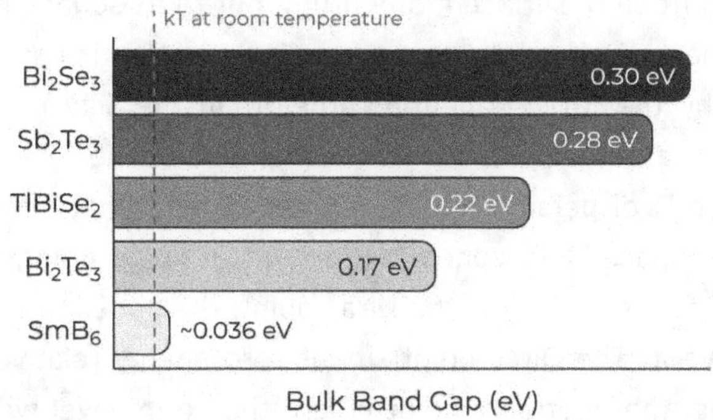

The Single Dirac Cone: Topological Surface State

The feature that Priya showed Marcus on the ARPES monitor is called a Dirac cone, and it is the most important single image in this book. Understanding what it shows, why it has the shape it does, and what that shape implies for the electrons that occupy it is the pivot point around which every downstream application of topological insulators turns.

The Dirac cone is a plot of electron energy as a function of surface momentum. The two horizontal axes are the two components of in-plane momentum, kx and ky. The vertical axis is energy. In a conventional metal or semiconductor surface state, the dispersion relation that maps momentum to energy is roughly parabolic: energy goes as momentum squared divided by twice the effective mass, the same functional form as the kinetic energy of a classical particle. The effective mass captures how the curvature of the band structure near a band extremum modifies the electron's response to applied forces.

The topological surface state has a fundamentally different dispersion: linear rather than parabolic. Energy is proportional to the magnitude of surface momentum, not to its square. This is the mathematical structure of a massless relativistic particle, described by the Dirac equation rather than the Schrodinger equation for a parabolic band. The name Dirac cone refers to the shape this dispersion traces in three-dimensional energy-momentum space: two cones meeting at a single point, the lower cone for states below the Dirac point, the upper cone for states above it. The Dirac point sits at zero energy relative to the crossing, the neutrality point where the Fermi level would sit in an undoped system.

The physical origin of the linear dispersion is the strong spin-orbit coupling in the heavy-atom compounds that host topological insulators. Bismuth, tellurium, and selenium are heavy elements with large spin-orbit energies. In the bulk, this spin-orbit coupling induces band inversion, yielding a nontrivial Z2 topology. At the surface, the same coupling enforces the linear dispersion and locks the electron's spin rigidly to its momentum direction. The connection between heavy-element spin-orbit coupling, band inversion, topological classification, and linear Dirac dispersion is not accidental. All four are manifestations of the same underlying physics, which is why the topological insulator family is reliably found in heavy-element chalcogenides.

Diagram 6.5 - Dirac Cone ARPES Surface State

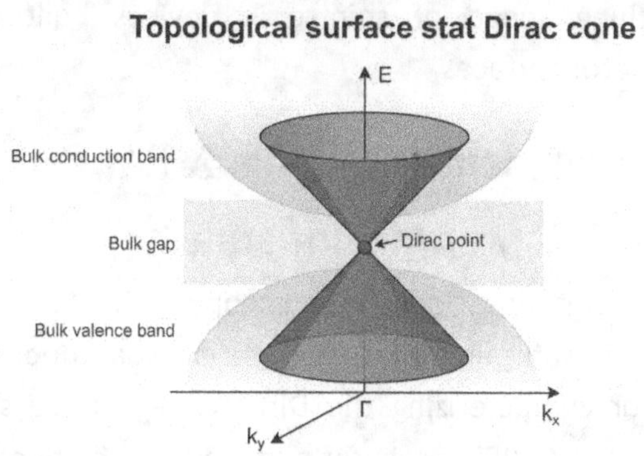

What makes the single Dirac cone of a strong topological insulator physically special is its odd number. Graphene has four Dirac cones per Brillouin zone, two valleys times two for spin, and this even number means that graphene is not a topological insulator: its cones can be gapped by perturbations that mix the two valleys. A topological insulator surface has a single Dirac cone, an odd number, which cannot be gapped by any perturbation that preserves time-reversal symmetry. There is no partner cone on the same surface to pair with and fill the gap. The bulk-boundary correspondence forbids removing the state without a bulk phase transition. The odd number is topological protection made manifest in the band structure.

The bulk gap in an ARPES measurement of Bi2Se3 spans roughly 0.15 eV below to 0.15 eV above the Dirac point. The surface state bands, the two bright lines forming the X on Priya's monitor, have a slope corresponding to a Fermi velocity of approximately five times ten to the fifth meters per second, about 0.2 percent of the speed of light, and roughly ten times larger than the Fermi velocity at the top of the copper valence band. This high Fermi velocity means that surface-state electrons respond to applied voltages more quickly than those in conventional metallic conductors, with implications for the potential switching speed of spintronic devices built from topological insulator surfaces.

ARPES: The Measurement That Confirms a Topological Insulator

Angle-resolved photoemission spectroscopy, ARPES, is the primary tool for confirming that a material is a topological insulator and for characterizing the Dirac cone surface state. Understanding what ARPES measures and why it is the right tool for this job is essential for anyone evaluating claims about topological insulator materials, because without ARPES data, assigning a topological phase is a theoretical prediction rather than an experimental confirmation.

The principle of ARPES is the photoelectric effect at high resolution. Ultraviolet or soft X-ray photons from a synchrotron or helium lamp strike the sample surface in ultra-high vacuum. When an electron in the crystal absorbs a photon, it escapes the solid and travels to a hemispherical electron analyzer, which measures its kinetic energy and emission angle. By conservation of energy and momentum, these quantities map back to the electron's binding energy and in-plane crystal momentum before photoemission. The result is a map of electron spectral weight as a function of energy and in-plane momentum, which is precisely the band structure projected onto the surface Brillouin zone.

Diagram 6.6 - ARPES Measurement Geometry

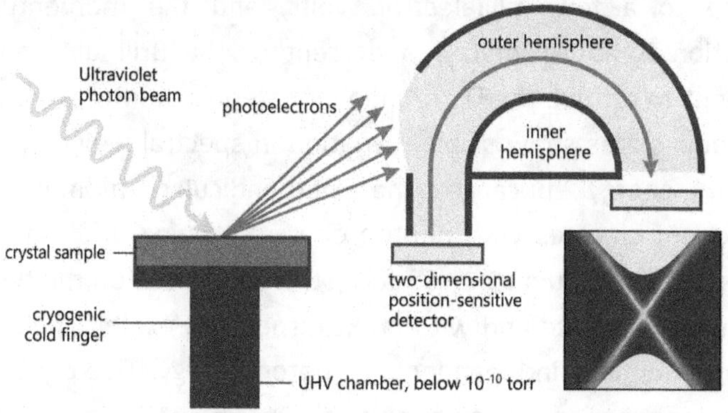

For a topological insulator, an ARPES measurement at the cleaved surface reveals several features that together constitute definitive identification. First: the bulk valence and conduction band edges appear as diffuse spectral weight above and below the gap, while the gap itself shows strongly suppressed weight. Second: inside the gap, a pair of sharp linearly dispersing bands cross at a single point, the Dirac point. The linearity of the dispersion and the existence of a single crossing point, rather than an even number, are the signatures of a topological surface state rather than a trivial surface resonance. Third: spin-resolved ARPES, in which photoelectron spin polarization is analyzed with a Mott detector, reveals that the spin direction rotates by 2 pi as the momentum direction traverses the Fermi surface around the Dirac point, providing a direct signature of spin-momentum locking.

ARPES has limitations that are important for device engineers to be aware of. It is a surface-sensitive technique that probes only the topmost few nanometers, an advantage for seeing surface states but a limitation for characterizing the bulk interior. It requires ultra-high vacuum and low temperatures, so it is a characterization tool rather than a process monitor. The energy resolution of state-of-the-art synchrotron ARPES is in the range of one to a few millielectron volts, and the momentum resolution is approximately a percent of the Brillouin zone, sufficient to resolve the Dirac cone in materials of interest. Bulk electronic states show strong variation in spectral weight with photon energy because the perpendicular momentum component changes with photon energy, probing different kz values in the Brillouin zone. Surface states, localized on the two-dimensional surface and with no kz dispersion, exhibit spectral weight essentially independent of photon energy. This photon-energy independence is an additional experimental criterion for identifying a genuine surface state, thereby completing the fingerprint alongside single-Dirac-cone dispersion and time-reversal-invariant spin texture.

Spin-Momentum Locking and Backscattering Suppression

The second most important property of the topological surface state, after the Dirac cone itself, is spin-momentum locking: the rigid coupling between the direction of an electron's momentum and the direction of its spin. In the Bi2Se3 surface state, an electron moving in the positive kx direction has its spin pointing in the positive ky direction, perpendicular to its motion in the surface plane. As the momentum direction rotates around the Fermi surface, the spin direction rotates in lockstep. This is the helical spin texture of the topological surface state.

To understand why spin-momentum locking suppresses backscattering, consider what happens when a surface state electron encounters an impurity. In a conventional conductor, an impurity can scatter the electron in any direction, including directly backward, which is the most resistance-generating event. In the topological surface state, backward scattering requires the electron to reverse its momentum, which, by the locking constraint, requires simultaneously reversing its spin. But time-reversal symmetry forbids spin-flip scattering from a non-magnetic impurity: the time-reversed partner of an electron with momentum k and spin up is an electron with momentum negative k and spin down, and Kramers' theorem says these are degenerate states that non-magnetic scattering cannot mix. Backscattering is forbidden.

Diagram 6.7 - Spin-Momentum Locking Fermi Surface

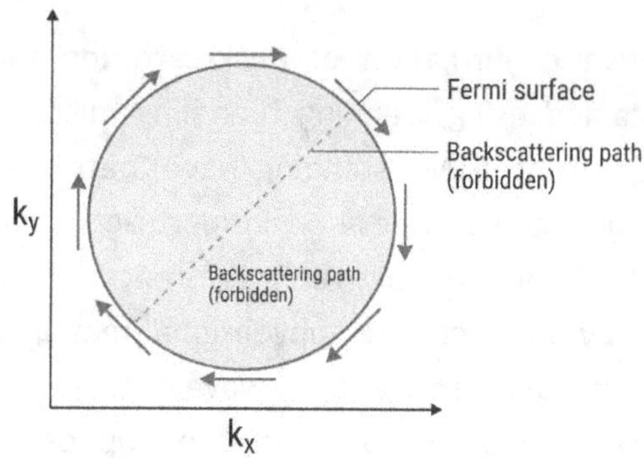

The engineering consequence of backscattering suppression is a significant reduction in resistivity from non-magnetic disorder. In a conventional thin metal film, surface roughness, grain boundaries, and point defects each contribute to resistivity through backscattering. In the surface state of a topological insulator, these imperfections contribute far less. This is not the same as perfect conduction: forward and sideways scattering are still allowed and still produce finite resistivity. But the dominant mechanism in many practical disordered systems is backscattering, so suppressing it yields a measurable reduction in surface resistance relative to a conventional metal film with comparable carrier density.

The protection against backscattering from non-magnetic disorder does not extend to magnetic disorder. A magnetic impurity breaks time-reversal symmetry locally, lifts the Kramers degeneracy at the Dirac point, and opens a gap in the surface state spectrum. For spin-injection device applications, this magnetic proximity effect is a feature rather than a defect: the coupling between the surface state and a ferromagnet's exchange field drives the spin-transfer torque that the device exploits. For topological qubit applications, magnetic contamination is a primary concern, driving the stringent cleanliness requirements of Axiom's MBE process.

Quantitative confirmation of backscattering suppression has been obtained using scanning tunneling microscopy (STM). In constant-current STM, standing-wave patterns in the local density of states reveal quasiparticle interference, the constructive and destructive interference of electron waves scattered by a defect. In a conventional metal, standing waves appear at all scattering wavevectors, including the backscattering wavevector connecting opposite sides of the Fermi surface. STM measurements of topological insulator surfaces show a standing-wave pattern absent at the backscattering wavevector and present at all scattering wavevectors connecting states with compatible spin orientations. This spatial-domain observation directly confirms what ARPES reveals in momentum space.

Bulk-Surface Challenge: Fermi Pinning, Compensation

The central materials engineering problem for topological insulator devices is to make the bulk truly insulating while keeping the surface states at the Fermi level. This sounds like a standard materials purity problem, and it is in part, but it has a specific character that distinguishes it from impurity control in conventional semiconductor fabrication.

As-grown Bi2Se3 crystals are almost always n-type with a carrier concentration from ten to the seventeenth to ten to the nineteenth per cubic centimeter, because selenium vacancies form readily during crystal growth at typical growth temperatures and act as effective donors. The result is a Fermi level sitting well inside the conduction band, meaning the bulk carries a large electron density that shunts the surface state. The surface state exists, as ARPES confirms, but it is buried beneath a much larger bulk-conductance signal.

Diagram 6.8 - Fermi Level Pinning in Bi2Se3

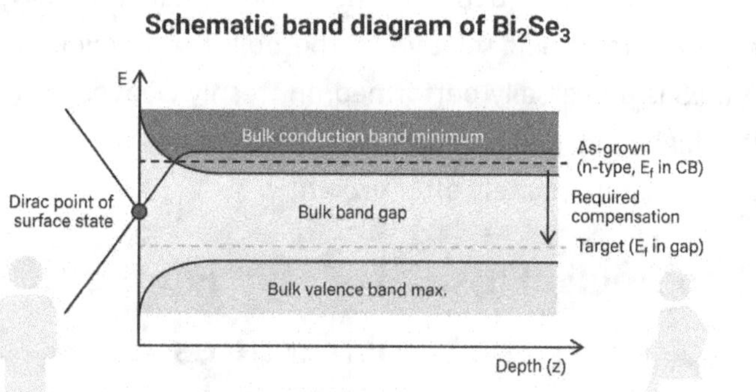

A Schematic band diagram of Bi_2Se_3 illustrating energy state, as a w function of the surface.

The most commonly used compensation strategy is to substitute calcium or other acceptors for bismuth on the bismuth sites, or to add antimony to create a Bi2-xSbxSe3 alloy, in which Sb content shifts the Fermi level toward the gap. In thin films grown by MBE, independent flux control of each element produces nearly stoichiometric material with far lower defect concentrations than bulk crystals, and electrostatic gating through a top or bottom gate can additionally shift the Fermi level in situ. The goal is to place the Fermi level within the bulk gap, where only the surface state contributes to conduction.

Two additional complications compound the challenge. First, Fermi-level pinning at interface trap states can resist electrostatic gating, much as interface traps in the silicon dioxide system shift the threshold voltage in MOSFET devices. Identifying and passivating these traps in topological insulator heterostructures is an active area of interface engineering, and it is why Axiom's materials team characterizes every new heterostructure with both ARPES and capacitance-voltage measurements before committing to a device process. Second, air exposure causes oxygen and water molecules to adsorb on the surface, thereby bending the bands near the surface, shifting the Dirac point relative to the bulk Fermi level. This is why ARPES is universally performed on freshly cleaved surfaces in ultra-high vacuum, and why device-relevant films are encapsulated immediately after growth.

Topological Insulator Thin Films and Heterostructures

Bulk crystals are useful for characterization but impractical for devices. The device-relevant geometry is a thin film, typically grown by MBE on a lattice-matched substrate, with a thickness ranging from a few quintuple layers to a few tens of nanometers. How the topological surface state evolves with film thickness and which substrate and overlayer choices are compatible with it are critical design decisions for topological insulator device engineering.

When a Bi2Se3 thin film is thin enough that the top and bottom surfaces are within quantum-mechanical tunneling distance of each other, approximately six quintuple layers or about six nanometers, the surface states on the two faces hybridize. Hybridization opens a gap at the Dirac point, splitting the single Dirac cone into two branches separated by an energy gap that grows as the thickness decreases. Below the critical hybridization thickness, the film no longer hosts a gapless topological surface state. For device applications that require the gapless Dirac cone, film thickness must exceed approximately six to eight quintuple layers in Bi2Se3.

Diagram 6.9 - Surface State Hybridization vs Film Thickness

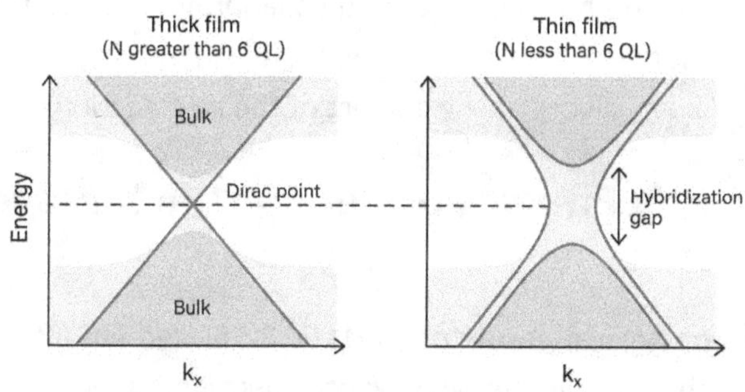

Substrate choice matters significantly for MBE growth. Bi2Se3 has a hexagonal surface periodicity of 4.14 angstroms, and suitable substrates include silicon (111), sapphire (0001), and mica, each with different lattice mismatches and consequences for crystallinity. Silicon 111 is attractive for its compatibility with standard semiconductor fabrication; sapphire is attractive for its very low electrical conductivity, which eliminates substrate shunting of the topological surface state. MBE growth of Bi2Se3 at substrate temperatures between 200 and 300 degrees

Celsius yields step-flow growth, producing the smoothest films with the lowest defect densities.

Heterostructures combining topological insulators with other materials create properties neither material has alone. The TI-ferromagnet heterostructure, with a thin magnetic layer such as EuS or a chromium-doped topological insulator on the TI surface, breaks time-reversal symmetry at the surface and magnetically gaps the Dirac cone. In the appropriate geometry, this produces the quantum anomalous Hall effect, in which a quantized Hall conductance of 1 quantum is observed in the absence of an external magnetic field. The quantum anomalous Hall effect was first observed in 2013 in magnetically doped thin films of topological insulators at Tsinghua University, confirming a prediction made by Zhang, Yu, and collaborators in 2010. The TI-superconductor heterostructure, the proximity system central to Axiom's work, is the subject of the next section.

Proximity Effect: Cooper Pairs in Surface States

When a topological insulator surface is placed in intimate contact with a conventional s-wave superconductor, Cooper pairs from the superconductor leak across the interface by Andreev reflection and penetrate the topological insulator, inducing superconducting pairing correlations in the surface state. This proximity-induced superconductivity is not the same as making the topological insulator a superconductor: the bulk band gap is still present, the topological surface state is still there, and the superconducting coherence is confined to the near-interface region. But the pairing is happening in a state with spin-momentum locking.

Conventional s-wave superconductivity pairs electrons with opposite momenta and opposite spins: one electron with momentum k and spin up, one with momentum- k and spin down. When this pairing is induced by proximity in a surface state where spin and momentum are locked, the pairing is between electrons whose spin directions are determined by their momenta. An electron at momentum k has its spin fixed perpendicular to k by the locking, and its time-reversed partner at negative k has its spin in the opposite perpendicular direction. The result is a pairing of states that are their own time-reversed partners, in a highly constrained, symmetry-enforced way, with no analog in conventional proximity-effect systems.

Diagram 6.10 - TI-Superconductor Proximity Structure

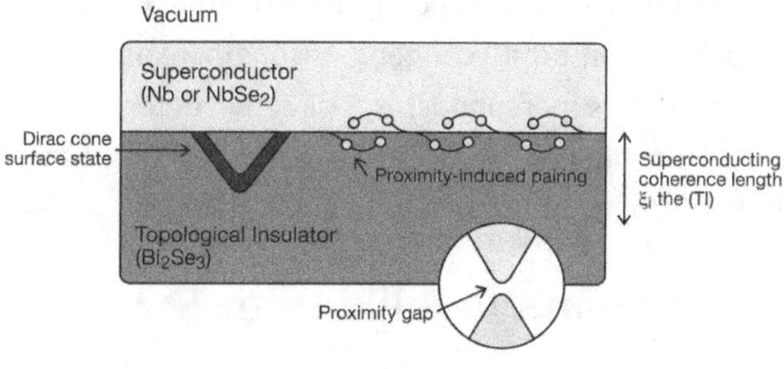

The theoretical significance of superconducting pairing in a spin-momentum-locked Dirac state was established in a 2008 paper by Fu and Kane at the University of Pennsylvania. Fu and Kane showed that the effective low-energy description of the proximity-induced superconducting state on the surface of a topological insulator is mathematically equivalent to that of a spinless p-wave superconductor, which supports Majorana zero modes at its vortex cores or boundaries. A Majorana zero mode is a quasiparticle that is its own antiparticle, exists at zero energy, and has non-Abelian exchange statistics: physically exchanging two Majorana modes performs a unitary operation on the combined quantum state that is not simply a phase factor. These properties make Majorana zero modes the proposed building blocks of topological qubits in Microsoft's and Axiom's qubit architectures.

The experimental search for Majorana zero modes in Fu-Kane devices is developed fully in Chapter 8. For the present chapter, the key point is that the proximity effect on a topological insulator surface is fundamentally different from conventional proximity-induced superconductivity in a normal metal. The spin-momentum locking converts what would be a trivial superconducting proximity effect into a topological superconducting state that supports Majorana physics. Every material parameter of the topological insulator, its bulk gap, Fermi velocity, spin-orbit coupling strength, and interface quality with the superconductor, directly determines the properties of the induced topological superconducting state and therefore the viability of the resulting qubit platform.

What Can We Build With This?

The topological insulator is the first class of topological material with a well-characterized, reproducible, manufacturable surface state. The device opportunities it opens span three distinct application areas at different stages of maturity.

The most near-term application is the spin-injection device. Because the topological surface state carries a spin-polarized current, the current flowing in the surface state applies a spin-transfer torque to an adjacent ferromagnetic layer. The efficiency of this spin-orbit torque, measured as the ratio of spin current to charge current, is significantly higher in the topological surface state than in conventional heavy-metal spin Hall layers used in today's STT-MRAM devices. Early experimental measurements in TI-ferromagnet bilayers have confirmed torque efficiencies in the range of one to several, compared to 0.1 to 0.3 for the best conventional heavy-metal layers. A practical TI-based STT-MRAM element would allow lower write currents and lower power consumption. Reaching this goal requires solving the Fermi-level pinning problem in thin films and demonstrating reproducible interface quality with ferromagnetic overlayers, both of which are engineering problems with well-defined targets.

The second application is low-power interconnects exploiting backscattering suppression. A thin film of Bi2Se3 with the Fermi level in the bulk gap carries current predominantly in the topological surface state, which is resistant to backscattering from non-magnetic disorder and has a high Fermi velocity. The resistance per unit length would be lower than that of a conventional metal film of comparable thickness, because backscattering-driven resistance dominates in narrow, thin-film metallic wires at current CMOS dimensions. Realizing this requires the same Fermi-level control as the spin device, plus the ability to pattern the TI film into wires at the five-to-ten nanometer scale without introducing edge disorder that would gap the surface state.

Diagram 6.11 - Spin-Injection Device Architecture

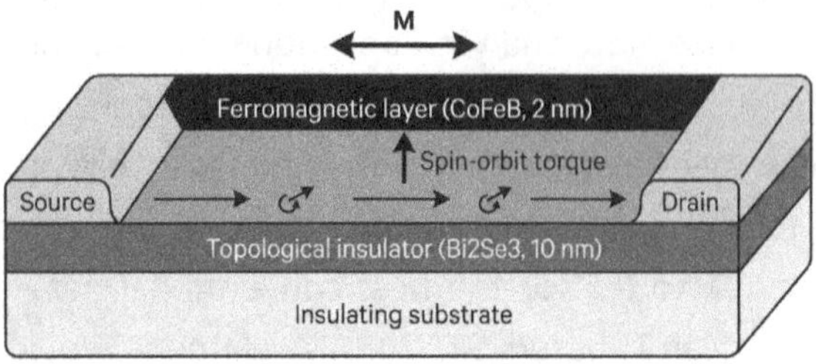

The third and most consequential application for Axiom's work is the Fu-Kane platform for topological qubits. A topological insulator thin film in proximity to a conventional s-wave superconductor, with electrostatic gating to control the surface state Fermi level and appropriate patterning to define the device geometry, is the physical substrate for inducing and manipulating Majorana zero modes. A single Majorana mode exists at zero energy. It is intrinsically protected from local perturbations because its information is encoded in the global parity of the superconducting state rather than in any local degree of freedom. Two spatially separated Majorana modes store a qubit of information in their joint parity state, with that information not locally accessible. Braiding pairs of Majorana modes performs quantum gates whose fidelity depends on the topology of the braiding path rather than on the precise timing or amplitude of control pulses, delivering intrinsic fault tolerance. The distance from Priya's ARPES Dirac cone image to a braided topological qubit is measured in materials quality, interface engineering, and device architecture. The physics is already in the data.

Takeaway

The Dirac cone that Priya showed Marcus is a measurable consequence of a topological invariant, the Z2 index of the bulk band structure, which the bulk-boundary correspondence requires. Its linear dispersion gives it a Fermi velocity that is ten times larger than that of copper. Its spin-momentum locking suppresses backscattering from non-magnetic disorder. Its topological protection means that the surface state persists as long as the bulk is in the topological phase and time-reversal symmetry is preserved, regardless of surface roughness or atomic-scale disorder, within the limits of perturbation theory. These are not approximate advantages. They are symmetry-enforced properties.

The materials challenge of making the bulk truly insulating is real and not yet fully solved. Still, it is an engineering problem with a defined target: Fermi level in the bulk gap, achieved through compensation doping, electrostatic gating, or stoichiometric MBE growth. The measurement challenge of confirming the topological phase via ARPES is well understood. The device-geometry challenge of growing thin films, controlling interfaces, and patterning at the nanometer scale is an active research focus in every major topological materials laboratory, including the team Priya leads.

Marcus's recognition moment, the realization that the protection is intrinsic to the material rather than imposed by external error correction circuitry, is the correct insight to carry forward. Every chapter from here builds on it. The topological insulator is the simplest realization of a material whose useful properties are guaranteed by topology. The topological superconductor, which Chapter 7 approaches through the broader landscape of topological semimetals and Chapter 8 enters directly, takes that guarantee and extends it to quantum information.

Diagram 6.12 - Chapter 6 Concept Map

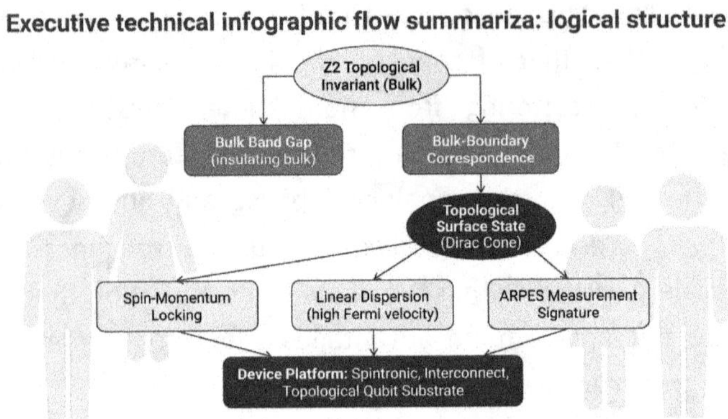

7 Beyond Insulators

The whiteboard in Axiom Quantum's theory suite covers most of the east wall, and by mid-morning, it is filled with something resembling a heavily annotated periodic table. Sasha Korolev has color-coded it by symmetry class: blue for time-reversal-protected phases, green for crystalline-symmetry phases, and red for magnetic phases in which time-reversal is broken on purpose. Priya Nair stands to his left, adding labels from memory, filling in the material examples beside each topological class with the confidence of someone who has grown these crystals and read their ARPES spectra herself. The board is not a taxonomy for its own sake. It is a navigational map, and the two of them are building it because the question of which materials to prioritize at Axiom has become urgent.

Marcus Webb walks in from the fabrication side, still wearing the cleanroom smock he forgot to remove. He looks at the board, reads a few of the labels, and turns to Sasha. "Topological insulators, I understand now. Protected surface states and the Dirac cone at the surface are conducive to proximity coupling with a superconductor. But you have seven other boxes up there. Which of these can we actually build with? Which ones are engineering bets, and which ones are still physics experiments?" Sasha caps his marker. "That is exactly the right question. Each of these classes has a different engineering story. The insulator was the first chapter. This is everything that came after, and some of it is more useful for us than the insulator itself."

This chapter systematically answers Marcus's question. For each material class beyond the topological insulator, the opening question is what the engineering opportunity is, not what the physics is. What can this material do that a conventional material cannot? What device function does that property enable? What fabrication constraints does it impose? The physics follows from those questions. By the end of the chapter, the board on the wall is readable not as a catalog of exotic states but as a structured set of engineering options, each with its own readiness level and its own path toward a device.

Why It Matters

Topological insulators were the proof of concept that topology could protect electronic states in a real material at experimentally accessible temperatures. That proof mattered enormously, but it narrowed the perception of what constitutes topological materials. For several years after the experimental confirmation of Bi2Se3 and Bi2Te3, the phrase topological material in an engineering context was nearly synonymous with topological insulator, as though the first confirmed example were the only example. The past decade has dismantled that equivalence. We now have experimentally confirmed phases that include bulk-conducting semimetals, magnetic insulators with quantized Hall conductance in zero external field, higher-order phases with protected states on hinges and corners rather than on surfaces, and crystalline phases in which the relevant symmetry is the crystal structure itself rather than time-reversal invariance.

The hardware stakes differ by class. For a quantum computing engineer, the most relevant question is which materials can contribute to a topological qubit architecture. The answer extends beyond the insulator-superconductor interface to include Weyl semimetals with proximity coupling and magnetic topological insulators, where the quantized Hall state eliminates the need for an external magnet. For a semiconductor engineer working on post-silicon transistor technology, the relevant question is which materials provide electron mobility beyond gallium arsenide or indium antimonide. There, the answer is Dirac semimetals, specifically cadmium arsenide, which holds the highest measured electron mobility of any known material. For a sensing engineer, the answer includes the anomalous Hall conductance of magnetic topological insulators and the chiral-anomaly transport in Weyl semimetals.

What each material class requires of the engineer is a clear understanding of what it does, why it does it, and the fabrication constraints that follow. That is the framework this chapter provides. The theoretical depth goes where it needs to go, no further, because Marcus's question was not about the elegance of the topological classification scheme. It was about what can be built.

Weyl Semimetals: Protected Bulk Transport

The topological insulator's defining engineering feature is its surface: a conducting channel that cannot be localized by disorder, protected by the topology of the bulk band structure. The Weyl semimetal offers something categorically different. Its defining engineering feature is what happens in the bulk. A Weyl semimetal is a material whose conduction and valence bands touch at discrete points in momentum space called Weyl nodes, and those touching points are topologically protected. No perturbation, no impurity, no structural distortion can open a gap at a Weyl node without either annihilating it with a node of opposite chirality or violating the material's fundamental symmetry. That robustness is a bulk property that shapes the material's transport behavior throughout its entire volume.

Near a Weyl node, electrons behave as Weyl fermions, massless relativistic quasiparticles first predicted by Hermann Weyl in 1929. Their energy dispersion is linear in all three momentum directions, and they carry a definite chirality, either left-handed or right-handed. The chirality of a Weyl node is a topological quantum number called the Chern number, defined as the integral of the Berry curvature, the curl of the Berry connection in momentum space, over any closed surface surrounding the node. A node with Chern number plus one is a source of Berry curvature; a node with Chern number minus one is a sink. Topology requires that sources and sinks come in pairs: Weyl nodes always appear in pairs of opposite chirality, and destroying one requires annihilating it with its partner, which demands a finite perturbation. Small perturbations, including disorder that would scatter electrons in a conventional metal, cannot touch them.

Diagram 7.1 - Weyl Node Pair in Momentum Space

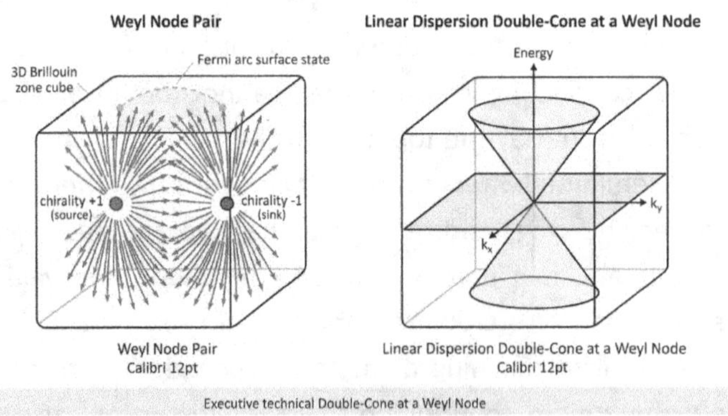

The topological protection of Weyl nodes gives rise to a distinctive surface state. On any surface of a Weyl semimetal, states connect a node of one chirality to the corresponding node of opposite chirality on the opposite surface. In the surface Brillouin zone, these states trace an open arc rather than a closed loop, hence the term "Fermi-arc surface states." A Fermi arc cannot exist in a conventional material because conventional surface states either close into loops or scatter into bulk states. The Fermi arc's topological anchor, the Weyl node it terminates at in the bulk, protects it from backscattering just as the topological insulator surface state is protected by time-reversal symmetry.

The first experimental confirmation came in 2015, when groups at Princeton, MIT, and in China simultaneously published angle-resolved photoemission spectroscopy data from tantalum arsenide, TaAs. ARPES fires ultraviolet photons at a crystal surface and measures the energy and momentum of the emitted photoelectrons, providing a direct image of the surface band structure. The TaAs spectra clearly showed the open Fermi arc, connecting the projected Weyl node positions across the surface Brillouin zone. Subsequent measurements confirmed Fermi arcs in niobium arsenide (NbAs), tantalum phosphide (TaP), and niobium phosphide (NbP), establishing the transition metal monopnictide family as the most thoroughly characterized Weyl semimetal class.

Diagram 7.2 - Fermi Arc ARPES Confirmation in TaAs

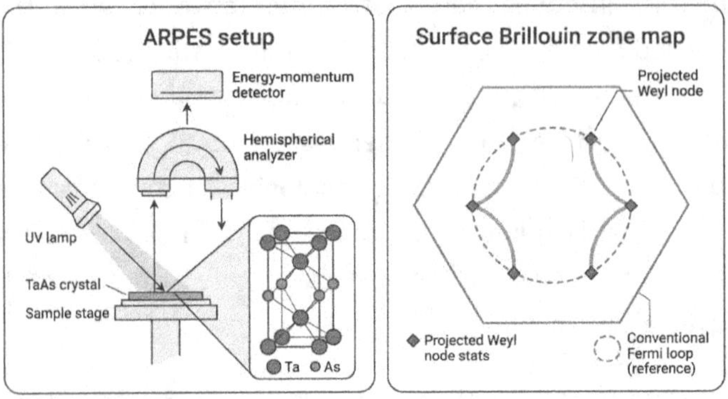

The engineering motivation for Weyl semimetals also rests on a bulk transport phenomenon called the chiral anomaly. When a magnetic field and an electric field are applied in parallel in a Weyl semimetal, charge carriers are pumped between Weyl nodes of opposite chirality through a process with no classical analog. This inter-node pumping reduces the effective scattering rate. It produces an anomalous decrease in resistivity as the parallel magnetic field increases, the opposite of what magnetoresistance does in a conventional metal. This negative longitudinal magnetoresistance has been measured in TaAs, NbAs, and several related compounds. It is not a delicate effect observable only near absolute zero: reports of the signature approaching room temperature in some materials considerably elevate its engineering relevance. A material whose bulk conductance responds to a parallel magnetic field through a topologically protected mechanism is a candidate for a magnetoresistive sensor element whose sensitivity derives from the band structure rather than the geometry of a thin-film stack.

Dirac Semimetals: Mobility for High-Frequency RF

A Dirac semimetal is, in one sense, two Weyl semimetals superimposed. Where a Weyl semimetal has nondegenerate Weyl nodes, each carrying a Chern number of plus or minus one, a Dirac semimetal has nodes where two Weyl nodes of opposite chirality occupy the same momentum point, producing a fourfold-degenerate Dirac point. The Dirac point is stable against hybridization because a crystal rotation symmetry prevents the overlapping nodes from gapping out. In the primary experimental candidates, the symmetry is rotational crystal symmetry, and the Dirac point lies on the high-symmetry axis of the Brillouin zone, where the symmetry is exactly preserved.

The engineering reason to care about Dirac semimetals is electron mobility. Cadmium arsenide, Cd3As2, holds the highest measured bulk electron mobility of any known material. Values above ten million square centimeters per volt-second have been reported in high-quality single crystals at cryogenic temperatures, and values above one million square centimeters per volt-second have been measured at room temperature in optimized specimens. Gallium arsenide, the standard high-mobility semiconductor for microwave transistors, achieves roughly 8,000 square centimeters per volt-second at room temperature. Cd3As2 is more than two orders of magnitude higher. The physics is the linear Dirac dispersion: electrons near a Dirac point behave as effectively massless quasiparticles, and massless carriers scatter far less efficiently from impurities and phonons than conventional parabolic-band electrons with a finite effective mass.

Diagram 7.3 - Dirac Cone Dispersion and Mobility Comparison

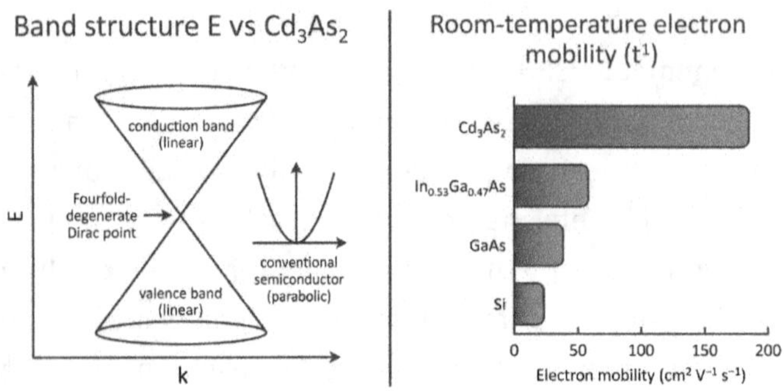

The-image of room-temperature electron mobilities (Calibri), 11pt

The experimental confirmation of Cd3As2 as a Dirac semimetal came in 2014, when ARPES measurements from multiple groups revealed linear surface band dispersion and confirmed the bulk Dirac point at the predicted position along the fourfold rotation axis. Sodium bismuthide (Na3Bi) was confirmed around the same time as a complementary platform. Both materials had been known for decades; their extreme mobilities had been documented in the 1960s and 1970s, but attributed to a narrow band gap rather than to Dirac physics.

For device engineering, the question is whether the mobility can be reproduced in a manufacturable transistor stack. Cd3As2 is a soft material that is resistant to standard dry-etch processes, and its cadmium content raises environmental concerns regarding commercial deployment. Thin-film growth by molecular beam epitaxy on GaAs and CdTe substrates has been demonstrated by groups at Purdue, the University of Minnesota, and in Japan, with mobilities that still substantially exceed those of III-V alternatives at comparable carrier densities. Groups at MIT and Purdue have demonstrated Cd3As2 thin-film transistors operating at hundreds of gigahertz in prototype form, competitive with the fastest available InP high-electron-mobility transistors. The path to high-volume manufacturing is not clear yet, but the trajectory is encouraging.

Nodal-Line Semimetals: Extended Band Crossings

Weyl and Dirac semimetals have point-like band crossings. A nodal-line semimetal is a material where the conduction and valence bands cross along a one-dimensional curve, forming a line or ring of touching points in momentum space. The topological protection of this crossing line arises from a combination of time-reversal and inversion symmetry, and the associated surface states take a characteristic form called a drumhead surface state: a flat band that fills the interior of the projected nodal ring in the surface Brillouin zone, as a drum skin stretched across a circular rim.

Drumhead surface states are flat bands, and flat bands concentrate a large density of states at the Fermi energy on the material surface. A high surface density of states amplifies superconducting pairing in the presence of even weak attractive interactions, a phenomenon predicted to produce surface superconductivity at temperatures far above those of the bulk material. This prediction, consistent with experimental hints in ZrSiS, PbTaSe2, and Ca3P2, represents a route to superconducting surface states engineered independently of bulk superconducting order, a potentially useful degree of freedom for proximity-effect device design.

Diagram 7.4 - Nodal Ring and Drumhead Surface State

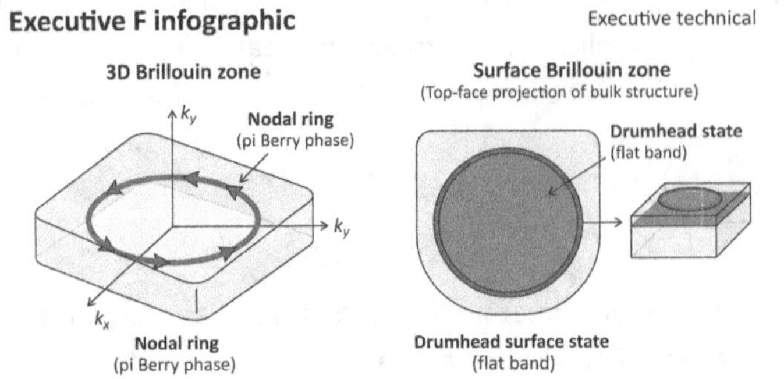

Caption: The Brillouin zone with ond nodal ring relind flat-band rainin the surface Brillouin zone.

ZrSiS is the most accessible nodal-line semimetal platform: its nodal-line structure has been confirmed by ARPES and quantum oscillation measurements, and it is reasonably air-stable. It can be cleaved cleanly, without the ultrahigh-vacuum precautions required for some topological insulator surfaces. Several groups have reported proximity-induced superconductivity in ZrSiS placed in contact with a conventional superconducting electrode. Sasha assesses that nodal-line semimetals are a research priority rather than a near-term device platform: the flat-band superconductivity prediction is compelling but not yet confirmed with the spectroscopic clarity of a confirmed topological phase. The engineering advantage over proximity-coupled topological insulators has not been established quantitatively. The concept is worth tracking, but not yet worth committing to a roadmap.

Magnetic TIs: Zero-Field Dissipationless Transport

Magnetic topological insulators produce the quantum anomalous Hall effect, abbreviated QAH: a state in which a material conducts electricity along its edges with a precisely quantized Hall conductance of e squared over h without any

applied magnetic field. In a conventional quantum Hall system, achieving this quantization requires an external magnetic field of several tesla applied to a two-dimensional electron gas at millikelvin temperatures. The QAH effect removes the magnet entirely. Time-reversal symmetry breaking is provided internally by magnetic order in the material, and the quantized edge state appears at zero field as long as the magnetic order is maintained. That distinction is a direct engineering consequence: no cryomagnet, no alignment requirements, no field coil current source.

The first experimental demonstration came in 2013, when a team at Tsinghua University, led by Ke He, Yayu Wang, and Qi-Kun Xue, reported quantized Hall conductance in zero magnetic field in thin films of chromium-doped (Bi, Sb)2Te3. In this system, chromium ions substituted into the topological insulator lattice provide the magnetic exchange interaction that breaks time-reversal symmetry and opens a magnetic exchange gap at the surface Dirac point. When the Fermi level lies inside that gap, the surface state is topologically nontrivial with a Chern number of one, and a single chiral edge mode appears on each edge with conductance exactly equal to e squared over h. This is not approximate. The quantization is exact, guaranteed by topology, and measured to one part in ten thousand in the best experiments.

Diagram 7.5 - Quantum Anomalous Hall Edge State Schematic

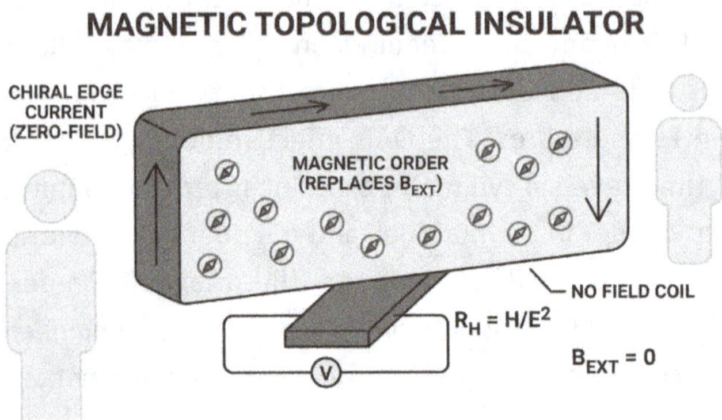

The primary limitation of Cr-doped (Bi, Sb)2Te3 is its temperature range. The quantized Hall state appears only below about 100 millikelvin because the magnetic exchange gap is small and doping disorder degrades the surface-state mobility. Both problems point to an intrinsic magnetic topological insulator in which magnetic order is built into the crystal structure without doping. That material is MnBi2Te4, manganese bismuth telluride, which was predicted to be an intrinsic magnetic topological insulator in 2018 and experimentally confirmed in 2019 and 2020 by groups in China, Germany, and the United States. MnBi2Te4 has a layered van der Waals structure in which each septuple layer consists of a Te-Bi-Te-Mn-Te-Bi-Te sandwich: the manganese layer provides magnetic order, the bismuth telluride outer layers provide the topological band inversion. QAH quantization has been confirmed in MnBi2Te4 thin films at temperatures up to approximately 1.5 kelvin, still cryogenic but meaningfully above the Cr-doped system.

Diagram 7.6 - MnBi2Te4 Crystal Structure and Magnetic Order

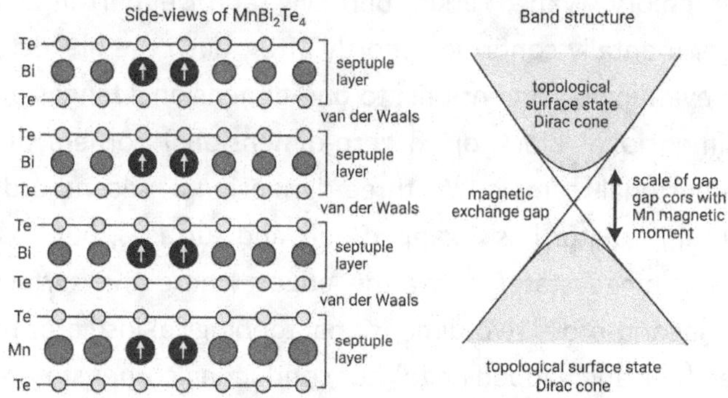

The magnetic memory application of MnBi2Te4 illustrates how QAH physics translates directly into a device specification. In a thin film of a magnetic topological insulator, the magnetization direction determines which edge carries the chiral current and therefore the sign of the quantized Hall resistance. Flipping the magnetization flips the Hall resistance between plus h over e squared and minus h over e squared by exactly one conductance quantum per transition. This binary switching between two precisely quantized states, driven by a magnetic-field pulse and read electrically as a Hall voltage, constitutes a topologically protected memory bit. Unlike a conventional magnetic random access memory cell, where the resistance difference depends on device geometry and magnetic anisotropy, the QAH memory state's resistance difference is fixed by fundamental constants. Topological protection operates directly as a device specification.

Higher-Order TIs: Topology on Hinges and Corners

First-order topological insulators support protected conducting states on their surfaces, one dimension lower than the bulk. Higher-order topological insulators, predicted by Schindler,

Cook, Vergniory, Wang, Parkin, Bernevig, and Neupert in 2018 and experimentally confirmed shortly after, push the protected state to even lower dimensions: to one-dimensional hinges of a three-dimensional block or to zero-dimensional corners of a two-dimensional sample. A three-dimensional second-order topological insulator has a gapped bulk and surfaces, but hosts conducting hinge states along the edges where the surfaces meet. A second-order two-dimensional topological insulator has a gapped bulk and gapped edges but conducting corner states.

Hinge and corner states are protected by crystalline symmetry, typically a rotation or mirror symmetry, rather than time-reversal invariance alone. The topological invariant is a bulk crystalline index rather than the Z2 invariant of the time-reversal-protected insulator. Experimental confirmation has come from bismuth crystals showing hinge states imaged by scanning tunneling microscopy, from SnTe under specific termination conditions, and from engineered acoustic metamaterials and photonic crystals, where the geometry can be designed rather than discovered.

Diagram 7.7 - Hinge States on a 3D Topological Insulator Block

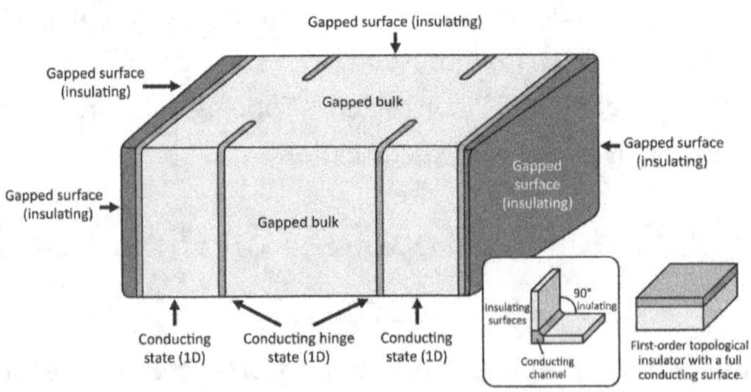

Captions I— executive ing hinges in azy for first-order topologict insulator flap in Calibri 12pt.

The engineering interest in higher-order topological insulators is in the geometry of the protected state. A first-order topological insulator's surface state covers an entire two-dimensional face, useful for broad-area proximity coupling but geometrically unconstrained. A hinge state is a one-dimensional conducting channel running along a specific crystal edge, topologically protected against perturbations that preserve the crystalline symmetry. If that geometry can be controlled by sample preparation, a higher-order topological insulator provides a built-in wire with topological protection: a one-dimensional conductor whose immunity to scattering is guaranteed by crystal symmetry rather than engineered by nanofabrication. The prospect of self-localized, topologically protected one-dimensional channels is sufficiently compelling that Sasha has flagged higher-order topological insulators as a watch-list item even though the material control is not yet at the level required for qubit device integration.

Quantum Anomalous Hall: Metrology and Qubits

The QAH effect and its material platform in MnBi2Te4 were introduced in the preceding section. Two engineering directions from QAH physics warrant separate treatment because their device implications extend beyond memory applications: resistance metrology and topological qubit architecture.

The quantized Hall conductance in a QAH insulator is exact to the precision of the measurement, fixed by fundamental constants e and h, and appears at zero magnetic field. Resistance metrology laboratories have recognized this immediately: a Hall resistance standard at zero field would eliminate the superconducting magnet infrastructure currently required for quantum Hall resistance calibration, reducing a room-sized instrument to a compact cryostat. The temperature limitation, currently around 1.5 kelvin in the best MnBi2Te4 specimens, is the only barrier to further improvement. Theoretical estimates suggest a well-optimized magnetic topological insulator could support QAH at tens of kelvin if the magnetic exchange gap can be increased while keeping bulk carrier density low. These requirements compete: doping changes that maximize the exchange gap tend to introduce bulk carriers that short out the edge state. Engineering both simultaneously is the central materials challenge in this space.

Diagram 7.8 - Chern Number and Quantized Hall Conductance

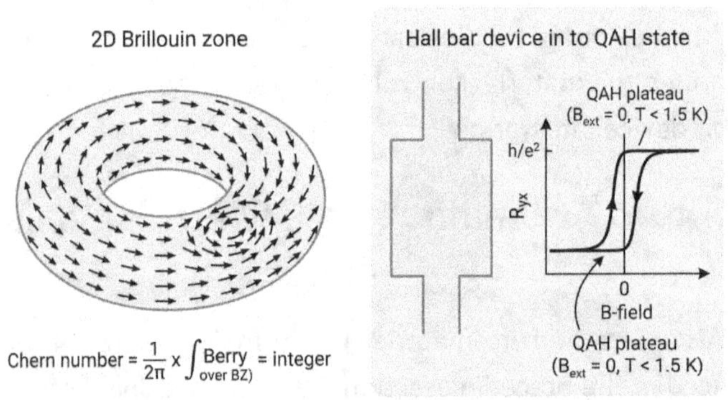

The topological qubit architecture connection was predicted by Qi, Hughes, and Zhang in 2010: the single chiral edge mode of a QAH insulator, when coupled to a conventional s-wave superconductor, splits into a pair of Majorana modes at the domain boundaries between superconductor-covered and superconductor-free regions of the edge. This platform has only one chiral mode per edge, reducing the risk of accidental Andreev bound states that can mimic the Majorana signature in multi-mode geometries. Chapter 9 covers this architecture in detail. The key point here is that the architecture's viability depends directly on QAH insulators with sufficiently large gaps to protect the Majorana mode above the qubit operating temperature, which is precisely the materials-engineering challenge the field is working to resolve.

Topological Crystalline Insulators: Symmetry Switches

Every topological insulator discussed so far is protected by time-reversal symmetry: the topological invariant is defined with respect to time-reversal, and the surface state is protected as long as time-reversal holds. Topological crystalline insulators are a distinct symmetry class. Their protection comes from a spatial symmetry of the crystal, typically a mirror or rotation symmetry, and their surface states exist on crystal surfaces that preserve that spatial symmetry. This distinction has a direct engineering consequence: the surface state of a topological crystalline insulator can be switched off by breaking the relevant crystal symmetry through applied strain, surface modification, or tuning of alloy composition. A topological insulator surface state cannot be switched off by strain because it is protected by time-reversal symmetry, which persists through strain and alloy disorder.

The primary experimental platform is tin telluride (SnTe). Hsieh, Liu, and collaborators predicted in 2012 that SnTe is a topological crystalline insulator protected by mirror symmetry, and ARPES measurements confirmed the presence of topological surface states at the predicted momentum positions. The topological invariant is a mirror Chern number, an integer counting how the band structure winds around the mirror-invariant planes in the Brillouin zone. SnTe is a IV-VI compound with the rock salt crystal structure, growable by MBE on BaF2 and related substrates, and less toxic than the bismuth telluride family. Its companion alloy systems, Pb1-xSnxTe and Pb1-xSnxSe, provide composition-tunable routes through a topological phase transition, placing the transition point at a composition that is lattice-matched to existing substrates.

Diagram 7.9 - SnTe Topological Crystalline Insulator and Strain Switching

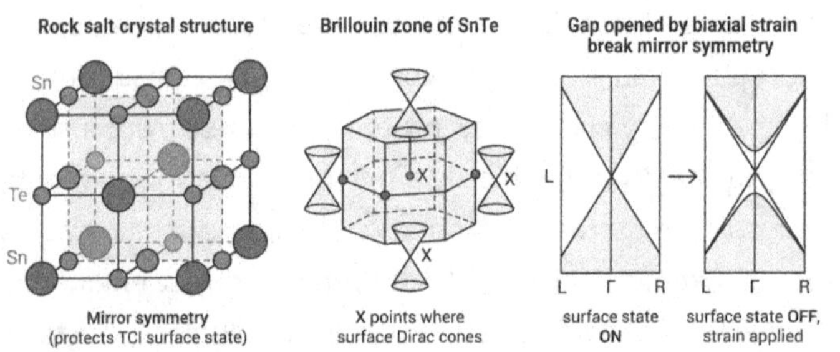

Rock salt crystal structure of 'oote SnTe of a. mirror symmetry' #D9E8F5

The topological transistor concept based on SnTe operates by applying gate-controlled strain to a thin film, opening a gap at the Dirac crossing point and switching the surface state from conducting to insulating. The switching is driven by a symmetry change rather than a conventional electrostatic band bending, making it qualitatively different from a MOSFET: the device transitions between two topologically distinct states, not between an inverted and a depleted channel. Whether this provides a practical speed or power advantage over conventional transistors at manufacturable dimensions remains an open question. Still, the concept has motivated sustained investment in the growth of SnTe thin films and in strain engineering.

The ability to tune through a topological phase transition by alloy composition rather than by an external field gives the Pb-Sn-Te and Pb-Sn-Se families a materials-engineering flexibility unavailable in binary compounds. Both alloy families have been grown by MBE and chemical vapor deposition, and their topological surface states have been characterized by ARPES in the TCI phase. The Bilbao Crystallographic Server's topological materials database lists dozens of additional TCI candidate compounds within the same symmetry class, providing experimentalists with a prediction-driven search list to work through.

The Tenfold Way: A Map, Not a Catalog

The classification on Sasha's whiteboard has a formal theoretical basis. In 2008 and 2009, Schnyder, Ryu, Furusaki, and Ludwig, and, independently, Kitaev, published a complete classification of all possible gapped topological phases protected by any combination of time-reversal symmetry, particle-hole symmetry, and chiral symmetry in any spatial dimension. This classification, called the tenfold way or the periodic table of topological insulators and superconductors, organizes all possible phases into ten symmetry classes, each of which can be either trivial or nontrivial in each dimension, with nontrivial phases characterized by integer or Z2 topological invariants depending on the symmetry class. The topological insulator of Chapter 6 is the Z2 insulator in symmetry class AII in three dimensions. Topological superconductors, the subject of Chapter 8, occupy the symmetry classes with particle-hole symmetry, and their topological invariants directly predict the existence of Majorana zero modes.

Diagram 7.10 - Periodic Table of Topological Phases (Tenfold Way)

Topological Invariant - Calibri 11pt

Symmetry Class	1D	2D	3D	4D		Time-Reversal	Particle-Hole	Chiral Symmetry
A	Trivial		Z	Trivial	A	T_n	p^h	Gh
AIII	Trivial	Z QAH ($MnBi_2Te_4$)	Trivial	Trivial	AIII	0	0	1
AI	Trivial		Z_2	Trivial	AI	−1	0	0
BDI	Trivial	Trivial	Z_2	Trivial	BDI	−1	−1	1
D	Z Kitaev chain (Majorana)	Trivial	Z_2	Trivial	D	0	−1	0
DIII	Trivial	Trivial	Z_2 TSC	Trivial	DIII	0	−1	1
AII	Trivial	Trivial	Z_2 TI Z_2 TI (Bi_2Se_3)	Trivial				
CII	Trivial	2Z	Z_2	Trivial				
C	Trivial	2Z	Z_2	Trivial				
CI	Trivial	2Z	Z_2	Trivial				

Topological invariant – 16:9 horizontal in with executive technical tone

For a hardware engineer, the value of the tenfold way lies in its use as a navigational tool. When a paper claims a new topological phase, the symmetry class tells you which invariant is relevant, which boundary states are predicted, and whether the phase survives time-reversal breaking (relevant if you need to apply a magnetic field in device operation) or particle-hole symmetry breaking (relevant for superconducting proximity coupling). Knowing that the QAH system lives in class A, characterized by an integer Chern number, tells you immediately that magnetic field application does not destroy the topological phase and that edge states come in a definite integer multiple of the conductance quantum per edge. That reading is available from the table without calculation.

The expansion of the tenfold way to include crystalline symmetries and gapless topological phases, carried out by Ando, Fu, Shiozaki, and collaborators, has produced a much larger classification encompassing hundreds of phases in three dimensions. The Topological Materials Database, maintained by groups at Princeton and in Madrid, has applied this extended classification computationally to thousands of known compounds, producing a prediction-driven target list for experimentalists. The field no longer operates by lucky discovery. It operates by prediction followed by verification, which is a mature engineering methodology, and the density of confirmed predictions is increasing every year.

What Can We Build With This?

Running through the material classes in this chapter with an engineer's eye yields a structured set of near-term device opportunities, each with a distinct readiness level and fabrication bottleneck.

Weyl semimetals, specifically TaAs and NbAs, are the most mature topological semimetal class from a single-crystal characterization standpoint. The leading near-term application is magnetic field sensing, exploiting the chiral-anomaly-induced negative magnetoresistance signal. A sensor element whose sensitivity derives from the topology of the Weyl bulk band structure would be physically distinguishable from conventional magnetoresistive sensors and potentially more robust to thermal drift. The fabrication challenge is thin-film integration: TaAs single crystals are well characterized, but TaAs thin films of device-relevant quality have only recently begun to emerge from MBE groups. The path from characterization-quality films to device-quality contacts and reproducible transport is the current engineering frontier.

Fermi arc surface states in Weyl semimetals offer a longer-range opportunity for high-mobility surface electronics. The Fermi arc is a high-mobility one-dimensional channel anchored to the Weyl node in the bulk. Devices that exploit Weyl semimetallic surface transport for high-frequency applications have been analyzed theoretically and sketched as prototypes. The mobility advantage over conventional III-V surfaces has not yet been convincingly demonstrated in a manufacturable geometry, but the theoretical motivation is clear.

Diagram 7.11 - Engineering Opportunities from Beyond-Insulator Material Classes

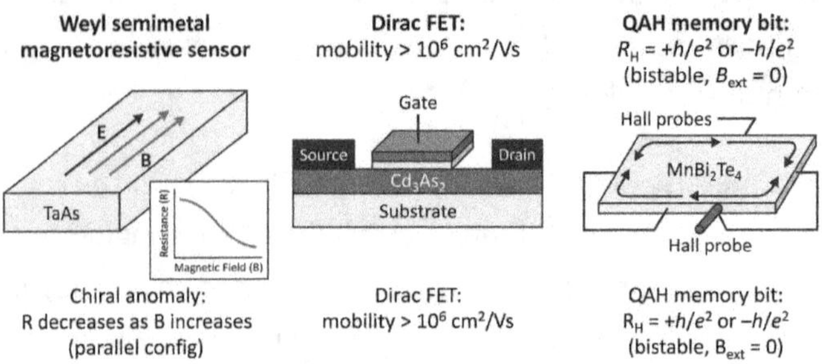

Cadmium arsenide for high-frequency transistors is the most commercially viable near-term opportunity. The mobility figures are measured values, not theoretical predictions. The question is whether they can be reproduced in a manufacturable thin-film process that integrates gate dielectrics, provides ohmic contacts, and protects against atmospheric degradation. Prototype frequencies in the hundreds of gigahertz are competitive with the fastest InP devices. The toxicity profile and material fragility of Cd3As2 remain unresolved challenges for commercial fabrication, but the performance motivation is compelling enough to sustain development efforts.

Magnetic topological insulator systems offer two near-term applications. The QAH memory device, read out as a quantized Hall voltage and written by a magnetic field pulse, has topological protection, guaranteeing stability against thermal noise up to the temperature at which the QAH gap closes. The

QAH resistance metrology application would eliminate the superconducting magnet infrastructure currently required for quantum Hall resistance calibration. Both require QAH materials that quantize above liquid helium temperature, which is the organizing challenge of the field.

Topological crystalline insulators offer a strain-switchable surface state for transistor architectures. The basic concept has been demonstrated spectroscopically but not yet in a gated device with reproducible on-off switching. Higher-order topological insulators offer the longest time horizon but the most architecturally distinctive opportunity: a material that self-organizes topologically protected one-dimensional hinge channels that no amount of nanolithography can replicate. Both classes are watch-list items at Axiom rather than active device programs, which is the right stance given their current experimental maturity.

Diagram 7.12 - Technology Readiness Map for Beyond-Insulator Material Classes

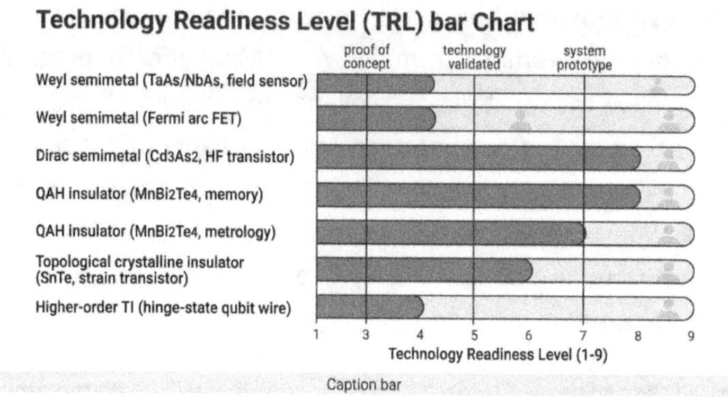

Takeaway

The material classes in this chapter share a common architecture: topology encodes a protection guarantee into the electronic structure, and that guarantee translates into a device specification that conventional materials cannot match. The engineering distinction between classes is which boundary carries the protected state and which symmetry protects it. Weyl semimetals protect bulk transport through chirality. Dirac semimetals exhibit extreme mobility due to massless dispersion. Quantum anomalous Hall insulators quantize edge conduction without a magnet. Topological crystalline insulators make surface states symmetry-switchable. Higher-order topological insulators confine protection to hinges and corners. Each of these is a different answer to a distinct engineering question, which is why Sasha's whiteboard needs all seven boxes, not just one.

Fabrication readiness varies widely across the class. Weyl and Dirac semimetals have the most mature single-crystal characterization and the clearest near-term device applications. Still, the gap between bulk crystal physics and manufacturable thin-film device geometry remains real. Magnetic topological insulators have the most direct relevance to qubit architectures, but are gated by the temperature at which QAH quantization persists. Topological crystalline insulators and higher-order topological insulators are at the forefront, with compelling theoretical structure and promising experimental hints, but not yet demonstrated device function.

What all of these classes share is a theoretical organizing framework: the tenfold way and its crystalline symmetry extensions. That framework is a predictive tool that materials theorists are using to identify topological phases in existing compounds and to design new compounds with targeted properties. The Topological Materials Database lists thousands of predicted topological compounds; the experimental community is working through that list, and confirmed predictions outnumber refuted ones every year. The engineering community's job is to be ready when the materials mature, and being ready requires understanding the map.

The next chapter turns to topological superconductors, the material class that connects the physics surveyed here to the qubit architecture that Axiom is building toward. Superconductivity is a symmetry-breaking phase in its own right. When it is topologically nontrivial, the combination of broken symmetry and topological protection produces Majorana fermions, quasiparticles that are their own antiparticles and that obey non-Abelian braiding statistics. Understanding how Weyl semimetals, QAH insulators, and higher-order topological insulators serve as substrates for that topological superconducting phase is the bridge between the materials in this chapter and the device Axiom is trying to build.

8 Superconductivity

The cryostat in Bay 4 was running at fourteen millikelvin when Priya Nair waved Marcus Webb over. A steel vacuum can, bristling with coaxial cables and DC lines, sat inside a dilution refrigerator beneath its pulse-tube pre-cooler. On the laptop propped against the granite vibration-isolation table, a single plot glowed: resistance on the vertical axis, temperature on the horizontal, and a curve that ran gently downward from the upper left and then, at a precise temperature just under nine kelvin, dropped cleanly and without ceremony to zero. Not near zero. Zero.

"That is the niobium-titanium nitride film we deposited last week," Priya said. "Forty nanometers. Below Tc, the resistance is not small. It is not negligible. It is zero. The material has reorganized itself into a collective quantum state in which no scattering mechanism can dissipate energy. You are not measuring a very good metal. You are measuring something categorically different." Marcus had worked with superconducting materials before, had soldered niobium joints, and shimmed Josephson junction boards. Still, he had always treated superconductivity as a specification rather than a phenomenon—zero resistance below Tc. Apply the field carefully. Do not exceed the critical current. Now the vertical drop felt like something that required explanation.

"So why do we need fifteen millikelvin?" he asked. "This film transitions at nine kelvin." Priya turned to face him. "What we are making requires temperatures where the thermal energy is far below a different energy scale entirely. Not the Josephson energy of a junction. The topological gap of a Majorana mode. And to understand why that gap is smaller, why it is more fragile, and why it is worth engineering around, you need to understand what superconductivity actually is, from the condensate up." She pulled a stool to the bench. "Let me start at the beginning."

Why It Matters

Superconductivity is the prerequisite for topological quantum computing. Every serious topological qubit platform requires a superconducting component. The superconductor is not peripheral hardware: it supplies the quantum correlations from which the topological phase is constructed. To understand why topological superconductors host Majorana modes, you first need to understand what a conventional superconductor is doing microscopically, why its gap is topologically trivial, and what change to the gap structure makes it non-trivial. That chain of reasoning runs from the phonon-mediated Cooper pairing mechanism all the way to the Fu-Kane proximity-effect proposal, and every step is load-bearing.

Superconductors are also the substrate of the best-understood quantum computers currently operating. IBM, Google, IQM, and Rigetti all build on superconducting transmon qubits from aluminum or niobium Josephson junctions. Understanding why those qubits require millikelvin temperatures and what their physical limitations are provides context for the architectural bet that Axiom and Microsoft are making: that topological protection in a different class of superconducting material can deliver fault tolerance with lower overhead than the error-correcting codes required by conventional transmons. And beyond quantum computing, superconductors underlie quantum-limited amplifiers, SQUID magnetometers, and the microwave readout chains of every cryogenic quantum processor in existence.

Cooper Pairs and the BCS Mechanism

The Bardeen-Cooper-Schrieffer theory, published in 1957 and awarded the Nobel Prize in 1972, explains superconductivity as arising from a phonon-mediated attractive interaction between electrons. In a normal metal, electrons scatter off lattice defects, phonons, and each other, and that scattering is the microscopic origin of electrical resistance. BCS showed that when the lattice-mediated attraction between electrons near the Fermi surface exceeds their screened Coulomb repulsion, they pair up into composite objects called Cooper pairs, and the entire population of Cooper pairs condenses into a single macroscopic quantum state from which no scattering can extract energy.

The phonon-mediated attraction is best understood through the mattress analogy. An electron moving through the positive-ion lattice creates a slight dimple by attracting nearby ions. The lattice takes finite time to relax back, and during that relaxation, the local excess of positive charge attracts a second electron. The second electron is drawn toward the region the first has already vacated: an effective attraction mediated by a phonon, retarded over the Debye frequency timescale. Cooper showed in 1956 that even an arbitrarily weak such attraction binds a pair below the Fermi surface into what is now called a Cooper pair. The Fermi sea is essential because it restricts pairing to momenta near the Fermi surface and eliminates the kinetic-energy competition that would otherwise prevent binding in free space. Cooper pairs consist of two electrons with equal and opposite momenta and opposite spins, the (k up, minus-k down) singlet configuration known as s-wave pairing.

The BCS ground state is a coherent superposition of Cooper pairs sharing a single macroscopic quantum phase. The key quantity is the superconducting order parameter delta, with units of energy, sometimes called the superconducting gap. Delta represents the energy cost to break a Cooper pair: any perturbation below 2 delta cannot disrupt the condensate, which is why superconductors are immune to the scattering processes that dissipate energy in normal metals. The BCS gap equation gives delta approximately equal to 1.76 times the Boltzmann constant times Tc. For aluminum, delta is roughly 180 microelectronvolts (Tc near 1.2 kelvin); for niobium, roughly 1.5 millielectronvolts (Tc near 9.2 kelvin). The operating temperature of superconducting devices must be kept well below 2 delta to avoid thermally breaking pairs and suppressing the condensate.

In a conventional BCS superconductor, the order parameter is the same for all momenta k at the Fermi surface: delta(k) equals a constant. This is s-wave pairing, with the full rotational symmetry of an s orbital. An s-wave gap is topologically trivial: you can continuously deform it to zero without any topological obstruction: no winding, no Chern number, no Z2 invariant. The path from this trivial gap to a topologically nontrivial one is the central materials-engineering problem in topological superconductivity.

Diagram 8.1 - Cooper Pair Formation via Phonon Mediation

Phonon-mediated Cooper pairing

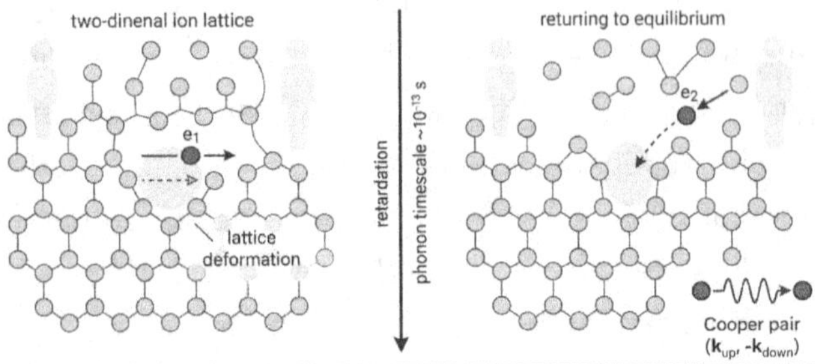

Phonon-mediated Cooper pairing: electron e1 deforms the lattice; e2 is attracted to the residual positive charge before the lattice relaxes.

The Meissner Effect and the SC Operating Envelope

The Meissner effect, discovered by Walther Meissner and Robert Ochsenfeld in 1933, is the expulsion of magnetic flux from the bulk of a superconductor as it cools through Tc. This is not simply a consequence of zero resistance. A perfect conductor with zero resistance would prevent changes in magnetic flux by Lenz's law, but it would not expel an already-present field as it transitioned. A superconductor does both: it expels pre-existing fields and prevents new flux from entering. The mechanism is spontaneous surface currents that generate a field that cancels the applied external field inside the material. The competition between the energy cost of expelling the magnetic field and the condensation energy gained by entering the superconducting state defines the critical field Hc, above which the material returns to normal.

Type I superconductors, including most pure elements such as aluminum, lead, and mercury, undergo a sharp transition from full Meissner expulsion to the normal state at a single critical field Hc. Type II superconductors, including alloys such as niobium-titanium (NbTi) and compound materials such as

Nb3Sn, have two critical fields: a lower Hc1 below which the Meissner state holds, and an upper Hc2 above which the material is normal. Between Hc1 and Hc2, the superconductor enters the Abrikosov vortex state, in which quantized tubes of magnetic flux penetrate the material. Each vortex carries exactly one flux quantum h over 2e, approximately 2.07 femtowebers, where the factor of 2e rather than e is a direct signature of Cooper pairing. The coherence length xi sets the vortex core radius, and the circulating supercurrents decay over the London penetration depth lambda.

For topological superconductor engineering, the Type I versus Type II distinction is not academic. Tuning into the topological phase in semiconductor-superconductor nanowire devices requires an applied axial magnetic field. A Type I superconductor would immediately quench under that field. The aluminum shell used in InAs nanowire platforms is thin, and thin-film confinement shifts aluminum's effective behavior toward Type II, making it compatible with the applied fields required for topological phase tuning. The operating envelope of any superconducting device is bounded simultaneously by Tc, Hc2, and the critical current density Jc. Axiom's dilution refrigerator sets the base temperature safely below Tc; the external vector magnet is calibrated below the thin-film critical field; and all current biases remain well below Jc.

Diagram 8.2 - Type I vs. Type II Superconductor Phase Diagrams

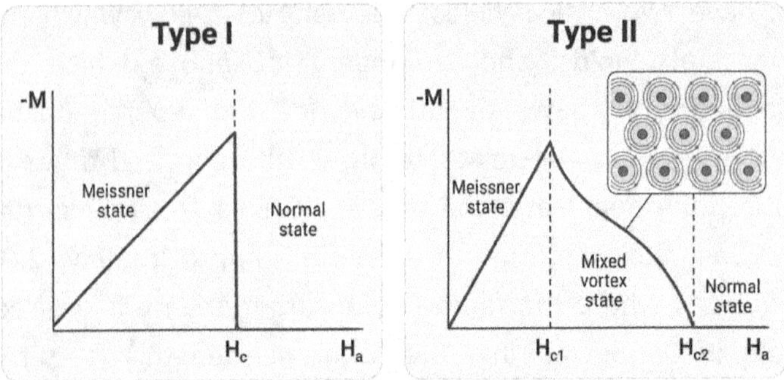

Type I expels all flux up to H_c; Type II allows quantized vortex penetration between H_{c1} and H_{c2}.

Diagram 8.3 - Superconductor Critical Operating Envelope (T, H, J Phase Diagram)

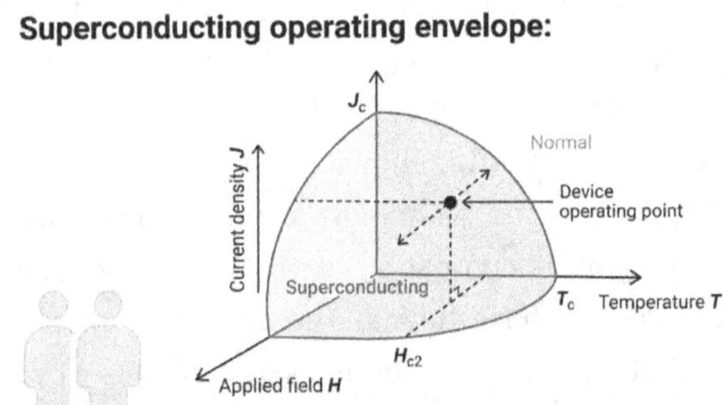

Superconducting operating envelope: device must stay inside the surface defined by T_c, H_{c2}, and J_c simultaneously.

The Josephson Effect and Superconducting Qubits

In 1962, Brian Josephson predicted that Cooper pairs could tunnel through a thin insulating barrier separating two superconductors, thereby producing a supercurrent without an applied voltage. The DC Josephson effect gives a supercurrent I equal to Ic times the sine of the phase difference phi between the two superconductors, where Ic is the critical current of the junction. This sine dependence is non-linear, and that nonlinearity is what makes Josephson junctions the active element of superconducting qubits.

A resonant LC circuit has a harmonic spectrum of equally spaced energy levels: you cannot isolate a two-level qubit because driving at the 0-to-1 frequency also drives the 1-to-2 transition. The Josephson junction's sinusoidal current-phase relation gives an effective inductance proportional to 1 over cos(phi), which changes as phi changes. This non-linear inductance makes the energy spectrum anharmonic: the 0-to-1 spacing differs from the 1-to-2 spacing by an amount called the anharmonicity. A microwave drive tuned to the qubit frequency does not resonantly excite higher transitions, isolating the two-level subspace. This is the physical principle behind the transmon qubit used by IBM, Google, and Rigetti.

The transmon qubit is a Josephson junction shunted by a large capacitor to reduce sensitivity to charge noise, operating at 15 to 20 millikelvin with a transition frequency of 4 to 6 gigahertz. Coherence times in the best current devices reach milliseconds, limited by dielectric losses in the substrate materials, quasiparticle poisoning from Cooper pairs broken by stray high-energy photons, and flux noise from magnetic-field inhomogeneity in the junction loop. Each loss mechanism is a direct consequence of superconducting physics. Improving transmon coherence is fundamentally a materials engineering problem, and the techniques required, controlling oxide barriers at the angstrom level, minimizing surface contamination, optimizing substrate surface preparation, are the same techniques that underlie every other superconducting device platform. The AC Josephson effect provides the world's most precise voltage standard: a constant voltage across a junction drives an oscillating supercurrent at 484 megahertz per microvolt, a conversion so reproducible that the SI volt is now defined through the Josephson constant, 2e/h.

Diagram 8.4 - Josephson Junction Structure and Transmon Qubit Energy Spectrum

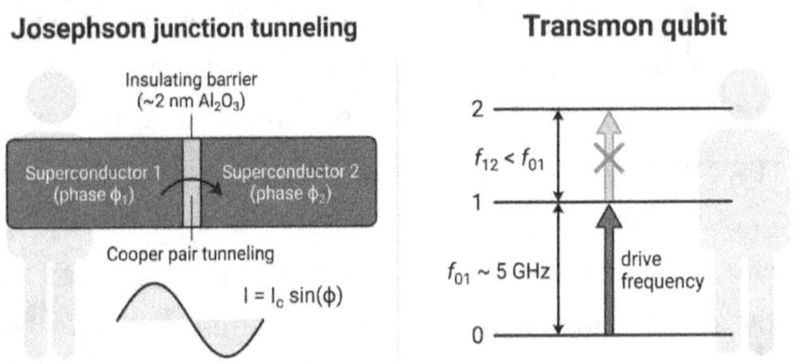

Josephson junction tunneling (left) and anharmonic transmon qubit spectrum (right): the non-linear inductance separates the 0-to-1 and 1-to-2 transition frequencies, isolating the qubit subspace.

Unconventional Superconductors: High-Tc and Gap Symmetry

In its original form, BCS theory describes s-wave superconductors with a uniform, nodeless gap. Materials with stronger electronic correlations can form pairs with higher angular momentum, producing order parameters that vary in momentum space with d-orbital or p-orbital symmetry. These are unconventional superconductors, and their physics differs from BCS theory in ways that directly matter for topological superconductivity.

The high-temperature cuprates, discovered by Georg Bednorz and Alex Müller at IBM Zurich in 1986 and awarded the Nobel Prize the following year, shattered the expectation that superconductivity above 30 kelvin was impossible. YBa2Cu3O7 (YBCO) has a Tc of 93 kelvin, well above the boiling point of liquid nitrogen at 77 kelvin. Bi2Sr2CaCu2O8 (BSCCO) reaches 85 kelvin. The pairing symmetry of the cuprates is d-wave, specifically d(x2-y2): the order parameter changes sign four times around the two-dimensional Brillouin zone, producing four nodes where delta(k) vanishes. Quasiparticles near these nodes cost negligible energy, so low-energy excitations exist even deep in the superconducting state. This nodal structure is the reason cuprates have not been successfully used as qubit substrates despite their high Tc: the gap-protected immunity of s-wave superconductors is lost along nodal directions, and the coherence properties required for qubit operation depend critically on a fully gapped spectrum.

Iron-based superconductors, discovered in 2008 by Hideo Hosono's group, include compounds such as LaFeAsO(1-x)F(x), BaFe2As2, and the iron chalcogenide FeSe, with Tc values from 6 kelvin for bulk FeSe to over 100 kelvin reported for single-layer FeSe films on SrTiO3 substrates. The pairing mechanism is generally attributed to spin fluctuations, producing an s+-gap in which the order parameter changes sign between electron and hole Fermi-surface pockets. Several iron-based superconductors, particularly FeTe(1-x)Se(x), appear to be intrinsic topological superconductors. Scanning tunneling microscope measurements of FeTe(0.55)Se(0.45) by Wang and colleagues in 2018 reported zero-energy bound states in vortex cores consistent with Majorana modes, making this material family a subject of active experimental study alongside the proximity-engineered platforms.

More relevant to the Axiom platform is p-wave pairing, in which Cooper pairs carry orbital angular momentum of one unit. Spinless p-wave superconductors in one dimension are the canonical model of a topological superconductor, as Alexei

Kitaev showed in his foundational 2001 paper. In two dimensions, a chiral p-wave superconductor hosts chiral Majorana edge modes at its boundary, analogous to the edge states of a quantum Hall insulator. The challenge is that no confirmed clean bulk p-wave superconductor is available in a form suitable for fabrication. Sr2RuO4 has long been the leading candidate, but recent NMR measurements have cast serious doubt on its p-wave assignment. This is why practical topological superconductivity has converged on proximity engineering: assembling the ingredients of a topological gap from individually trivial components.

Diagram 8.5 - Gap Symmetry in Momentum Space: s-wave, d-wave, and chiral p-wave

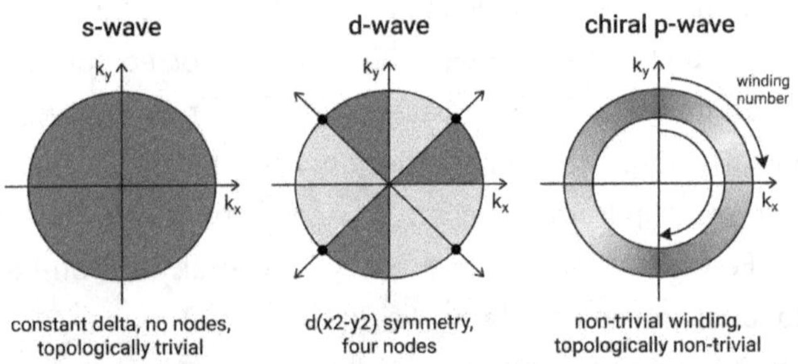

Gap symmetry determines topological character: s-wave is trivial, chiral p-wave carries a non-trivial topological winding

Topological Superconductors and Majorana Zero Modes

The concept of a topological superconductor extends the bulk-boundary correspondence from topological insulators into the superconducting context. In a superconductor, the relevant spectrum is the Bogoliubov-de Gennes (BdG) quasiparticle spectrum, which describes electrons and holes together in a particle-hole symmetric space, and which has a gap equal to the superconducting order parameter. If the topology of the BdG Hamiltonian is non-trivial, the bulk-boundary correspondence requires zero-energy states at any boundary between the topological superconductor and a trivial phase. These zero-energy boundary states are Majorana fermion modes, quasiparticles that are their own antiparticle: the creation and annihilation operators for a Majorana mode are identical. The zero energy of the mode is protected by particle-hole symmetry combined with the topological invariant of the bulk, and no local perturbation preserving particle-hole symmetry can move these modes away from zero energy without closing the bulk gap.

The ten-fold way, the classification of all topological phases of matter by symmetry class developed around 2008 to 2009 by Schnyder, Ryu, Furusaki, Ludwig, and Kitaev, organizes superconductors by the symmetries they possess. Class D, which has particle-hole symmetry but no time-reversal symmetry, is the relevant class for spinless p-wave superconductors in one dimension. In class D in one dimension, the topological invariant is a Z2 number (0 or 1), and the non-trivial phase hosts an unpaired Majorana zero mode at each end of a finite wire. Kitaev's 1D chain model is the prototype of this phase. A tight-binding Hamiltonian describes it with a nearest-neighbor p-wave pairing term, and it supports a topological phase whenever the chemical potential is inside the band defined by the hopping parameter. In that topological phase, zero-energy Majorana modes appear at the ends regardless of the wire length, provided the length exceeds a few coherence lengths. This length-independence is the mathematical signature of non-locality: the Majorana mode is not a localized electronic state but a non-local degree of freedom distributed across the entire wire.

The quantum information consequence of Majorana non-locality is that two Majorana modes at the ends of a single wire define one fermionic state of occupation number zero or one, and the superposition of these two occupation states encodes one qubit. Because neither end of the wire contains the full qubit on its own, a local perturbation at one end cannot measure or corrupt the qubit without simultaneously disturbing the other end, which is separated by the full wire length. The energy splitting between the two occupation states decays exponentially with the wire length divided by the coherence length, making the qubit exponentially insensitive to local noise as the wire is extended. This is topological protection: not perfect immunity, but exponential suppression of error rates, which changes the scaling economics of fault-tolerant quantum computation.

Diagram 8.6 - Kitaev Chain and Majorana End Modes

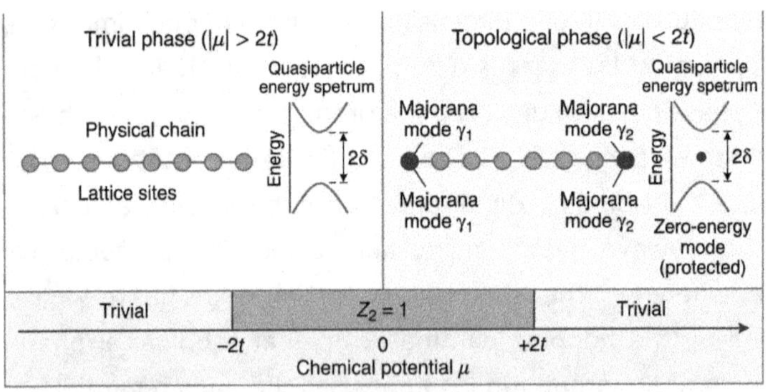

Kitaev chain in one dimension: the topological phase hosts Majorana zero modes at both ends, protected by the bulk gap and particle-hole symmetry.

The Fu-Kane Proposal: TI Proximity Effect

The theoretical breakthrough that made topological superconductivity accessible to experiment came in 2008, when Liang Fu and Charles Kane at the University of Pennsylvania showed that proximity coupling an ordinary s-wave superconductor to the surface of a three-dimensional topological insulator engineers a topological superconducting phase without requiring any intrinsically topological superconductor. The required materials were already in hand: a thin film of niobium or aluminum deposited on the surface of Bi2Se3 or Bi2Te3. The proximity effect, in which Cooper pairs tunnel from the superconductor into the TI surface state and induce a pairing amplitude there, does the rest.

The mechanism rests on the special structure of TI surface states. As established in Chapter 6, the surface of a 3D topological insulator hosts a single Dirac cone in which electron spin is locked perpendicular to momentum by strong spin-orbit coupling. Electrons moving in opposite directions carry opposite spins, exactly the configuration for Cooper pairing. When the Fermi level is tuned to the Dirac point and s-wave pairing is induced by proximity, the Dirac cone is gapped, but the resulting state is not a trivial superconductor. The non-trivial Berry phase of pi from the Dirac cone cannot be removed by smooth deformation: the gapped surface state is topologically equivalent to a spinless p-wave superconductor in two dimensions, with a Chern number of one-half. Vortices in the superconducting order parameter on this surface each bind a single Majorana zero mode in their core.

The engineering appeal of the Fu-Kane proposal is its separation of concerns. The s-wave superconductor provides pairing via well-understood BCS physics in materials like niobium, with a reliable gap and critical field. The topological insulator supplies the non-trivial Berry phase from the spin-orbit physics of bismuth. Neither ingredient needs to be unusual on its own. The topological superconducting phase emerges from the interface. Experimental evidence has been reported in several systems, including Nb-Bi2Te3 junctions, through zero-bias conductance peaks in scanning tunneling microscope measurements of magnetic vortex cores. A true Majorana mode in a vortex core produces a sharp peak in differential conductance at zero bias, but distinguishing it from trivial Caroli-de Gennes-Matricon bound states requires energy resolution below a fraction of a millielectronvolt and measurement temperatures below one kelvin. This experimental challenge has made the unambiguous identification of Fu-Kane Majorana modes an ongoing program.

Diagram 8.7 - Fu-Kane Proximity Effect: TI Surface State and s-wave Superconductor

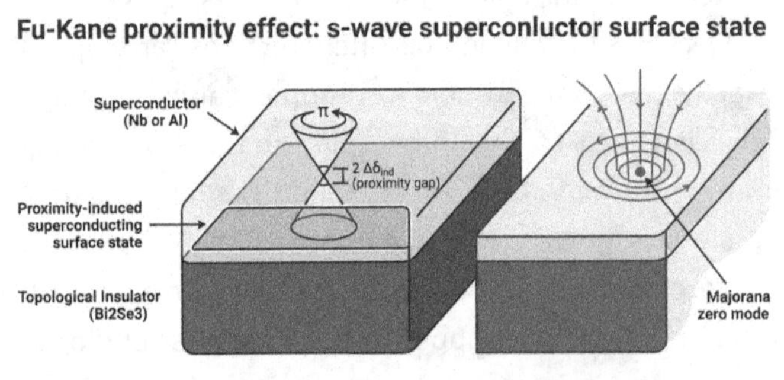

Fu-Kane proximity effect: s-wave superconductor induces pairing into the spin-momentum-locked Dirac surface state of a topological insulator, engineering a topological superconducting phase with Majorana modes in vortex cores.

Lutchyn-Oreg: Semiconductor-SC Nanowires

The most experimentally advanced topological superconductor platform is the semiconductor-superconductor nanowire, proposed independently in 2010 by Roman Lutchyn, Jay Sau, and S. Das Sarma at the University of Maryland, and by Yuval Oreg, Gil Refael, and Felix von Oppen at the Weizmann Institute. A semiconductor nanowire with strong spin-orbit coupling (InAs or InSb), covered by an s-wave superconductor (aluminum), and subjected to an axial magnetic field can enter a topological superconducting phase with a Majorana zero mode at each end. The three ingredients are precisely specified: the semiconductor provides spin-orbit coupling, the aluminum shell provides the pairing by proximity, and the axial field drives the topological transition by lifting spin degeneracy.

The mechanism follows from the interplay of three energy scales: Rashba spin-orbit coupling, Zeeman splitting from the axial field, and the proximity-induced superconducting gap. Rashba spin-orbit coupling in InAs, arising from broken inversion symmetry at the semiconductor-superconductor interface, separates spin-up and spin-down states in momentum space: electrons at positive k carry predominantly spin-up character, whereas electrons at negative k carry predominantly spin-down character. The axial Zeeman field splits these bands into energy levels. When the Zeeman energy exceeds the square root of the sum of the chemical potential squared and the induced gap squared, the system passes through a topological phase transition. Below that threshold, the system is a trivial superconductor. Above it, the system is topological with Majorana modes at its two ends. The phase boundary in the parameter space of chemical potential and Zeeman energy is a hyperbola defined by the induced gap, giving the device engineer a quantitative map of which combinations of gate voltage and applied field correspond to topological operation.

The key fabrication advance that enabled device-quality nanowires was the epitaxial growth of aluminum on InAs by Krogstrup and colleagues at the Niels Bohr Institute in 2015. In epitaxial growth, the aluminum crystal lattice matches the InAs lattice atom-by-atom, producing an interface free of the oxide and disorder layers present in evaporated contacts. The epitaxial interface yields an induced gap of 200 to 300 microelectronvolts and, crucially, a hard gap with no subgap density of states. A soft gap, arising from interface disorder, would populate subgap states that hybridize with and destabilize any candidate Majorana mode. The first zero-bias conductance peaks in InAs nanowires were reported by Kouwenhoven's group at Delft in 2012. Still, subsequent measurements revealed that peaks consistent with Majorana signatures could also arise from disorder-induced quasi-Majorana states, pairs of Andreev bound states accidentally degenerate near zero energy. Distinguishing a true topological Majorana mode from a quasi-Majorana requires two-end measurements that verify non-locality: a true Majorana produces correlated zero-bias signatures simultaneously at both ends of the wire, because its two components are spatially separated. A quasi-Majorana, being spatially overlapping, does not produce this correlation.

Diagram 8.8 - Semiconductor-Superconductor Nanowire Platform and Topological Phase Diagram

Executive technical infographic

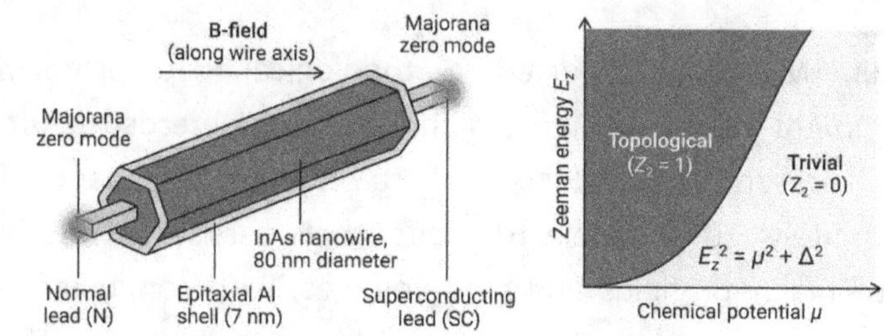

An executive technical infographic: have nent phise to chamoetrott InAs nanowire.

Microsoft's Topological Qubit Program

Microsoft has pursued topological quantum computing through its Station Q program, founded by Michael Freedman in 2005, and through partnerships with Delft University, the Niels Bohr Institute, and dedicated hardware teams in Redmond and Copenhagen. The engineering argument for topological qubits rests on an overhead comparison. In the conventional transmon route, physical qubit error rates of 0.1 to 1 percent per gate require encoding each logical qubit into hundreds to thousands of physical qubits, using surface codes, to meet the error rates needed for useful algorithms. At the scale of one million physical qubits needed for a useful fault-tolerant algorithm, the engineering challenge in control electronics, cabling, and refrigeration is immense. The topological bet is that Majorana modes provide intrinsic protection, reducing or eliminating that overhead. Because the encoded information is non-local, distributed between the two ends of a wire separated by a micron or more, local perturbations at either end cannot corrupt it without a correlated error at both ends. The probability of such a correlated error is exponentially suppressed by the wire length divided by the Majorana coherence length, potentially reducing the physical-to-logical qubit ratio from thousands to tens or hundreds.

In 2023, Microsoft reported a topological gap protocol measurement on a two-dimensional InAs-Al heterostructure device, presenting evidence of a topological gap of approximately 20 microelectronvolts that persists across a range of magnetic fields and gate voltages, with conductance signatures at both ends consistent with Majorana behavior. The topological gap protocol was designed to distinguish topological from trivial signatures by simultaneously measuring the phase diagram as a function of multiple control parameters, going beyond single-parameter sweeps. Critical scrutiny of the community has focused on whether two-terminal measurements suffice to prove non-locality without a direct entanglement measurement between the two ends. This debate reflects the genuine difficulty of unambiguously identifying Majorana fermions on any platform. What is not disputed is that device quality, materials engineering, and measurement protocols have advanced substantially since 2012, and the roadmap from current devices to a functioning topological qubit, while long, is more technically specified than it was a decade ago. The editorial advice from the acquisitions team is correct: the reader should regard these chapters as a tool for evaluating whatever experimental claims exist at the time of reading, not as a snapshot of a single moment in a fast-moving field.

Diagram 8.9 - Microsoft Topological Qubit Device Geometry

Microsoft topological qubit device: schemiew

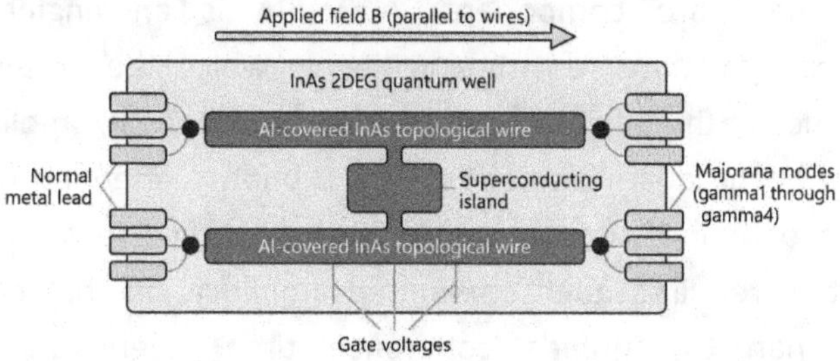

Microsoft topological qubit device: four Majorana modes at the ends of two proximity-coupled InAs-Al wire segments, forming a qubit encoded in non-local joint parity.

What Can We Build With This?

The engineering outputs of superconductivity span a hierarchy from mature commercial products to research-stage topological platforms, and understanding each layer is the practical payoff of this chapter.

Superconducting transmon qubits are the most deployed quantum computing hardware in existence. IBM and Google use aluminum Josephson junctions to run their processors, fabricated on silicon or sapphire substrates. The materials engineering bottleneck in every current-generation transmon processor is dielectric loss in the oxide and surface layers surrounding the junctions: two-level system noise in these layers limits qubit coherence time. The improvement from microsecond to millisecond coherence times over the past decade has been driven almost entirely by advances in materials and fabrication, not by circuit redesign. This is applied superconducting materials science at the production scale, and it requires the same interface control and surface-chemistry understanding that underlie every other quantum material in this book.

Traveling-wave parametric amplifiers (TWPAs) are a second critical hardware component. A TWPA is an engineered Josephson junction transmission line in which the non-linear inductance of the junctions provides parametric gain, amplifying a signal at the quantum limit of half a photon of added noise. Single-shot qubit readout with fidelity sufficient for error correction requires quantum-limited amplification that occurs faster than the qubit's coherence time. Every quantum computing system below the fault-tolerance threshold depends on TWPAs or Josephson parametric amplifiers (JPAs) in the readout chain. Fabricating the junction arrays in a TWPA requires critical current uniformity across hundreds of junctions to within a few percent. This process control challenge sits at the intersection of thin-film deposition, e-beam lithography, and oxide engineering.

SQUID magnetometers are the most sensitive magnetic field sensors in existence. A DC-SQUID consists of two Josephson junctions in a superconducting loop, with the loop's critical current modulated by the flux threading the loop with periodicity of one flux quantum. Operating at a sensitive bias point yields magnetic field noise at the femtotesla-per-root-hertz level for millimeter-scale pickup loops, orders of magnitude below that of any semiconductor sensor. SQUIDs underlie clinical magnetoencephalography (MEG) systems for brain imaging, geophysical surveying systems, and precision magnetic anomaly detection. They are mature commercial technologies, but achieving the lowest noise figures still requires sub-angstrom control of the junction-barrier thickness to match critical current.

Topological qubits based on Majorana zero modes represent the longest-range application in this hierarchy. The operating requirements are more demanding than for transmon systems: 15 to 20 millikelvin base temperature, a vector magnetic field of 0.5 to 1 tesla in the device plane, and magnetic shielding of the qubit region at the nanotesla level because the topological gap is sensitive to local field variations that shift the Zeeman energy across the phase boundary. The dilution refrigerator for a Majorana qubit system must integrate a superconducting vector magnet, mu-metal shielding layers, and a vibration-isolation system more stringent than that required for transmons, while maintaining thermal conductance from the cold plate to the qubit chip at the sub-femtowatt level. The cryogenic hardware engineering of a topological qubit system is a distinct discipline from that of a transmon system, driven entirely by the physics of the proximity gap and the topological phase boundary.

Diagram 8.10 - Traveling-Wave Parametric Amplifier (TWPA) Architecture

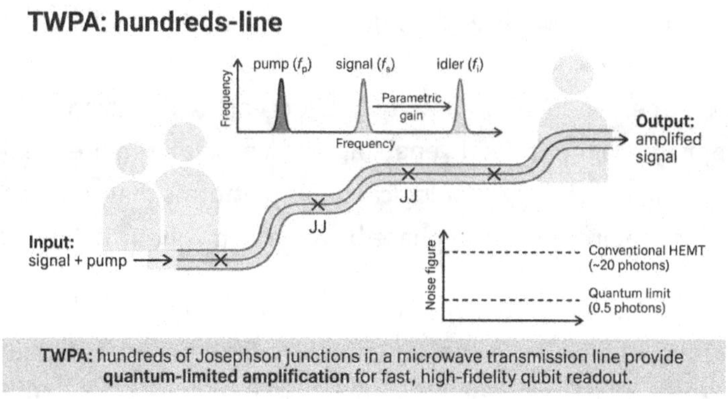

Diagram 8.11 - SQUID Magnetometer Architecture and Sensitivity Comparison

DC-SQUID

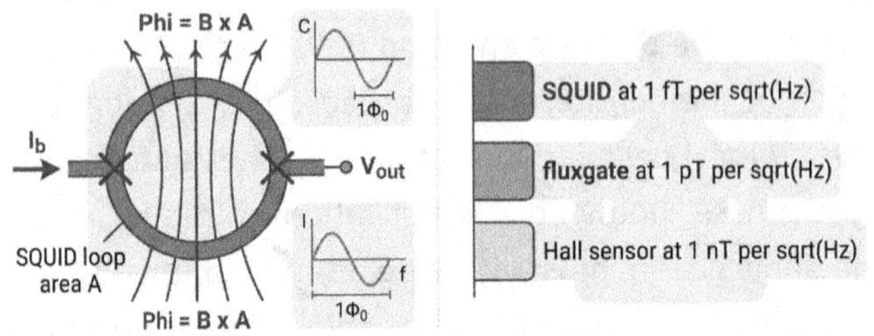

DC-SQUID: two Josephson junctions in a superconducting loop modulated by magnetic flux; sensitivity orders of magnitude beyond any semiconductor magnetic sensor.

Takeaway

Superconductivity is a collective quantum state in which phonon-mediated attraction binds electrons near the Fermi surface into Cooper pairs that condense into a macroscopic phase-coherent condensate. The BCS gap protects the condensate against perturbations smaller than 2 delta. The Josephson effect provides the non-linear inductance behind superconducting qubits, the quantum-limited amplification behind TWPAs, and the world's most precise voltage standard. Type II superconductors allow quantized vortex penetration in an applied magnetic field, enabling devices that require field compatibility, including topological qubit platforms that must be tuned into their topological phase by an axial magnetic field.

The distinction between conventional and topological superconductivity lies in the gap structure in momentum space. An s-wave gap is topologically trivial: uniform, nodeless, and deformable to zero without obstruction. A chiral p-wave gap, or topologically non-trivial gap, has a winding that cannot be removed, mandating zero-energy Majorana modes at any boundary between the topological and trivial phases. Because no fabricable bulk p-wave superconductor exists in a proven form, the practical route is proximity engineering: combining a conventional superconductor with a material that provides strong spin-orbit coupling and the right Fermi-surface topology. The Fu-Kane proposal uses TI surface states. The Lutchyn-Oreg platform uses InAs nanowires with epitaxial aluminum shells. Both arrange topological superconductivity from individually trivial components, modularizing the engineering challenge.

Every cryogenic hardware decision at Axiom is traceable to the physics in this chapter. The dilution refrigerator base temperature is set by the thermal energy scale needed to preserve the proximity gap. The vector magnet specification is set by the field required to drive the topological phase transition without quenching the aluminum shell. The magnetic shielding architecture is set by the nanotesla sensitivity of the topological phase boundary to stray fields. Understanding the physics behind these constraints is what separates an engineer reading a cryogenic specification from one who can derive it.

Majorana modes in nanowires and TI heterostructures are, so far in this discussion, static objects: bound to wire ends or vortex cores, protecting quantum information through non-locality. The next chapter asks what happens when those modes are moved. Braiding Majorana modes in a controlled way implements quantum gate operations whose outcome depends only on the topology of the worldlines traced by the modes in space-time, not on the specifics of the braid. This topological protection of the gate operation itself, extending protection from information storage to information processing, is the deepest engineering argument for the topological qubit architecture, and it is the subject of Chapter 9.

Diagram 8.12 - Cryogenic Hardware Stack for Topological Qubit Operation

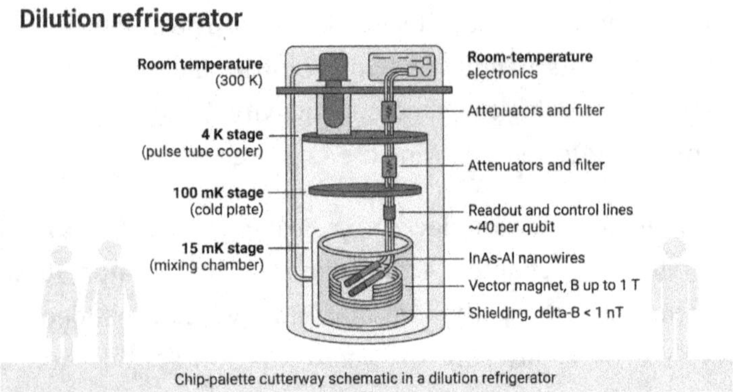

9 Topological Quantum Computing

The whiteboard in Conference Room B had been accumulating equations for three days. Sasha Korolev had started with the Kitaev chain Hamiltonian, written in notation only he and Priya could read at a glance. Priya had added the material stack schematic below: an indium arsenide nanowire with cross-sectional dimensions in nanometers, an aluminum shell in blue, and gate electrodes drawn as rectangles beneath it.

Marcus Webb arrived on the third morning, set down his coffee, and stared at the board for two full minutes. Then he picked up a red marker, drew a box around the entire diagram, and labeled it QUBIT. He drew an arrow to a blank region on the right and wrote GATE. A second arrow pointed to another blank region: READOUT. He turned to Sasha and Priya. "Walk me through how this thing actually computes. Where does the qubit live, how do you flip it, and how do you know it flipped?"

Sasha pointed to the two ends of the nanowire schematic. "The qubit lives here, and here. Not at either location alone. Across both of them together. That is the topology." He added a worldline diagram beside the nanowire: two curved lines crossing in a stylized braid, labeled braid = gate. Marcus looked at the braid, then at the stack of materials, then back at the braid. He reached for his notebook. That moment of recognition, when everything from Chapters 3 through 8 converges into a single device, is what this chapter is about.

Why It Matters

Quantum computing has a decoherence problem. Every physical qubit, whether a superconducting transmon, a trapped ion, or a spin in silicon, interacts with its environment. Thermal fluctuations, electromagnetic noise, and stray fields push the qubit state toward a classical mixture, destroying the superposition and entanglement that make quantum computation powerful. The standard engineering answer is active error correction: encode one logical qubit in hundreds to thousands of physical qubits, continuously measure error syndromes, and apply corrections faster than errors accumulate. This works, but the overhead is severe enough that a million-qubit fault-tolerant machine could require tens of millions of physical qubits.

Topological quantum computing proposes a different answer. Rather than building fragile qubits and layering elaborate error correction on top, it proposes building qubits that are structurally resistant to local perturbations from the outset. The protection comes from the topology of the qubit encoding: the quantum information is stored non-locally, distributed across two spatially separated locations, and a perturbation at either location alone cannot access the full quantum state. This is not a software trick. It is a materials science argument that the right architecture, built from the right materials, can reduce error-correction overhead to a small fraction of what conventional approaches require.

This chapter covers qubit encoding, the gate mechanism, the physical platforms, the honest scorecard of what has been achieved and what remains to be demonstrated, and the comparative engineering picture relative to leading conventional architectures. By the end, the reader will be equipped to evaluate any claim about topological qubit hardware as an engineer.

The Qubit Decoherence Problem and Topological Protection

To understand why topological protection matters, precision is required about what decoherence is at the device level. A qubit is a two-level quantum system that can exist in a superposition of ground and excited states, with complex coefficients encoding both the probability amplitude for each outcome and the phase relationship between them. Decoherence is the process by which that phase relationship is destroyed through coupling to the environment. Two processes contribute: energy relaxation, characterized by the timescale T1, in which the qubit decays from the excited to the ground state by emitting a phonon or photon; and dephasing, characterized by T2, in which the phase is scrambled by fluctuating fields without energy exchange. The ratio of gate time to coherence time determines whether a computation is feasible.

The key distinction for topological protection is between local and non-local errors. A local error acts on a single physical location: a photon absorbed by the qubit, a phonon exchanged with the substrate, or stray magnetic flux. Conventional qubits are maximally vulnerable to local errors because the entire quantum state resides at one physical location. Topological encoding distributes the quantum state across two physically separated locations in a specific way, making the logical qubit state invisible to local operators at either location. A perturbation acting only at one end of a topological wire cannot distinguish between the two states of the logical qubit, because the information distinguishing those states does not reside at either end alone.

Diagram 9.1 - Decoherence Mechanisms in Qubit Architectures

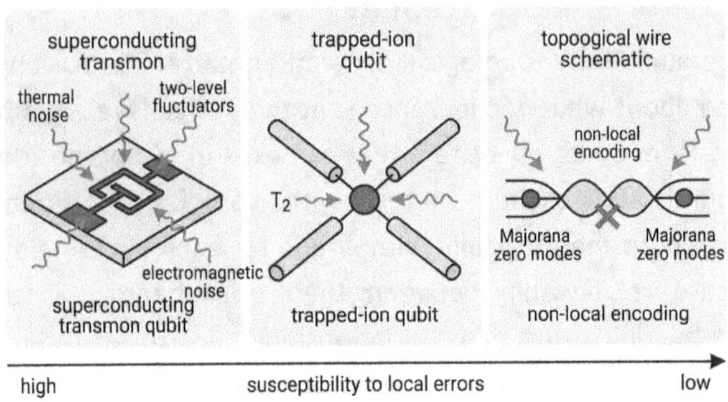

The degree of protection scales with the physical separation between the two Majorana modes and decays exponentially over a length scale set by the wire's superconducting coherence length. A wire that is long compared to the coherence length achieves exponentially small coupling between the two ends and therefore exponentially small susceptibility to local errors that might hybridize the Majorana modes and lift the ground state degeneracy that encodes the qubit. This is the hardware bet: making the wire physically larger directly and exponentially reduces the error rate. That is a fundamentally different engineering scaling relationship from that of conventional qubits, where making the qubit physically larger generally increases susceptibility to noise.

Anyons: Abelian and Non-Abelian

Particles in three-dimensional space are either bosons or fermions, a dichotomy enforced by topology: any path traced by one particle around another can be continuously deformed and shrunk to a point, constraining the exchange phase to 0 or π. In two-dimensional space, this constraint is lifted. The path of one particle encircling another cannot be shrunk to a point without crossing the other particle's trajectory, meaning exchange statistics in two dimensions are not restricted to plus one or minus one. Particles obeying this relaxed constraint are called anyons.

Abelian anyons acquire an arbitrary complex phase upon exchanging two of them. The exchange operation commutes: exchanging particle A with particle B yields the same phase as exchanging particle B with particle A. Fractional quantum Hall states host abelian anyons, confirmed through shot noise and interferometry. But abelian anyons cannot be used for universal quantum computation. All information is encoded in phases; phase addition limits computational power to a subset of quantum operations.

Non-Abelian anyons are the computationally powerful case. When two non-Abelian anyons are exchanged, the quantum state undergoes a unitary rotation in a higher-dimensional Hilbert space, and exchange operations do not commute. Exchanging particle A around B and then B around C gives a different result than performing those exchanges in reverse. The non-commutativity is what makes non-Abelian anyons useful for computation: the sequence of exchanges acts as a sequence of quantum gates, and the gate applied depends on the topology of the braid, not on the exact path taken.

Diagram 9.2 - Abelian vs. Non-Abelian Anyon Exchange Statistics

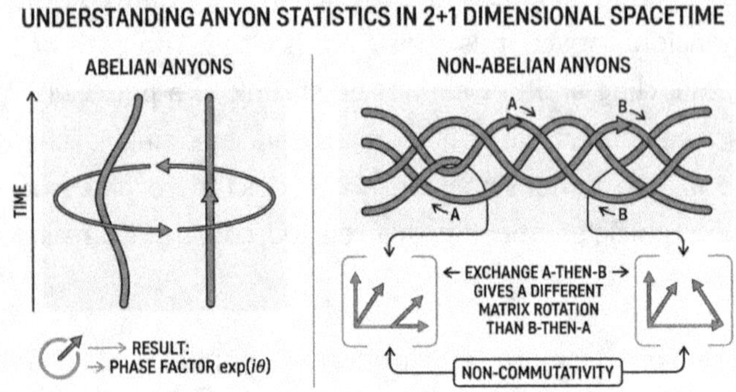

The ground state of a system of non-Abelian anyons is degenerate: multiple states share the same energy, and the space of degenerate ground states is the Hilbert space where qubits are encoded. For Majorana zero modes, the specific type of non-Abelian anyon most relevant to current hardware: two modes produce a twofold-degenerate ground-state encoding of one qubit; four modes give a fourfold-degenerate space encoding of two qubits. The topological gap protects the ground-state degeneracy: creating any excitation requires finite energy, and thermal fluctuations cannot create excitations unless the thermal energy is comparable to the gap.

Majorana Zero Modes as Non-Abelian Anyons

Ettore Majorana's 1937 proposal that a fermion could be its own antiparticle was a mathematical curiosity for decades before it acquired engineering relevance. In condensed matter physics, Majorana physics has a tractable form: quasiparticles, collective excitations of a many-body system with the same mathematical structure as Majorana fermions. These quasiparticles appear at the boundaries of topological superconductors as zero-energy modes, called Majorana zero modes, which are the hardware-relevant objects for topological quantum computing.

The physical meaning of a Majorana zero mode is clearest in its creation operator. For a conventional fermionic mode, the creation and annihilation operators are distinct. For a Majorana mode, the creation operator equals its own adjoint: creating and annihilating the mode are the same operation. Physically, a Majorana mode is half of a conventional fermionic mode. Two Majorana modes together make up one conventional fermionic mode, and the quantum number distinguishing occupied from unoccupied is the qubit degree of freedom.

In a physical device, two Majorana zero modes appear at the two ends of a finite-length topological superconductor wire. The ground state is two-fold degenerate: the shared fermion is either occupied or unoccupied, corresponding to the two logical qubit states. Because the modes are spatially separated, the qubit state is non-local. A local perturbation at one end acts on the Majorana mode there, but it cannot change the qubit state because the qubit state depends on the relationship between both ends. The coupling between ends is exponentially suppressed by the wire length, making the qubit exponentially protected against local perturbations.

Diagram 9.3 - Majorana Zero Modes at Wire Ends

Majorana zero mode: (nninicolagnat metapo)

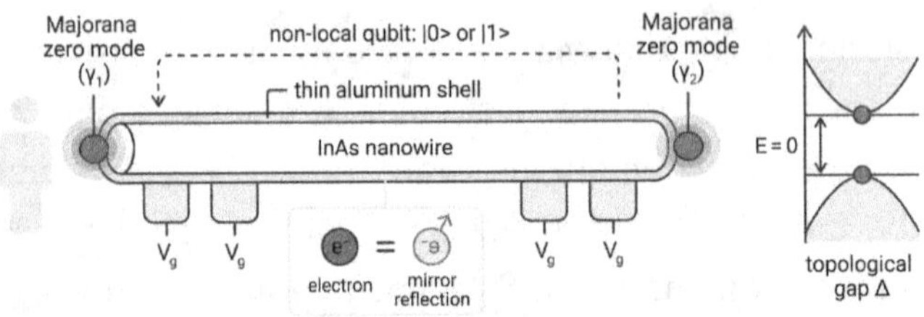

A clean minimistor to guide a Majorana quasiparticle schematic

The key experimental signature of Majorana zero modes is a zero-bias conductance peak in tunneling spectroscopy. A normal-metal probe connected to one end of the wire through a tunnel barrier exhibits a conductance gap in a trivial superconductor. A topological superconductor with Majorana zero modes shows a conductance peak at exactly zero bias, because tunneling into or out of a Majorana mode is resonant regardless of bias sign. The ideal peak has a height quantized to 2e^2/h, a value set by the same topology that protects the mode. The robustness of this peak with respect to changes in gate voltage and magnetic field serves as a diagnostic of the topological phase.

The experimental history of this signature is complicated and instructive. Zero-bias conductance peaks in semiconductor-superconductor nanowires were first reported in 2012 by Mourik and colleagues at Delft, with similar results from multiple groups shortly after. For several years, these peaks were interpreted as evidence for Majorana zero modes. Subsequent theoretical and experimental work revealed that similar peaks arise from trivial mechanisms: Andreev bound states localized at the tunnel junction, and quantum dot states accidentally tuned to zero energy. Distinguishing a genuine topological Majorana mode from these trivial mimics motivated the development of more demanding diagnostic protocols, including the topological gap protocol and nonlocal conductance measurements.

Braiding Statistics: Worldline Crossings as Gates

Braiding in topological quantum computing refers to a precise physical operation: moving one Majorana mode around another such that the worldlines traced in spacetime form a braid pattern. The quantum gate applied depends only on the topology of the braid, specifically which worldline passes over which at each crossing, not on the speed of the moves or the exact path. This is the same principle as a knot's topology: a trefoil knot is a trefoil knot regardless of whether the rope is taut or loose. The topological protection is direct: any local perturbation that does not change the topology of the worldlines cannot change the gate applied.

The mathematical framework for braiding is expressed in terms of exchange operators. For Majorana modes labeled by index j, the operator exchanging mode j with mode j+1 generates a rotation in the degenerate ground state space. These operators do not commute: exchanging modes 1-2 and then 2-3 yields a different result than performing those exchanges in reverse order. This non-commutativity is the non-Abelian statistics. Composed braiding operations build up a unitary matrix in the qubit space, implementing the quantum gate corresponding to that braid.

The gates accessible through Majorana braiding include the Hadamard and controlled-phase gates, but not the T gate, which promotes the Clifford group to universality. This limitation means that a Majorana-based quantum computer cannot run arbitrary algorithms using only topologically protected operations. It requires a supplemental operation, typically magic state injection, to implement the T gate. The supplemental operation is not topologically protected and introduces a conventional error rate. The engineering argument does not require all gates to be topologically protected: it requires that the dominant error channel be addressed by topology, while remaining non-topological gates are handled by conventional error correction operating on a much smaller residual error budget.

Diagram 9.4 - Braiding Worldlines in Spacetime

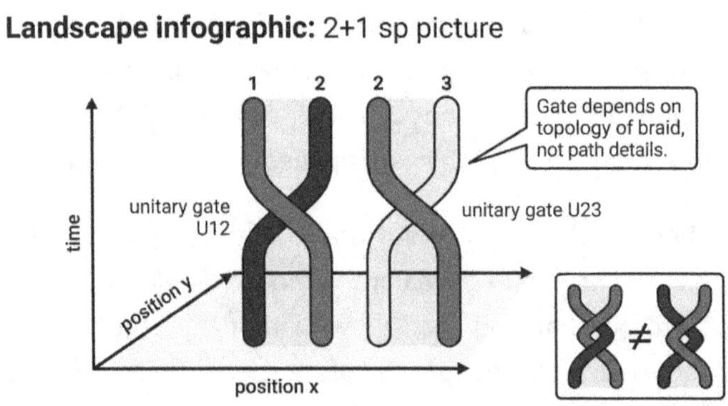

In a one-dimensional wire, Majorana modes sit at the two ends and cannot pass through each other without fusing rather than braiding. The solution is a two-dimensional network. If multiple wires are connected at T-junctions, Majorana modes can be transferred between wires via gate-voltage operations that shuttle them through the junction. The topological charge of a Majorana mode is conserved during movement, and the braiding operation is effected by moving one mode through the network in a route that encloses another. This is physically realized by tuning gate voltages to open and close sections of the wire network, thereby defining a moving topological region that carries the Majorana mode.

Majorana Wires: Semiconductor-SC Hybrids

The most experimentally advanced platform for Majorana zero modes combines a semiconductor nanowire with strong spin-orbit coupling and a conventional s-wave superconductor deposited epitaxially on the wire surface. The semiconductor provides spin-orbit coupling and gate-voltage-tunable electron density. The superconductor provides the pairing potential via the proximity effect, in which Cooper pairs tunnel into the semiconductor, inducing a gap in its quasiparticle spectrum even though the semiconductor is not intrinsically superconducting. When a magnetic field is applied along the wire axis, the interplay among spin-orbit coupling, the induced gap, and Zeeman splitting drives the wire into a topological phase transition. Above a critical field, the wire enters the topological superconducting phase with Majorana zero modes at its ends.

The semiconductor of choice in current hardware programs is indium arsenide, selected for its large spin-orbit coupling, low effective electron mass, and the availability of high-quality epitaxial growth. Indium antimonide offers even larger spin-orbit coupling but presents more challenging fabrication constraints. The superconductor of choice is aluminum, selected for its small coherence length, which sets the energy scale of the topological gap, and its compatibility with semiconductor processing. The Al-InAs interface quality is critical: disorder at this interface creates subgap states that mimic the Majorana zero-bias conductance signature while not being topological, and these trivial states were a major source of false positives in early experiments.

Diagram 9.5 - InAs-Al Nanowire Platform Cross-Section

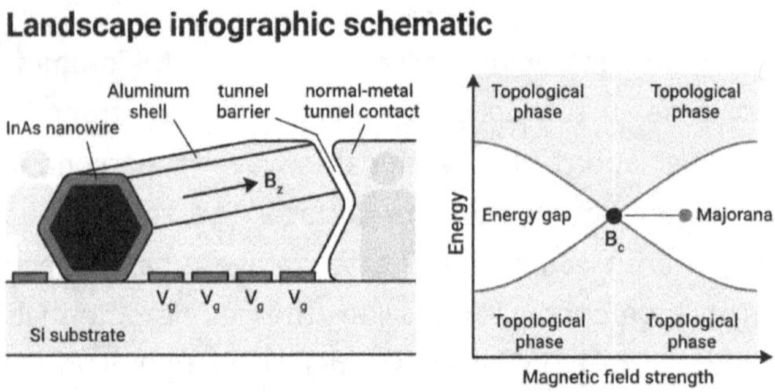

The fabrication sequence for the InAs-Al Majorana device requires precision in nanofabrication at several critical steps. InAs nanowires are grown by molecular beam epitaxy, producing single-crystal wires with diameters of 70 to 150 nanometers. The aluminum shell is deposited by MBE at low temperature, immediately after wire growth, without breaking vacuum, to achieve the epitaxial interface quality required for a clean subgap spectrum. The wires are then transferred to a substrate and placed across pre-patterned gate electrode arrays. A selective etch removes aluminum from a short section, creating the tunnel junction at one end. The entire device operates at millikelvin temperatures in a dilution refrigerator, necessary both to maintain the superconducting state and to suppress thermal excitation of subgap states above the topological gap.

The topological phase diagram of the InAs-Al system in the space of gate voltage and magnetic field has been mapped experimentally by several groups, most extensively at Microsoft and Delft. The topological phase occupies a region of intermediate electron density above a critical magnetic field, where Zeeman splitting exceeds the induced superconducting gap, and the system transitions from a trivial to a topological phase. The closing and reopening of the bulk gap, as observed in two-terminal conductance measurements, trace the boundaries. The experimental protocol for distinguishing a topological gap from a trivial gap involves probing both ends simultaneously and verifying that the gap closes at the same parameters from both sides, a signature of the bulk topological phase transition.

T-Junctions, 2D Braiding, and Measurement Schemes

A single Majorana wire cannot perform quantum computation. Computation requires multiple qubits that can be entangled, and gates that act on qubit pairs. Extending the wire architecture to multi-qubit computation requires a two-dimensional network of wires connected by junctions, and the braiding operations implementing quantum gates must be defined on this network. The T-junction is the fundamental building block: a branching point where three wire segments meet, allowing a Majorana mode to be transferred from one wire to another via a sequence of gate-voltage operations. By cycling the topological phases of the three segments, a Majorana mode can be moved from either horizontal arm to the vertical arm and back, constituting half of a complete braiding operation.

A full braiding operation requires two T-junction moves in sequence, with one Majorana mode encircling the other through the network. The result is a unitary gate determined by the topology of the overall path, not by details of the individual moves. The physical implementation requires adiabaticity: moves must be slow compared to the gap energy divided by Planck's constant, but fast compared to decoherence timescales. For a 100-microelectronvolt gap, the adiabaticity time is roughly 40 picoseconds, and with a coherence time of microseconds, there is a comfortable window. Achieving this window in practice requires both a sufficiently large gap and a sufficiently long coherence time, and both are active engineering challenges.

Diagram 9.6 - T-Junction Braiding Network

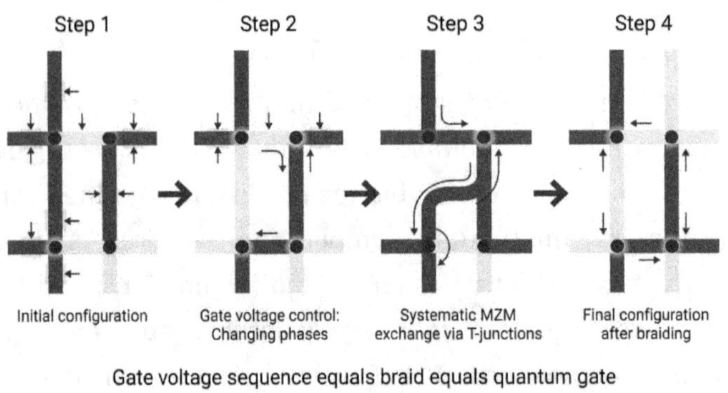

Measurement-based topological quantum computing offers an alternative to physically moving Majorana modes. In this approach, qubits encoded in Majorana modes need not be transported. Instead, joint parity measurements on pairs of Majorana modes from different qubits are performed, and the sequence of measurement outcomes defines an effective braid in the space of logical states. The advantage is that the physical operations required are measurements rather than adiabatic moves, which are potentially faster and easier to control. Measuring the joint parity of two Majorana modes from different qubits is equivalent to performing a partial Bell measurement, and sequences of such measurements implement Clifford group gates on the logical qubits. Combined with magic-state distillation for the T gate, this yields a complete set of gates for universal quantum computation.

The hardware requirement for a parity measurement is a coherent coupling between two Majorana modes in different wire segments, typically implemented via a superconducting island that connects them. Electrons can tunnel from one wire to the other through the island, and the energy depends on the system's total parity. By monitoring the resonant frequency of a microwave resonator coupled to the island, the joint parity can be read out without measuring individual qubit states. This is a dispersive readout, the same technique used in superconducting transmon qubit readout, adapted to the Majorana context. The measurement-based framework is closer to the conventional quantum error correction framework than to the pure braiding picture, making it more accessible to hardware teams with backgrounds in superconducting qubits.

Diagram 9.7 - Measurement-Based Parity Readout

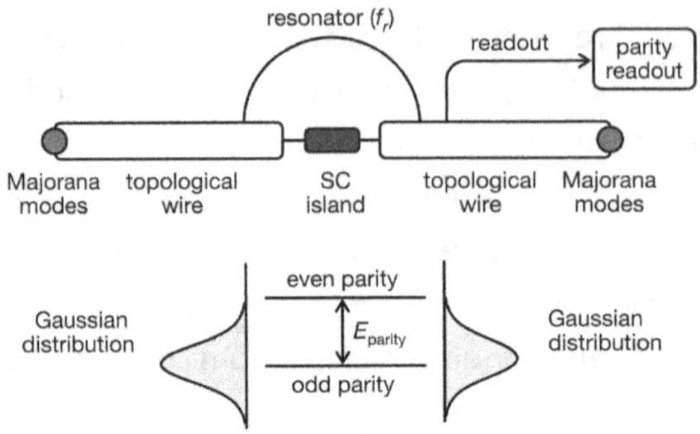

Microsoft's StationQ Program: An Engineering Bet Assessment

Microsoft's topological qubit program is the most sustained and heavily resourced effort in the field, spanning more than 15 years from the founding of Station Q, a collaborative research center at the University of California, Santa Barbara, to the current Azure Quantum topological qubit roadmap. Understanding this program's trajectory is itself an exercise in engineering risk assessment: a case study in how a major technology company evaluates a speculative hardware bet, commits resources over a long timeframe, and adjusts its claims as experimental evidence accumulates.

The foundational theoretical work stemmed from Alexei Kitaev's 2003 paper proposing topological quantum computation with non-Abelian anyons, and from the subsequent development of Majorana-based topological qubits by Kitaev, Nayak, Simon, Stern, and others. Microsoft's research investment accelerated after 2010, supported by theoretical proposals showing that topological Majorana phases could be engineered in semiconductor-superconductor systems rather than requiring exotic materials. The 2012 experimental report from Delft, which first observed a zero-bias conductance peak attributed to a Majorana mode in an InAs-Al nanowire, was celebrated as confirmation that the engineered Majorana platform was viable.

The 2021 retraction is essential to any honest engineering assessment. A Nature paper from a Microsoft-affiliated collaboration reported observing a topological gap using the topological gap protocol, which is designed to provide more rigorous evidence than a simple zero-bias peak. The paper was retracted after reviewers and independent researchers identified problems with the data analysis: raw data were inconsistent with a genuine topological gap, and data points had been excluded from the published analysis without disclosure. The retraction prompted a comprehensive re-evaluation of experimental standards in the field. The lesson for any hardware team is not that the science is wrong, but that the standards of evidence for demonstrating topological phases are stringent and require specific verification steps that a conventional conductance measurement alone cannot provide.

Diagram 9.8 - Microsoft Topological Qubit Program Timeline

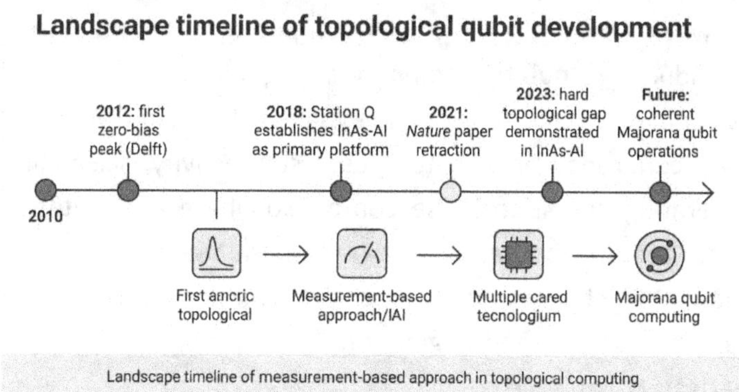

The 2023 results represent a more carefully documented milestone. Microsoft reported observing a hard topological gap in an improved InAs-Al device, where "hard" means the induced superconducting gap remains closed throughout the interior of the topological phase in both local and nonlocal conductance measurements, with no subgap features above the resolution limit. This measurement addressed concerns raised by the 2021 retraction using simultaneous two-end spectroscopy to verify the bulk origin of the gap. The result was received more positively as a genuine step toward the topological phase. The consensus view remains that demonstrating a hard gap is necessary but not sufficient for a topological qubit: additional steps include demonstrating Majorana-mode localization at the wire ends, measuring qubit coherence in the Majorana basis, and demonstrating a braiding or parity-measurement gate operation with sufficient fidelity for fault-tolerant computation.

The Competitor Landscape: Topological QC Against the Field

Topological quantum computing is one of four major hardware approaches to a fault-tolerant quantum computer, and fairly evaluating it requires understanding the engineering strengths and weaknesses of the competing architectures: superconducting qubits, trapped-ion qubits, neutral-atom qubits, and photonic qubits. Each makes different trade-offs between coherence time, gate speed, connectivity, scalability, and operating conditions. The comparison here is qualitative and architecture-focused rather than numerical, because specific figures change rapidly as each technology improves. In contrast, the physics and engineering principles underlying the comparison are durable.

Superconducting qubits, the approach taken by Google, IBM, and Rigetti, are the most mature competing architecture. They operate at millikelvin temperatures, like topological qubits. Still, their physical mechanism is different: a superconducting qubit is a nonlinear LC oscillator based on a Josephson junction, whose anharmonicity allows the two lowest energy levels to be addressed as the qubit subspace. Gate times are nanoseconds to tens of nanoseconds, coherence times are microseconds to hundreds of microseconds in state-of-the-art devices, and gate fidelities above 99.9 percent have been demonstrated for single-qubit operations. The physical qubit count has reached the hundreds to thousands, and the path to millions of physical qubits will require addressing significant challenges in cryogenic engineering, control-line routing, and frequency crowding. Surface code estimates suggest several hundred to several thousand physical qubits per logical qubit at current error rates.

Trapped-ion qubits, the approach taken by IonQ and Quantinuum, use individual ions in electromagnetic traps with qubit states encoded in long-lived electronic or hyperfine levels. Physical isolation from the environment gives coherence times of seconds to minutes. Single-qubit gate fidelities have exceeded 99.99 percent, the highest in any platform. The cost is speed: two-qubit gates driven by laser-mediated interactions take 0.1 to 10 milliseconds, six to eight orders of magnitude slower than superconducting gates. Scaling beyond a few hundred qubits in a single trap is limited by decreasing mode density and increasing susceptibility to heating. Large-scale systems connect multiple traps via photonic links, introducing additional latency and loss.

Diagram 9.9 - Quantum Computing Architecture Comparison

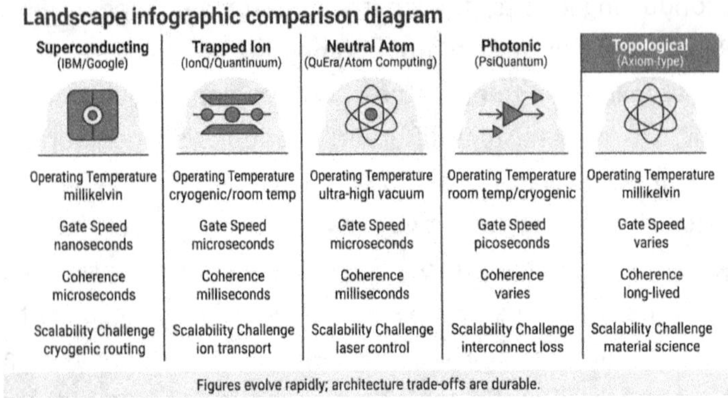

Neutral-atom qubits, championed by QuEra Computing and Atom Computing, are a rapidly rising architecture. Individual neutral atoms are trapped in arrays of optical tweezers at specific positions in free space. Two-qubit gates are implemented by exciting pairs into highly excited Rydberg states that interact via van der Waals forces. The key engineering advantages are natural scalability to thousands of physical qubits and reconfigurability of the qubit array between circuit layers. Gate fidelities have improved dramatically in recent years and are now competitive with trapped ions. The main limitations are gate speed, limited by the Rydberg interaction timescale to microseconds, and sensitivity to laser noise and atom loss.

Against this landscape, topological qubits occupy a specific position. They share the millikelvin operating temperature requirement with superconducting qubits. Their gate speed in the braiding picture is limited by the adiabaticity constraint, giving gate times in the range of microseconds to milliseconds. Their coherence advantage over superconducting qubits comes not from longer intrinsic coherence times but from reduced sensitivity to local noise channels, which could translate to a lower physical-to-logical qubit ratio if topological protection achieves its theoretical promise. The honest assessment is that topological qubits are behind leading conventional architectures in demonstrated qubit count, gate fidelity, and system-level integration, but ahead in the theoretical overhead reduction they could achieve if materials engineering challenges are solved. The topological approach trades near-term benchmarks for long-term scalability, and the payoff comes at the scale at which the error-correction overhead of conventional approaches becomes prohibitive.

Evaluation Framework: What a Hardware Claim Needs

The history of Majorana physics in experiments is one of results initially interpreted as topological but subsequently found to be consistent with, or better explained by, trivial mechanisms. This is the normal process by which physics establishes extraordinary claims. It means that any engineer encountering a claim about topological qubit hardware needs a framework for evaluating what the claim actually demonstrates, what it leaves open, and what the path from that demonstration to a working qubit looks like.

The first level of evidence is a zero-bias conductance peak in tunneling spectroscopy. This is the entry-level signature associated with a Majorana zero mode, but as experimental history demonstrates, it arises from multiple mechanisms. A genuine topological zero-bias peak should have height quantized at 2e squared over h, be robust against changes in gate voltage and magnetic field within the topological phase, and appear at both ends of the wire simultaneously when the geometry allows both ends to be probed. A peak that appears only at one end, has height well below the quantized value, or shifts with gate voltage inconsistently with a topological phase transition, is more likely a trivial Andreev bound state or quantum dot resonance.

The second level is the topological gap protocol: systematically measuring device conductance as a function of both gate voltage and magnetic field, constructing the full phase diagram, and verifying that the apparent topological region exhibits consistent properties at both ends of the phase diagram. The Microsoft 2021 retraction concerned a topological-gap protocol measurement, and the 2023 results were a revised protocol with improved two-end consistency. Passing the protocol demonstrates that the material stack is in the topological phase under certain conditions. The qubit demonstration requires additional steps.

Diagram 9.10 - Topological Phase Diagnostic Hierarchy

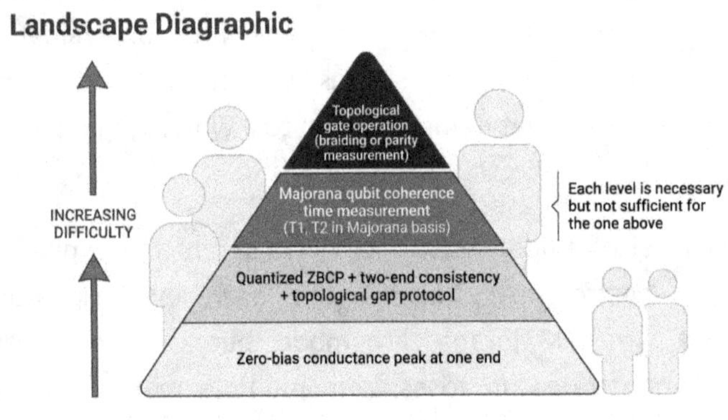

The third level is qubit coherence: demonstrating that the Majorana encoding actually extends qubit lifetime compared to a conventional qubit in the same device. This requires operating the device as a qubit and measuring T1 and T2 times in the Majorana basis. A definitive measurement of the coherence time of a topologically protected Majorana qubit, clearly exceeding that of a comparable conventional qubit in the same device, is the next major milestone the field is working toward. The fourth and highest level is a gate operation with topological character: demonstrating that a braiding or parity measurement operation has been performed, that the gate fidelity is consistent with topological protection, and that the operation has the non-Abelian character expected from Majorana braiding. The reader who internalizes this four-level hierarchy can evaluate any hardware announcement as an engineer, placing each claimed result in context regardless of when it is made.

What Can We Build With This?

Marcus Webb stepped back from the whiteboard, notebook full of diagrams: the wire cross-section, the T-junction network, the braid worldlines, the parity measurement circuit. He had been asking the same question he always asked, in one form or another, for every physics concept that came through his engineering brain: what does this let me build that I could not build before? The answer, when it came, was not one device but a path. The topological qubit, built from an InAs-Al nanowire network and read out via dispersive parity measurements, is the device for which Marcus can now design a fabrication process. The fault-tolerant gate operation, implemented through parity measurements on a network of such qubits, is the operation his control electronics team is already planning for. The million-qubit machine is the endpoint of an engineering road with identified milestones and tractable problems at each step.

The near-term deliverable is a single topological qubit with demonstrated coherence time in the Majorana basis and parity-measurement fidelity. This is a device that can be fabricated with current nanofabrication technology, measured with current cryogenic electronics, and characterized with current spectroscopic protocols. It does not require a breakthrough in materials science, though it does require careful optimization of the InAs-Al epitaxial interface, the gate geometry, and the magnetic field configuration. The timeline, based on the field's current trajectory, is in the range of 1 to several years.

The intermediate deliverable is a small-scale topological quantum processor: a network of five to twenty topological qubits connected by measurable couplings, capable of running simple quantum algorithms with a logical error rate below the fault-tolerance threshold. This device requires advances in cryogenic wiring density, classical control electronics co-integration, and qubit-to-qubit coupling fidelity. At this level, the comparison with conventional superconducting and trapped-ion architectures becomes genuinely competitive: a small topological processor with low error rates and high connectivity could outperform a much larger conventional processor on specific algorithms in which error-correction overhead dominates.

Diagram 9.11 - Topological Qubit Device Architecture Roadmap

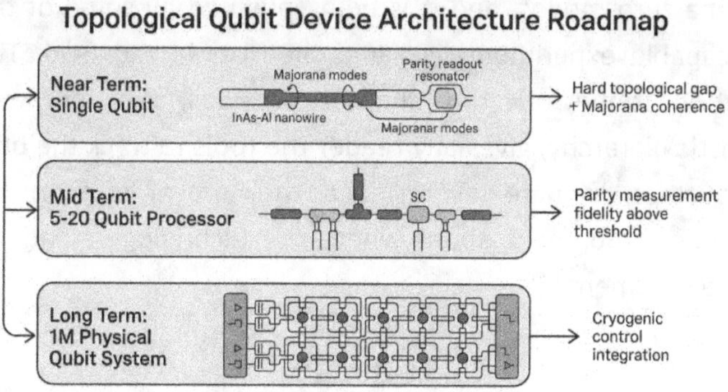

The long-term deliverable is what Axiom Quantum's business plan and Microsoft's Azure Quantum roadmap both converge on: a fault-tolerant quantum computer with a logical qubit count sufficient to run classically hard computations in chemistry, materials science, optimization, and cryptography. The specific physical qubit count required depends on the error rate of the Majorana hardware at the time of construction, and the exponential improvement in topological protection with device size means the engineering problem is tractable as fabrication improves. As the wire quality increases, the error rate drops exponentially, reducing the overhead for fault-tolerant encoding. The path to a million-qubit machine is a sequence of engineering milestones, each requiring the solution of defined materials science and device engineering problems, none of which violates any known physical law.

The topological qubit is not a guaranteed winner in the quantum computing race. It is the best that physical overhead reduction from topological protection, once demonstrated, will compound at scale, ultimately producing a fault-tolerant quantum computer with fewer physical qubits than any competing architecture can achieve. That bet is coherent and well-motivated by the physics of non-Abelian anyons and

Majorana zero modes, and it is being pursued by some of the most capable experimentalists and theorists in the field. The evaluation framework this chapter provides, the four-level diagnostic hierarchy, gives any reader the tools to track the best as it develops, evaluate new results as they appear, and form an independent judgment about where the technology stands at any given moment.

Takeaway

Topological quantum computing brings together everything this book has built: the Berry phase and topological invariants of Chapters 3 through 5, the topological surface states and edge modes of Chapters 6 and 7, the superconducting proximity effect and Majorana physics of Chapter 8, and the materials engineering developed throughout. The payoff is a specific hardware architecture, the topological qubit built from a semiconductor-superconductor nanowire network, and a specific engineering argument: that non-local Majorana encoding provides exponential protection against local errors, reducing the physical-to-logical qubit overhead in ways that could make fault-tolerant quantum computing feasible at a scale not achievable by conventional architectures.

The physics of non-Abelian anyons and braiding statistics is not speculation. It is a consequence of two-dimensional topology verified in fractional quantum Hall systems, and the engineered Majorana version of this physics has been observed in semiconductor-superconductor hybrids under controlled conditions. The engineering challenge is moving from spectroscopic signatures to operating qubits, from operating qubits to coherent gate operations, and from coherent gate operations to a fault-tolerant processor. Each step is a defined problem with known solution pathways. The materials science and device engineering required at each step are challenging but tractable. The timeline is uncertain; the direction is clear.

The four-level diagnostic hierarchy, from spectroscopic evidence to gate demonstration, is the tool the reader can carry forward in any future engagement with claims about topological quantum computing. Whether a result appears in a peer-reviewed journal, a company press release, or a conference presentation, the hierarchy provides a precise language for situating the result within the context of what is required for a genuine qubit demonstration. That language is what distinguishes an engineer who can evaluate hardware from an observer who can only report it.

Diagram 9.12 - Chapter 9 Concept Integration Map

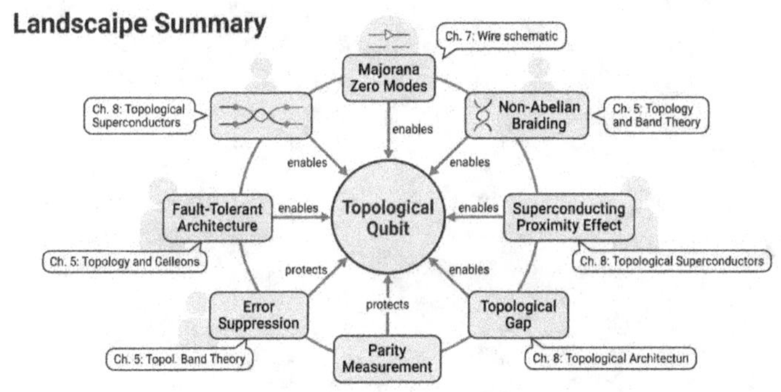

Caption: A Landscape summary diagram s style infographic with executive technical tone

The next chapter turns from computation to sensing. Quantum sensors built from topological materials detect magnetic fields, rotations, and gravitational gradients with sensitivities that are beyond those of classical sensors, and many sensing applications are closer to commercial deployment than to topological quantum computing. The materials physics is largely the same: topological surface states, edge modes, and proximity-engineered heterostructures. The engineering context is different: sensors operate in field conditions rather than dilution refrigerators, measure continuous physical quantities rather than performing discrete gate operations, and face different noise and calibration challenges. The payoff, as Yuki Tanaka will demonstrate, is devices that are already leaving the laboratory.

10 Quantum Sensors

The sensing lab on the fourth floor of Axiom Quantum smells faintly of diamond polish and isopropanol. Yuki Tanaka keeps it that way deliberately. On the center optical table sits a magnetometer module roughly the size of a deck of playing cards: no cryostat, no liquid-helium Dewar, just a compact gray box connected to a data-acquisition board by a ribbon cable. The monitor above it shows a real-time magnetic field trace scrolling at ten samples per second. Marcus Webb leans over the screen, watching.

Yuki slides a thin sheet of bismuth selenide under the probe tip without pausing the readout. The trace shifts. A small, steady offset appears, less than a hundred femtotesla, the magnetic signature of the induced current flowing through the sheet's topological surface state. "That is the stray field from the sample," she says. "The sensor is measuring it at room temperature, without a shielded room, and it has been running continuously for four days." Marcus straightens up. "Room temperature?" "The topological surface state does not need cryogenics," Yuki says. "That is the entire point of this division."

What Yuki is showing Marcus is the engineering argument that quantum sensing built on topological materials may reach the market before topological qubits do, and that the revenue it generates could fund everything else Axiom is trying to build. This chapter covers the physical principles that make quantum sensors categorically more sensitive than classical ones, the specific properties of topological materials that confer a sensing advantage, and the three measurement domains, magnetic fields, rotation, and timing, where those advantages are closest to displacing the state of the art.

Why It Matters

Precision measurement is one of the oldest and most commercially durable problems in engineering. Every GPS satellite depends on atomic clocks accurate to a few nanoseconds per day. Every MRI machine depends on magnetic field uniformity maintained to parts-per-million levels. Every inertial navigation system in a commercial aircraft depends on gyroscopes that accumulate less than a few degrees of heading error per hour. The sensors enabling these systems have been refined over decades, and the performance ceilings they approach are not engineering deficiencies but fundamental noise floors set by classical physics. Thermal noise, Johnson noise, shot noise: these are the irreducible backgrounds that no amount of better circuit design can overcome.

Quantum sensors break through that wall by operating at a different level of physics. Instead of measuring a classical electrical or mechanical response, a quantum sensor measures how a physical quantity perturbs a quantum state whose evolution can be tracked with precision limited only by the Heisenberg uncertainty principle and the quantum system's coherence time. The best quantum magnetometers detect fields as small as one femtotesla, one quadrillionth of a tesla, comparable to the field produced by a single neuron firing in the brain at a distance of a few centimeters. The best quantum clocks are accurate to better than one second in thirty billion years. These are not incremental improvements. They are a different category of measurement.

Topological materials bring a set of properties that address the practical limitations that keep quantum sensors expensive and confined to specialized installations. The canonical high-sensitivity magnetometer, the superconducting quantum interference device (SQUID), achieves femtotesla sensitivity but requires operation at temperatures below 4 K, liquid helium cooling, fixed installations, magnetically shielded rooms, and capital costs in the millions. Topological materials offer a pathway to equivalent sensitivity in devices that operate at room temperature, fit on a chip, and are fabricable using processes compatible with semiconductor manufacturing. That is Yuki Tanaka's engineering proposition, and it is why her sensing division at Axiom represents the company's most credible near-term revenue path.

The Physics of Quantum Sensing

Quantum sensing is better than classical sensing for a precise reason: quantum states are exquisitely sensitive to perturbations. A magnetic field that would produce a negligibly small voltage shift in a conventional resistor can nonetheless rotate the spin state of an electron, shift the energy levels of an atomic transition, or change the interference pattern of a superconducting loop. Measuring the change in the quantum state reveals the field with a precision limited not by electrical noise but by the quantum statistics of the measurement itself.

The three quantum-mechanical phenomena most exploited in practical sensors are superposition and interference, energy-level quantization, and flux quantization in superconductors. Superposition allows a quantum system to exist in a combination of two states simultaneously. When that superposition evolves under the influence of a physical quantity, the accumulated phase difference between the two components encodes the magnitude of that quantity. Quantization of energy levels means atomic transitions occur at frequencies fixed by quantum mechanics to extraordinary precision, making them the basis for atomic clocks and frequency references. Flux quantization in superconductors, where the magnetic flux threading a superconducting loop can only take integer multiples of the flux quantum (approximately 2.07 times ten to the negative fifteen weber), is the principle behind SQUIDs, which detect magnetic fields by counting flux quanta through a superconducting ring interrupted by Josephson junctions.

The sensitivity of any quantum sensor is determined by three parameters: the coupling strength between the measured quantity and the quantum state, the coherence time of that state (how long it maintains quantum properties before noise destroys the superposition), and the repetition rate of independent measurements. Sensitivity improves with the square root of the number of measurements. Coherence time is therefore the central materials engineering challenge in every quantum sensing platform, and it is where topological materials offer their most fundamental advantage: surface states protected by time-reversal symmetry and spin-momentum locking are inherently shielded against the backscattering and decoherence mechanisms that limit conventional solid-state sensors.

Diagram 10.1 - Quantum Sensing Physical Principles

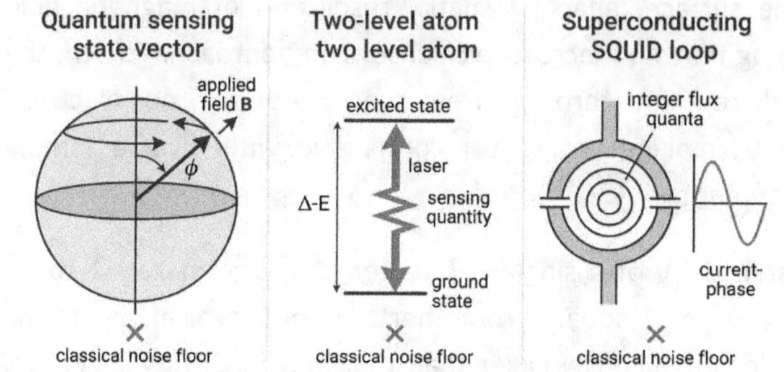

classical noise floor that the quantum sensing approach surpasises.

NV-Center Magnetometers: The Solid-State Workhorse

The nitrogen-vacancy (NV) center in diamond is the most developed solid-state quantum sensor and the platform closest to widespread commercial deployment. An NV center is a point defect consisting of a nitrogen atom substituting for a carbon atom adjacent to a vacant lattice site. This defect has a spin-1 electronic ground state whose energy-level splitting changes measurably in a magnetic field. The magnitude of that splitting, measured by driving transitions between the spin sublevels with microwave radiation and reading out the result via changes in photoluminescence under green laser illumination, encodes the local magnetic field experienced by the NV center.

The NV center's appeal stems from four properties. First, the defect is stable and optically addressable at room temperature, eliminating the cryogenic requirement that limits SQUIDs. Second, the spin coherence time T2 in high-purity, isotopically enriched diamond, grown with carbon-13 depleted below 0.01 percent, can exceed 1 millisecond at room temperature, an extraordinarily long time for a solid-state spin system. Third, single NV centers can be placed within a few nanometers of a sample surface, enabling spatial resolution of magnetic field mapping that no macroscopic sensor can approach. Fourth, the optical readout through free space requires no electrical contacts, making the sensor compatible with diverse sample environments.

The sensitivity of a single NV center is approximately 1 to 10 nanotesla per square root hertz under typical operating conditions, which is weaker than that of a SQUID by six orders of magnitude. The NV center's advantage is not sensitivity per sensor but the ability to form dense arrays that collectively achieve high sensitivity with spatial resolution without cryogenics. An ensemble of 10 to 12 NV centers per cubic centimeter achieves sensitivity in the 1 to 10 femtotesla-per-square-root-hertz range, comparable to that of a SQUID, in a compact, room-temperature package. Several companies, including Quantum Diamond Technologies, QZabre, and spin-outs from Delft University and MIT, are actively pursuing the manufacturing challenges: controlled NV center implantation yield, diamond growth purity, and miniaturized microwave and optical delivery.

Diagram 10.2 - NV Center Diamond Lattice and Sensing Protocol

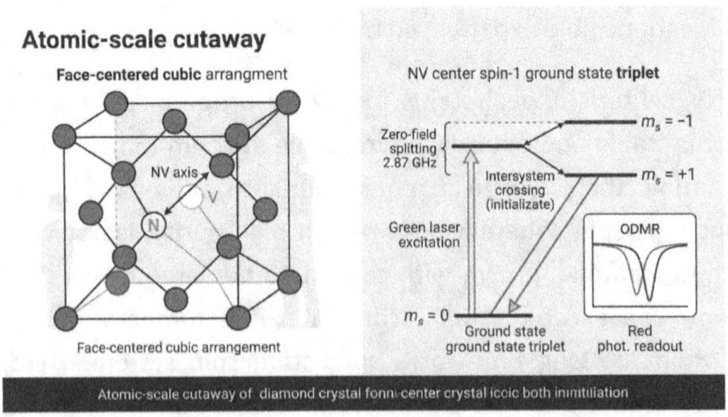

Topological Surface States as Sensing Elements

The NV center is a point defect in a conventional material. The topological surface state is categorically different: a conducting channel whose properties are determined by the global topology of the bulk band structure rather than any local defect, and whose response to magnetic perturbations is tied to fundamental quantum mechanical principles in a way that makes it inherently calibrated and immune to certain classes of noise. Recall from Chapter 6 the essential physics: Bi2Se3 is a material whose bulk is a band insulator but whose surface hosts a single Dirac cone of electronic states. The surface electrons' spin is locked to their momentum (spin-momentum locking), meaning an electron moving right has spin up and an electron moving left has spin down. This locking is enforced by time-reversal symmetry: as long as time-reversal symmetry is preserved, the Dirac cone cannot be gapped, and backscattering is suppressed.

The magnetic sensing mechanism works as follows. An applied magnetic field breaks time-reversal symmetry. When that protection is lifted, a gap opens at the Dirac point, which is proportional to the component of the field perpendicular to the surface. The opening of the gap changes the transport properties of the surface state: surface conductance drops and resistance rises. Measuring the change in resistance as a function of the applied field yields a magnetometer. The key engineering parameter is the surface-to-bulk conductance ratio: in stoichiometric Bi2Se3, selenium vacancies act as inadvertent donors, thereby populating the bulk conduction band and shunting the surface-state signal. Engineering solutions include compensation doping (addition of acceptor dopants to shift the

Fermi level into the bulk gap), thin-film geometry (reducing bulk volume relative to surface area), and material selection, particularly ternary compounds such as (Bi, Sb)2Te3, which allow independent tuning of bulk and surface carrier concentrations.

The quantum anomalous Hall effect (QAHE), first demonstrated in 2013 in chromium-doped (Bi, Sb)2Te3 thin films by Chang et al. at Tsinghua University, represents the most extreme expression of topological magnetic sensitivity. In the QAHE, a magnetic topological insulator exhibits a quantized Hall conductance of exactly e^2/h without an externally applied magnetic field. More recently, the intrinsic magnetic topological insulator MnBi2Te4, in which manganese atoms provide the magnetic order without chemical doping, has shown the QAHE at progressively higher temperatures, approaching room temperature. Two engineering applications follow: a portable resistance standard that realizes the universal value of h/e^2 without large magnets or cryogenics, and a threshold-detection magnetometer operating near the magnetic transition temperature, where small field perturbations can flip the magnetic order.

Diagram 10.3 - Topological Surface State Magnetic Sensing Mechanism

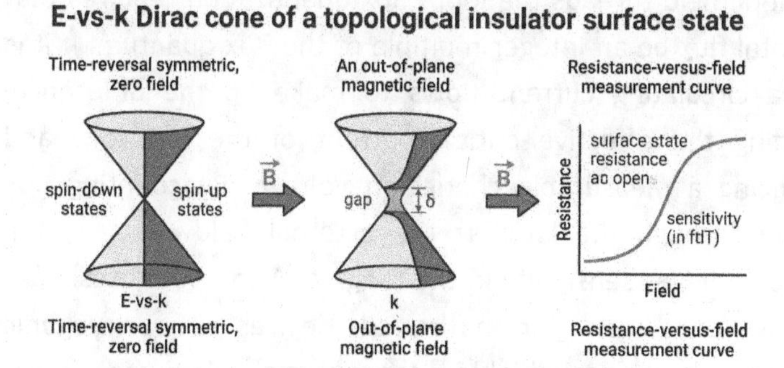

E-k Dirac cone of a topological insulator surface state - In infographic

Diagram 10.4 - Quantum Anomalous Hall Effect in Magnetic Topological Insulator

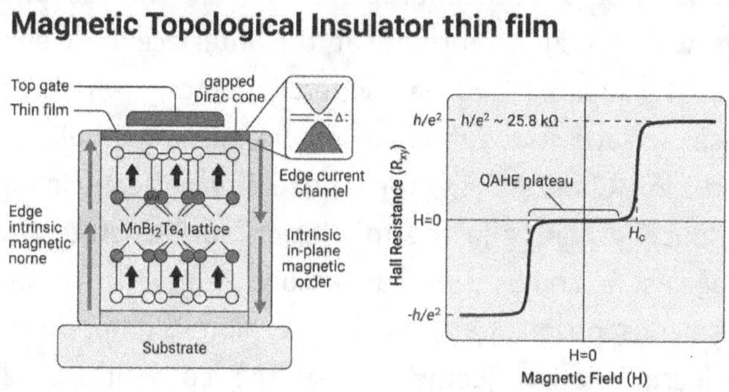

SQUIDs and the Topological SQUID Concept

The superconducting quantum interference device remains the gold standard against which all competing magnetometer technologies are measured. A SQUID consists of a superconducting loop interrupted by one or two Josephson junctions, each a weak link between two superconductors where Cooper pairs tunnel through a thin oxide barrier, maintaining superconducting coherence across the gap. When a magnetic field threads the loop, flux quantization requires that the total flux be an integer multiple of the flux quantum. If it is not, a circulating current flows to make up the difference, changing the effective critical current of the junctions and producing a measurable change in voltage. By counting flux quanta through the loop as the external field changes, the SQUID achieves sensitivity in the range of 1 to 5 femtotesla per square root hertz for optimized devices. The cryogenic requirement is unavoidable: conventional niobium SQUIDs become superconducting only below 9.3 kelvin, requiring liquid helium or closed-cycle cooling, which confines them to fixed installations.

The topological SQUID concept replaces conventional Josephson junctions with junctions formed at the interface between a topological insulator and a superconductor, where the topological surface states mediate the Josephson coupling. As discussed in Chapter 8, the proximity effect induces superconducting pairing in the topological surface state when placed against a conventional superconductor. The resulting topological Josephson junction can exhibit a 4-pi-periodic current-phase relation (compared to the conventional 2-pi periodicity) as a signature of Majorana-bound states at the junction, and its critical current is protected against certain classes of disorder by the topology of the surface state. Several groups have demonstrated signatures of the 4-pi-periodic Josephson effect in junctions using Bi2Se3, HgTe quantum wells, and the Weyl semimetal Cd3As2, but these demonstrations require millikelvin temperatures to suppress thermal fluctuations. At Axiom, Yuki's team is pursuing a hybrid approach that enhances a niobium SQUID at 4 kelvin using a topological insulator film to reduce flux noise, exploiting the surface state's unusually low noise contribution without requiring room-temperature superconductivity.

Diagram 10.5 - SQUID Schematic and Operating Principle

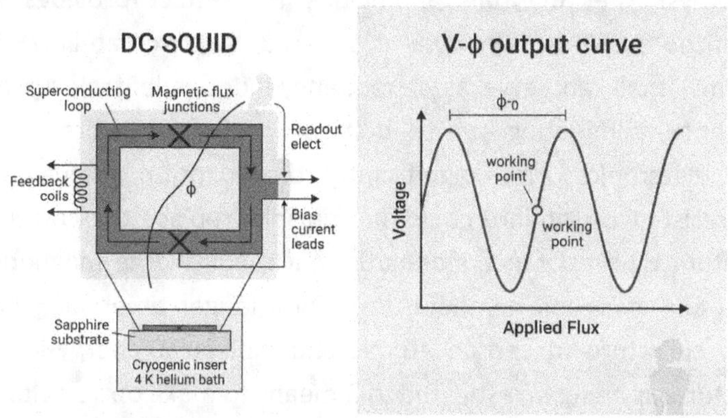

Atomic Clocks and Topological Frequency Standards

An atomic clock is not a mechanism that counts oscillations of a pendulum or quartz crystal; it is a frequency reference that locks an electronic oscillator to an atomic transition frequency fixed by quantum mechanics. The cesium-133 hyperfine transition at 9.192 631 770 gigahertz defines the SI second. Modern chip-scale atomic clocks (CSACs) based on coherent population trapping (CPT) in alkali metal vapor cells have achieved miniaturization to the cubic centimeter scale with power consumption below 100 milliwatts, maintaining frequency stability at 10 to the negative 10 over one second, approximately 1000 times more stable than a temperature-compensated quartz oscillator of the same size and power class. CSACs are deployed in GPS receivers requiring continued operation after satellite signal loss, in communications base stations, and in emerging chip-scale inertial measurement units that combine an atomic clock with MEMS gyroscopes and accelerometers.

Topology connects to atomic clock engineering through two pathways. The quantum anomalous Hall effect provides a quantized resistance (h over e squared, approximately 25.8 kilohms) that can serve as a frequency-independent electrical reference, eliminating one calibration uncertainty in precision clock electronics. More significantly, the quantum anomalous Hall resistance standard could, in principle, replace the current quantum Hall resistance standards that require large magnetic fields and cryogenic temperatures. On a longer timescale, the Berry curvature of certain atomic and molecular energy-level structures is being investigated as a means to make optical clock transitions more robust to magnetic-field noise. This residual error source limits the performance of optical lattice clocks. Optical lattice clocks, the most precise timekeepers ever built, achieve fractional frequency uncertainties below ten to the negative eighteen, equivalent to a clock that would not gain or lose a second in the age of the universe, and their miniaturization into field-deployable instruments would transform geodesy, navigation, and fundamental physics experiments.

Diagram 10.6 - Chip-Scale Atomic Clock Architecture

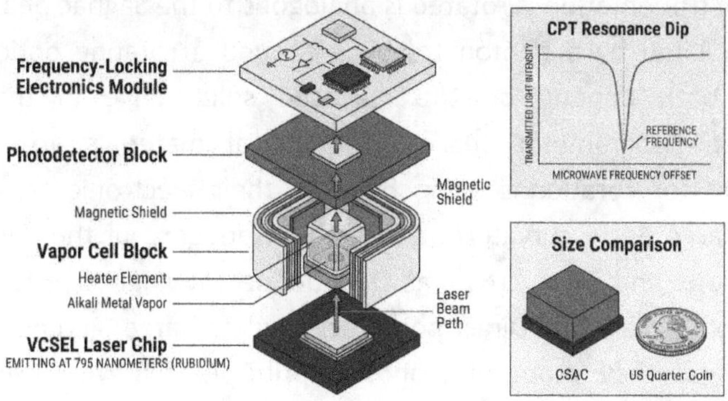

Gyroscopes, Sagnac, and Topological Rotation Sensing

A gyroscope measures rotation rate. In inertial navigation, knowing the rotation rate integrated over time to give the heading angle is the critical complement to knowing acceleration. The highest-performance gyroscopes currently deployed are fiber-optic gyroscopes (FOGs) and ring laser gyroscopes (RLGs), both exploiting the Sagnac effect: a rotating optical cavity splits the round-trip travel times of counter-propagating light beams by an amount proportional to the rotation rate, and the resulting phase difference (in a FOG) or frequency difference (in an RLG) is measured by optical interferometry. Navigation-grade FOGs achieve rotation rate sensitivity below 0.001 degrees per hour, sufficient for aircraft inertial navigation systems maintaining position knowledge to within a few hundred meters after hours of GPS-denied flight.

The connection between the Sagnac effect and topological physics is the Berry phase. As detailed in Chapter 5, the Berry phase is the geometric phase acquired by a quantum state as it is transported around a closed loop in parameter space. For a quantum system, the geometric phase accumulated as the system's orientation is rotated is analogous to the Sagnac phase accumulated by a photon traveling around a rotating optical loop: both depend on the enclosed solid angle in their respective parameter spaces. Topological materials are of interest for rotation sensing because their electronic states carry large Berry curvature, a direct consequence of the band inversions and Dirac crossings that define topological phases. Electrons near the Dirac point accumulate large geometric phases as they propagate, and, in principle, a device using topological surface-state electrons as the interfering waves in a Sagnac-type measurement could achieve greater phase sensitivity per unit area than a device using photons, because the electron mass provides a larger inertial response to rotation.

The practical challenge is coherence. Electrons in a topological surface state maintain quantum coherence over tens to hundreds of nanometers at low temperatures. Still, at room temperature, phonon scattering reduces the coherence length to a few nanometers, far shorter than what is needed to enclose a macroscopic area and accumulate a detectable Sagnac phase. The research priority is identifying topological materials with long room-temperature coherence lengths. Cadmium arsenide (Cd3As2, a Dirac semimetal with exceptionally high room-temperature mobility exceeding 10 to the 6 centimeters squared per volt-second) is the leading candidate, because high carrier mobility correlates directly with long room-temperature coherence lengths. A practical topological gyroscope operating at room temperature remains a research goal rather than a near-term product. Still, the physics gap between current demonstrations and the required coherence length is defined and quantified, which is the prerequisite for a credible engineering roadmap.

Diagram 10.7 - Sagnac Effect and Fiber-Optic Gyroscope Cross-Section

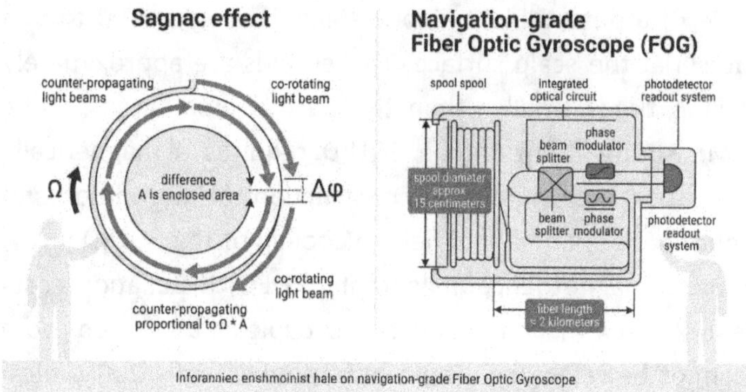

Diagram 10.8 - Topological Material Gyroscope Concept and Performance Comparison

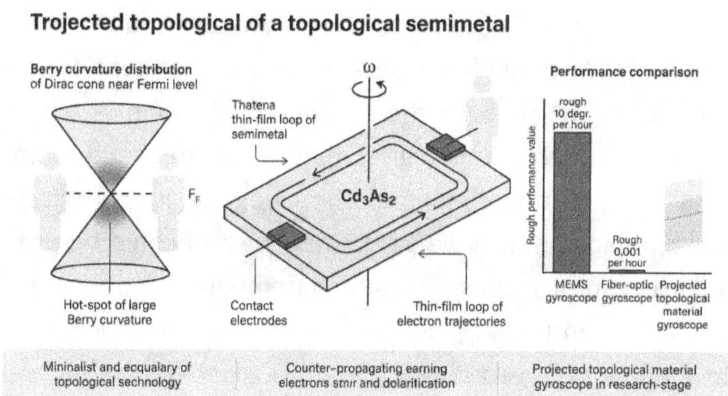

Medical: Magnetoencephalography and Cardiography

Of all the application domains for high-sensitivity magnetometers, medicine offers the most immediate commercial opportunity and the most clearly articulated performance requirement. The human brain and heart produce magnetic fields as direct consequences of the ionic currents driving neural and cardiac signaling. The typical magnetic field produced by a cluster of 50,000 neurons firing synchronously, the scale of a detectable epileptic spike, is roughly 100 to 500 femtotesla at the scalp surface. These fields are approximately one billion times smaller than the Earth's ambient magnetic field. Measuring them with a SQUID requires a magnetically shielded room, a multilayer construction of mu-metal and aluminum panels, and liquid helium cooling of the SQUID array. A complete magnetoencephalography (MEG) installation costs between 2 and 4 million dollars and occupies a dedicated room that cannot be relocated. There are approximately 200 clinical MEG systems installed worldwide, a tiny fraction of the neurological need.

The engineering case for room-temperature magnetometers in MEG is compelling because the performance requirement, approximately 10 to 100 femtotesla sensitivity with centimeter-scale spatial sampling over the full head, is within reach of optimized NV-center or topological material sensors, and room-temperature operation eliminates the cryogenic infrastructure that limits deployment. A wearable MEG system could be used in standard hospital rooms, accommodate pediatric populations where the conventional rigid SQUID helmet is impractical, and enable ambulatory recording of brain activity during natural movement. The neurological applications that become accessible with wearable MEG, such as pre-surgical epilepsy mapping outside the operating room, real-time brain-computer interface feedback during rehabilitation, and continuous monitoring for early detection of neurodegenerative conditions, represent a multi-billion-dollar clinical market currently inaccessible due to the cryogenic requirement.

Magnetocardiography (MCG) presents a more immediately achievable target. The heart's electrical currents produce fields of approximately 50 to 100 picotesla at the chest surface, roughly 1000 times larger than MEG signals. Room-temperature MCG with a sensitivity of 10 to 50 picotesla is achievable with current NV-center ensemble sensors, and several groups have demonstrated clinical-quality MCG recordings using NV-center arrays without shielded rooms, relying on active noise cancellation algorithms to subtract the ambient magnetic background. MCG can identify ischemic regions with three-dimensional localization that electrocardiography cannot provide, detect arrhythmia sources, and characterize fetal cardiac development in utero, where electrode contact is impossible. This is the closest quantum sensing application to clinical deployment, and it shares the same underlying room-temperature magnetometer engineering as wearable MEG.

Diagram 10.9 - MEG Helmet and On-Scalp Sensor Array Comparison

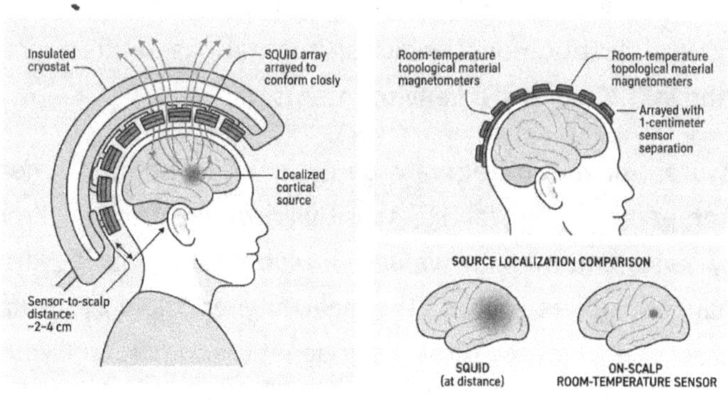

Caption-Magnetoencephalography (MEG) sensor helmet and spented 16:9 landscape layout

Geophysical, Navigation, and Defense Applications

Beyond medicine, high-sensitivity magnetometers and inertial sensors serve three defense and geophysical domains where topological sensing approaches are closest to displacing the state of the art. GPS-independent navigation is the most strategically significant. Every inertial navigation system (INS) integrates gyroscope and accelerometer outputs over time to provide position and heading without an external reference. The fundamental limitation is drift: integrating sensor noise produces heading and position errors that grow over time. A navigation-grade INS for aircraft maintains position accuracy to roughly 1 nautical mile per hour of GPS-denied operation; cheaper tactical-grade systems accumulate errors 10 to 100 times faster. The combination of a chip-scale atomic clock (timing), a quantum gyroscope (rotation rate), and a topological material magnetometer (heading reference against the geomagnetic field) in a handheld package is the defined requirement for next-generation GPS-independent navigation systems for autonomous vehicles, submarines, and aircraft operating in GPS-contested environments.

Underwater magnetic anomaly detection is a domain where room-temperature femtotesla sensitivity would provide direct military and commercial value. A submarine, as a large ferromagnetic object, distorts the local magnetic field by a small but detectable amount. Airborne magnetic anomaly detection (MAD) sensors currently use fluxgate or optically pumped vapor cell magnetometers with sensitivities of approximately 1 to 10 picotesla, sufficient to detect a submarine at ranges of 100 to 500 meters. A room-temperature femtotesla magnetometer would extend the detection range by one to two orders of magnitude, or, equivalently, allow detection from greater altitude, from safer altitudes for patrol aircraft, or through greater ocean depth. The engineering requirements for this application include robustness to vibration in a towed sensor pod, immunity to the aircraft's own electromagnetic interference, and operation across the full temperature range from polar to tropical deployments.

Mineral exploration and geophysical survey represent a large commercial market for precision magnetometry. Airborne magnetic surveys map variations in the Earth's crustal magnetic field to locate ore deposits, delineate geological structures for oil and gas exploration, and survey volcanic and geothermal regions. Survey magnetometers currently achieving 1-10 picotesla sensitivity measure only the total-field magnitude. A topological material sensor with femtotesla sensitivity and full vector-field measurement capability would improve geological resolution and enable deployment on small drones that cannot accommodate the weight and power consumption of current systems. This is the overlooked market where modest improvements in sensitivity and portability would immediately displace incumbent technology.

Diagram 10.10 - GPS-Free Navigation Sensor Suite Architecture

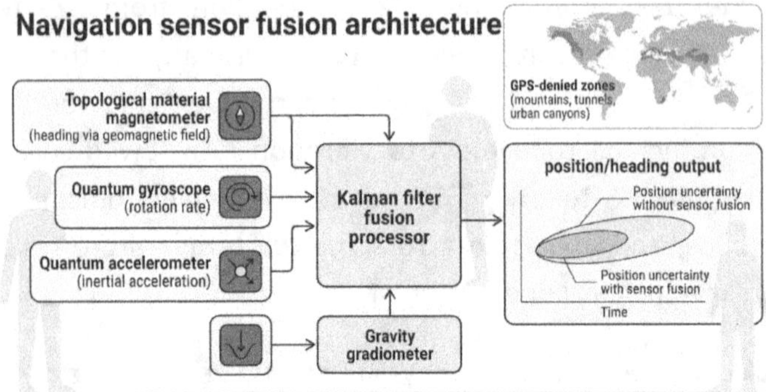

The powerful effect of quantum sensor inputs, through all advanced sensor-architecture

Practical Readouts and Electronics Integration

A quantum sensing element is only as useful as its readout. For NV-center magnetometers, the standard readout uses a 532-nanometer green laser to initialize and read out the NV spin state and a microwave source at approximately 2.87 gigahertz to drive spin transitions. The optical readout signal is small, typically 5 to 15 percent photoluminescence contrast between spin states, amid a large photon background. Shot noise in detecting this small contrast against the large background is the primary sensitivity limit. Engineering approaches to improve the signal include spin-to-charge conversion, which converts the spin state into a charge state before readout, yielding a much larger electrical signal; near-field optical techniques that enhance photon-collection efficiency; and resonant microwave cavities that amplify the transition signal.

For topological surface-state magnetometers, the readout is electrical: a change in the topological surface-state resistance in response to the applied field. This is simpler in principle than the optical readout of an NV center, but stringent requirements apply to contact resistance, sample quality, and low-frequency noise. 1/f noise from surface impurities is a significant issue in transport measurements of thin films of topological insulators. Lock-in amplification at frequencies above the 1/f noise corner, combined with surface passivation to reduce surface impurity density, is the practical engineering approach. The integration of quantum sensing elements with CMOS readout electronics is the critical bridge between laboratory demonstration and a manufacturable product. The sensing element is fabricated separately using its own process (chemical vapor deposition for diamond, molecular beam epitaxy for topological insulators) and then bonded to a CMOS readout chip through bump bonding or wire bonding. This hybrid integration approach sacrifices some noise performance compared to monolithic integration, but it is the practical manufacturing path at current levels of material maturity.

Diagram 10.11 - Topological Magnetometer Readout Electronics Signal Chain

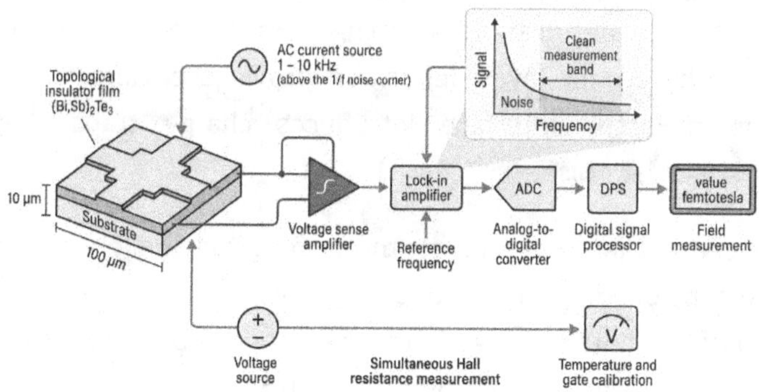

Fabrication Roadmap: From Lab to Manufacturable Device

Every topological sensing concept in this chapter faces the same manufacturing question: can the material properties demonstrated in a laboratory be reproduced at the wafer scale with acceptable yield and in processes compatible with existing semiconductor manufacturing infrastructure? For topological insulator thin films, the fabrication challenges are well-characterized. The first challenge is substrate compatibility: the best-performing Bi2Se3 and (Bi, Sb)2Te3 films are grown on lattice-matched substrates such as barium fluoride or graphene-terminated silicon carbide, neither of which is a standard CMOS substrate. Research into growth on silicon using buffer layers to manage the lattice mismatch is progressing. Still, it has not yet produced films with surface-dominated transport, where the ratio of surface to bulk conductance must exceed approximately 10:1 for sensing applications. The second challenge is surface passivation: Bi2Se3 surfaces are highly sensitive to atmospheric oxygen and water vapor. Capping with aluminum oxide deposited by atomic layer deposition provides encapsulation, but the dielectric interface introduces charge traps that contribute to 1/f noise.

For NV-center diamond sensors, the wafer-scale challenge is to achieve controlled NV-center depth profiles with high yield. The fraction of implanted nitrogen ions that produce optically active NV centers rather than other vacancy configurations is approximately 1-10 percent, which requires either high implant doses (that introduce lattice damage that shortens T2) or annealing processes that are not yet fully controlled at the wafer scale. Quantum Diamond Technologies and QZabre are addressing this yield problem by optimizing implant energy, dose, and anneal temperature, with recent reports of T2 times exceeding 100 microseconds in implanted samples. The honest engineering timeline for room-temperature topological material magnetometers with femtotesla sensitivity is five to ten years from the 2024 demonstrations, assuming continued investment at the current pace. The critical path items, surface-dominated transport at room temperature, CMOS-compatible deposition, and 1/f noise reduction, are materials engineering problems with known solution strategies. The uncertainty in the timeline is not whether they can be solved, but how long it will take to optimize the manufacturing processes.

Diagram 10.12 - Topological Sensor Technology Readiness Roadmap

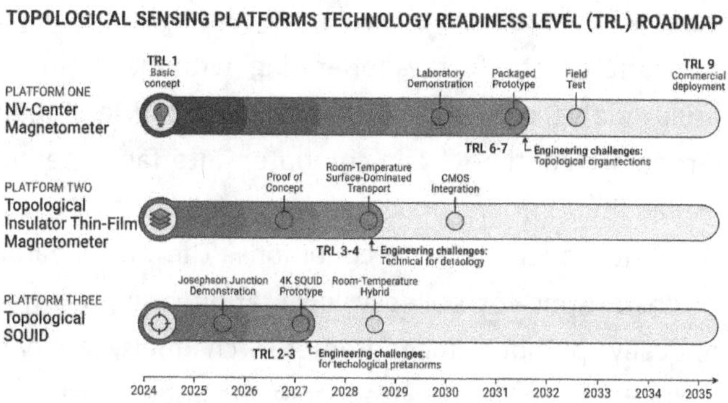

What Can We Build With This?

The near-term commercial answer begins with what is ready now. Room-temperature NV-center ensemble magnetometers with sensitivity in the 10 to 100 femtotesla per square root hertz range are achievable today in packaged form factors approaching those of a mobile phone camera module. The first markets to be disrupted are industrial: non-destructive testing of metallic components for stress cracks (currently performed with expensive SQUID arrays), current mapping in printed circuit boards and semiconductor packages (currently performed with magnetic force microscopy, which is slow and limited to small samples), and battery health monitoring in electric vehicle packs, where mapping current distribution in individual cells reveals degradation before it causes failure. These markets require 10 to 100 picotesla sensitivity at centimeter spatial resolution, a target well within the reach of 2024 NV-center sensor arrays, and they do not require the femtotesla sensitivity frontier.

The medium-term target most likely to generate a visible product launch that changes public perception of quantum sensing is wearable MEG for neurological monitoring. Ambulatory MEG based on on-scalp NV-center or topological material magnetometer arrays operating without a shielded room would enable pre-surgical epilepsy mapping in standard hospital rooms, real-time brain-computer interface feedback during rehabilitation, and continuous monitoring for early detection of neurodegenerative conditions. The first wearable MEG demonstrations for epilepsy localization, using arrays of 30-64 optically pumped magnetometer channels, appeared between 2019 and 2023. The step from those demonstrations to a clinical product is an engineering and regulatory challenge measured in years rather than decades, and the underlying sensing physics is the same room-temperature femtotesla magnetometer platform that enables clinical MCG.

The longest-horizon but highest-value target is GPS-independent navigation for autonomous systems. A chip-scale atomic clock providing precise timing, a quantum gyroscope providing rotational rate, and a topological-material magnetometer providing geomagnetic heading reference, combined in a package small enough for a smartphone, represent a navigation capability that does not currently exist at that scale or cost. A submarine navigating with centimeter-per-hour drift, a drone operating in GPS-denied urban environments with decimeter-scale position knowledge, an autonomous vehicle maintaining lane precision in tunnels: these are defined requirements for systems that militaries and transportation operators need today. The sensor suite to enable them is within reach of the engineering approaches described in this chapter.

At Axiom Quantum, Yuki's near-term product target is a topological-insulator thin-film magnetometer module operating at room temperature, with a noise floor below 1 picotesla per square root hertz, suitable for MCG cardiac imaging without a shielded room. The sensing physics is demonstrated. The fabrication challenges are the active engineering problems. The commercial target, a $50,000 MCG system deployable in any cardiology office rather than only in magnetically shielded installations, is the financial bridge that makes Axiom's topological qubit program viable. Marcus, watching the magnetic field trace scroll across the monitor in Yuki's lab, now understands this. The sensing division is not a distraction from the qubit work. Revenue makes Qubit work possible.

Takeaway

Quantum sensing is the domain where topological materials are most likely to reach commercial scale first. The key points to carry forward are these. Quantum sensors measure how a physical quantity perturbs a quantum state, and the sensitivity ceiling is set by the coherence time and coupling strength of that state, not by electrical noise. Topological materials contribute surface states with unusual coherence properties, large Berry curvature, and intrinsic sensitivity to time-reversal-symmetry-breaking fields, all of which translate to lower noise floors and more compact sensor architectures than conventional materials allow.

The engineering hierarchy runs from demonstrated to speculative: NV-center ensemble magnetometers are the most mature platform, with commercial products approaching clinical deployment for MCG. Topological insulator thin-film magnetometers have the best theoretical performance ceiling but require advances in surface-dominated transport and CMOS compatibility. Topological SQUIDs remain a research-stage concept. Each platform has a defined engineering pathway and is being pursued by identifiable teams at universities, national laboratories, and startups. The medical imaging market, specifically wearable MEG and point-of-care MCG, is the near-term commercial driver of miniaturization and ruggedization of quantum magnetometer technology. Defense and navigation provide the long-term, high-value demand that sustains investment. The geophysical survey market is an overlooked one where relatively modest improvements in sensitivity and portability would immediately displace incumbent technology.

Chapter 11 takes the sensing work out of the laboratory. It examines the full device stack: how topological materials for qubits, sensors, and other applications are integrated into manufacturable hardware, what the substrate, contact, and packaging challenges look like in practice, and what the timeline from material demonstration to manufacturable device product actually requires. The bridge from sensing physics to device engineering is shorter than it has ever been, and the details of that bridge are the subject of the next chapter.

11 Topological Materials for Real Devices

The wafer was the size of a pocket watch. Marcus Webb held it at the edge of the light, tilting it so the beam caught the bismuth selenide film deposited across its surface overnight in the MBE chamber down the corridor. From 1 meter away, a trained eye could see the interference color, confirming that the film had reached the target thickness. Marcus was not looking at the color. He was looking at a chip-scale crack running diagonally from the center toward the upper-right edge. This fracture developed during cooldown because the thermal expansion coefficients of the bismuth selenide film and the silicon substrate differed by 7 parts per million per degree Celsius. The crack was an integration problem, not a physics problem, and it had just killed three weeks of process development time.

He set the wafer in the inspection tray and looked at the process engineer across the bench. What is the yield-limiting step? She said: interface quality. The topological surface state is only as good as the interface between the topological insulator and the substrate. One monolayer of chemical disorder at that interface, and you have gapped the surface state. The conducting topological channel is gone. Marcus wrote that down. One monolayer. He thought about what that meant in terms of process control—angstrom-level cleanliness requirements at an interface formed at elevated temperature in a chamber approaching its maintenance interval. Priya Nair walked in from the hallway, still carrying the tablet she used to review the deposition logs, and Marcus held up the cracked wafer without a word. She looked at it for one second.

Welcome to topological materials engineering, she said. Then she pulled up a chair.

That scene at the integration bench is the organizing question of this chapter. The physics of topological insulators is well-established. What is not yet complete is the engineering knowledge to build a reliable, manufacturable device that exploits those properties in a production environment. This chapter is about the gap between a research-grade topological insulator sample and a manufacturable component: the specific fabrication problems, their known solution pathways, and the two application domains closest to commercial production beyond quantum computing and sensing.

Why It Matters

If you are building hardware, topological materials are relevant for one of three reasons. You may be working on quantum computing and need to understand what fabrication process actually produces a topological qubit substrate. You may be working on memory and have seen results showing that topological insulator surfaces switch magnetic bits at lower current density than any platinum or tantalum spin Hall layer your process team has tested. Or you may be working on process development and need to distinguish a topologically active film from one gapped by interface disorder. All three questions converge on the same fabrication physics, and this chapter develops that physics.

The practical stakes are significant. Spin-orbit torque magnetic random access memory, the application closest to production readiness among topological device types, could eliminate the write-energy penalty limiting conventional MRAM scaling. The write energy using a topological insulator spin source is lower than with a platinum spin Hall layer by a factor of three to ten, depending on material composition and interface quality, as measured by experimental groups at Samsung and Intel. That factor directly reduces power consumption in magnetic memory at advanced technology nodes and is the most sensitive to interface engineering. Getting the interface right is not a refinement. It is the technology.

Fabrication: Bulk Conductance and Surface Isolation

The first device engineering problem a topological insulator faces is a materials physics problem that appears as an electrical engineering problem: how do you isolate the topological surface-state contribution from the bulk? In an ideal topological insulator, the bulk semiconductor gap is sufficiently large to yield negligible conductance at the operating temperature. In a real film, the bulk is doped, either unintentionally by native defects such as selenium vacancies in bismuth selenide or intentionally to control the Fermi level, creating a parallel conduction channel that shunts the surface state. If the bulk conducts, the surface state is electrically invisible to external contacts.

Two compounding problems make interface control so demanding. Fermi level pinning occurs when a topological insulator surface contacts another material: charge transfer shifts the local carrier density, pulling the Fermi level into the bulk conduction or valence band rather than leaving it in the gap where the surface state lives. Gap opening occurs when interface disorder breaks the crystalline symmetry on which the topological surface state depends. Time-reversal symmetry protects the surface state from backscattering by non-magnetic perturbations. Still, it does not protect the state from being destroyed outright by a perturbation large enough to open an energy gap. Interface disorder of the wrong kind is exactly such a perturbation, which is why one monolayer of disorder is sufficient to kill the device function entirely.

Diagram 11.1 - Bulk vs. Surface Conductance in a Topological Insulator

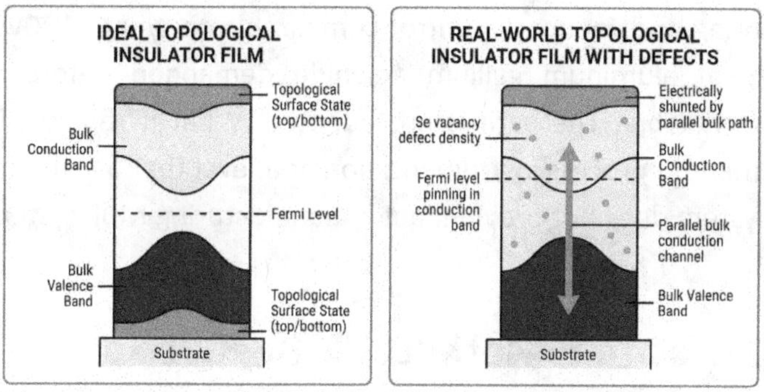

A ection infographic on onihe topological insulato: ıridscape with an executive tone

The materials-engineering solution to bulk conductance follows two parallel paths. Compensation doping adds p-type acceptors, most commonly calcium on bismuth sites, at a concentration calibrated to cancel the electron contribution from selenium vacancies. The manufacturing challenge is that the optimal calcium concentration depends on the selenium vacancy density, which varies with growth conditions, necessitating either tight control of growth parameters or a post-growth compensation step. The preferred path is alloy engineering using ternary compositions in the bismuth-antimony-telluride family, abbreviated BSTS. Antimony substitution moves the Fermi level toward the middle of the bulk gap by modifying the band inversion energy, and telluride-to-selenide substitution adjusts the gap magnitude. BSTS has produced the lowest bulk conductance values measured to date and is the current preferred direction for device-quality material.

The optimal BSTS composition for Fermi-level placement is sensitive to growth conditions. A two-percent shift in the antimony-to-bismuth ratio changes the Fermi level position by enough to matter for device operation. This is a process control problem that has been solved many times in III-V semiconductor manufacturing. Still, it requires in-situ monitoring and feedback control comparable to what MOCVD epitaxy of aluminum gallium arsenide demanded before it became reliable. The path is precedented. What it requires is investment in process instrumentation at a level that a research MBE system does not provide, but a manufacturing MBE system can.

Deposition Methods: MBE, CVD, and Exfoliation

Molecular beam epitaxy is the workhorse deposition technique for growing research-grade thin films of topological insulators. MBE evaporates elemental source materials from heated effusion cells inside an ultrahigh vacuum chamber maintained at pressures below one billionth of atmospheric pressure. The evaporated atoms travel in a directed beam and land on a heated substrate, incorporating into an epitaxial film one atomic layer at a time. The ultrahigh-vacuum environment eliminates gas-phase reactions that introduce contamination, and the low deposition rate of a fraction of a monolayer per second gives adatoms time to find equilibrium lattice sites before being buried by subsequent layers. Bismuth selenide films grown by MBE on sapphire or silicon with an appropriate buffer layer exhibit X-ray rocking curve widths comparable to those of bulk single crystals, and angle-resolved photoemission measurements confirm the characteristic Dirac-cone band structure of the topological surface state.

Diagram 11.2 - MBE Chamber Cross-Section for Topological Insulator Growth

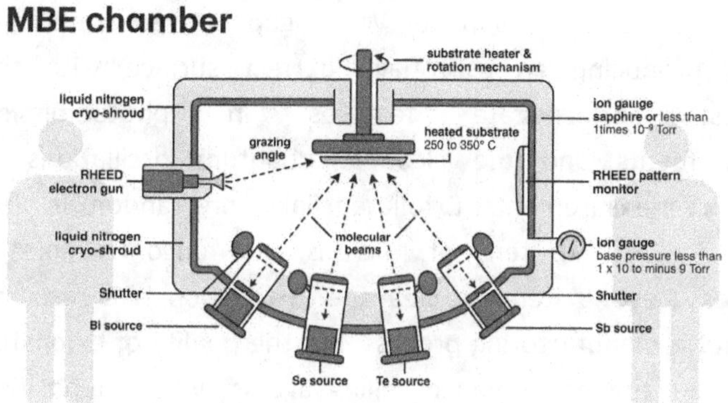

The limitations of MBE are its throughput and scalability. A typical system deposits one to two wafers per run with run times from several hours to overnight. Equipment cost is two to three million dollars per system. Maintenance intervals require breaking the vacuum, taking several days of pump-down, and outgassing. Chemical vapor deposition for topological insulators uses chalcogenide precursors combined with organometallic bismuth sources, enabling batch processing of multiple wafers simultaneously at rates one to two orders of magnitude faster than MBE. The penalty is film quality: CVD films exhibit higher defect densities, larger rocking-curve widths, and more variable surface-state band structures. Whether this quality gap is fundamental or can be closed by precursor chemistry and reactor design is an active research question. The analogous quality gap between MBE and MOCVD for III-V semiconductors was substantially closed over a decade of reactor development, suggesting that the CVD quality gap for topological insulators is an engineering problem rather than a physics constraint.

Mechanical exfoliation yields the highest-quality topological insulator flakes available for research. A bismuth selenide or bismuth telluride crystal is cleaved with adhesive tape, and the resulting thin flakes are transferred to a target substrate. The cleavage surface is a van der Waals gap between quintuple layers, producing an essentially perfect surface with the sharpest surface-state features in photoemission measurements and the cleanest quantum oscillations in transport measurements. Exfoliated flakes are random in size, typically a few to tens of microns, and uncontrollable in thickness beyond iterative cleavage. Exfoliation is a research tool, not a manufacturing process, but the quality of exfoliated flakes sets the performance ceiling against which deposition methods are measured.

Substrate Choice and Lattice Mismatch

Sapphire has a lattice mismatch with bismuth selenide of approximately 3% and a thermal expansion coefficient reasonably well matched to that of the film, making it the most commonly used research substrate. Silicon has a much larger lattice mismatch of approximately eleven percent, but CMOS integration requires silicon compatibility. The crack in Marcus's wafer was a thermal expansion mismatch crack, a consequence of depositing bismuth selenide directly on silicon without a buffer layer to grade the lattice constant and thermal expansion coefficient between the two materials. Buffer-layer engineering for topological insulators on silicon has centered on two material classes. Indium selenide buffer layers, specifically the layered van der Waals compound In2Se3, provide a crystallographic bridge between silicon and bismuth selenide.

Because bismuth selenide is itself a van der Waals material, the film can relax lateral strain by sliding at the van der Waals gap rather than accumulating dislocation density, thereby tolerating larger lattice mismatches than equivalently thick III-V films before crystalline quality degrades.

Diagram 11.3 - Substrate Lattice Mismatch and Buffer Layer Engineering

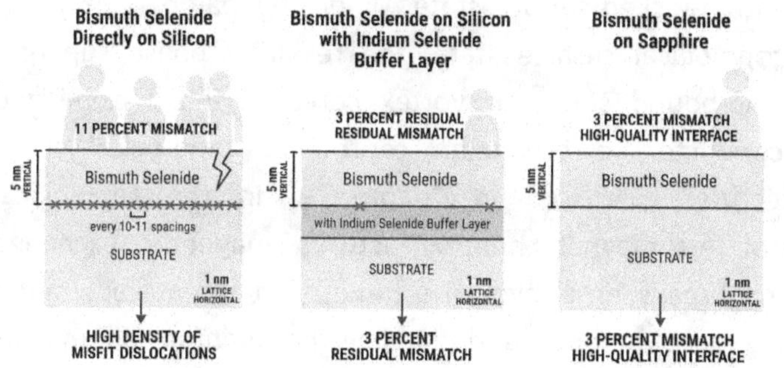

A strong central metarpor substrates for torological insulator configuration for topological insulato (Bi_2Se_3)

A second buffer-layer approach uses bismuth as a surfactant. A sub-monolayer of bismuth deposited on silicon before bismuth selenide growth terminates dangling bonds that would otherwise create a chemically reactive interface, reducing nucleation of amorphous BiSex oxide phases. The combination of a bismuth wetting layer with a subsequent low-temperature nucleation step at around 100 degrees Celsius, followed by higher-temperature growth at 300 degrees Celsius for the bulk of the film, has produced bismuth selenide films on silicon with rocking-curve widths approaching those of the best sapphire-grown material. A slow controlled cooldown rate remains required to prevent crack formation during post-deposition cooling, but the problem is manageable within the envelope of standard deposition process control.

Interface Engineering for Proximity Effects

The most compelling topological insulator device architectures require proximity coupling between the topological insulator and either a superconductor or a ferromagnet. In the topological insulator/superconductor heterostructure, Cooper pairs, the bound electron pairs that carry supercurrent and are characterized by their paired opposite momenta and spins, tunnel across the interface and induce a pairing gap in the spin-momentum-locked surface state. When this pairing gap opens in a topological surface state, the resulting phase supports Majorana-bound states at vortex cores in the proximitized superconductor, a prediction central to topological qubit architectures discussed in Chapter 9. In the topological insulator/ferromagnet heterostructure, magnetic exchange coupling breaks time-reversal symmetry in the surface state, gapping the Dirac point and enabling the quantum anomalous Hall effect, where quantized Hall conductance of exactly one quantum unit appears at zero magnetic field.

Diagram 11.4 - Topological Insulator Heterostructure Interface Engineering

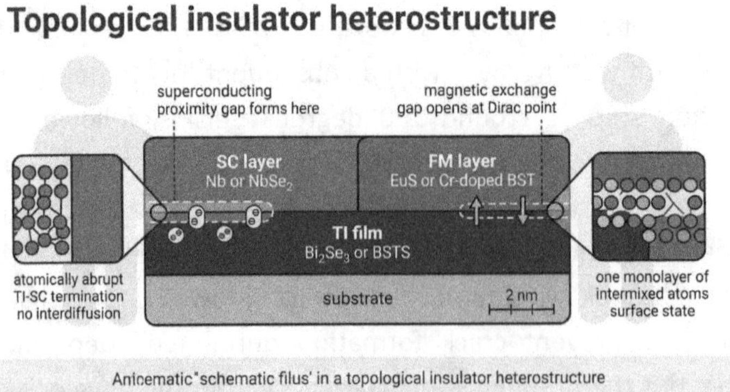

The tolerance requirement for both proximity heterostructures is the same: the interface must be atomically abrupt to within one monolayer. For niobium on bismuth selenide, the most studied TI-SC heterostructure, an interface transition zone of two to three monolayers has been shown to reduce the tunneling conductance signature of the proximity gap to below the measurement noise floor. Achieving atomic abruptness requires a deposition sequence minimizing thermal exposure after the initial bismuth selenide growth. Niobium reacts with selenium at temperatures above approximately 150 degrees Celsius, forming a niobium selenide phase that is not superconducting in the relevant temperature range and disrupts the topological surface state. The solution is in situ deposition: bismuth selenide growth is completed in the MBE chamber, the sample cools to below 150 degrees Celsius without breaking vacuum, and niobium is then deposited by magnetron sputtering from a module connected to the MBE chamber via an ultrahigh-vacuum transfer arm.

For the topological insulator/ferromagnet heterostructure, chromium-doped bismuth telluride can be grown in the same MBE system. Still, the chromium doping profile must be precisely controlled to avoid creating a magnetically inhomogeneous layer that introduces local time-reversal-symmetry-breaking fluctuations. This requires real-time monitoring of the chromium flux during growth, imposing additional demands on effusion cell hardware. The practical manufacturing consequence is that both TI-SC and TI-FM heterostructures require either in situ multimaterial deposition or specialized low-temperature ex situ deposition protocols, neither of which is currently offered as a standard process at a commercial semiconductor foundry.

Cryogenic Packaging and Thermal Management

Most confirmed topological insulator surface states operate reliably below 77 Kelvin, the boiling point of liquid nitrogen. The confirmed room-temperature topological insulators, including certain bismuth iodide compositions and the tin telluride family, exhibit surface-state signatures in photoemission measurements. Still, device-quality operation with surface-state-dominated transport is typically below 200 Kelvin for the most promising current candidates. This temperature constraint has direct consequences for packaging architecture: topological insulator devices that rely on the surface state require a cryogenic package, whether a liquid nitrogen- or helium-cooled module, a compact pulse tube cryocooler, or, for quantum computing applications, a dilution refrigerator operating below 100 millikelvin.

Diagram 11.5 - Cryogenic Package for Topological Device Integration

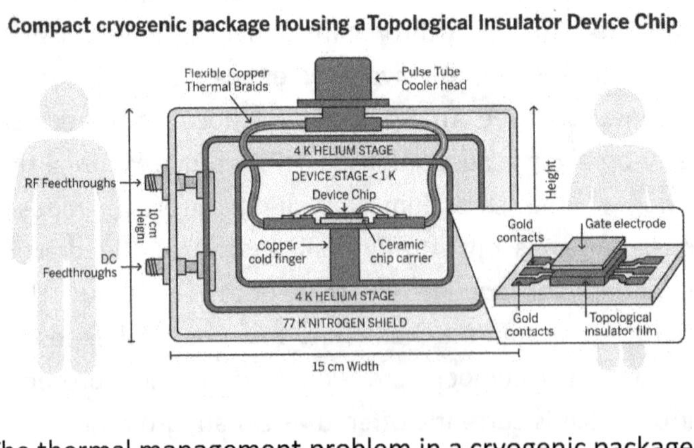

The thermal management problem in a cryogenic package is not heat removal from the device itself, which is negligible, but

thermal isolation between stages and thermal anchoring of electrical leads. Every current-carrying lead entering the cryostat at room temperature and connecting to the device at millikelvin temperatures carries a thermal load proportional to the conductor's thermal conductivity and cross-section. For a dilution refrigerator operating at 20 millikelvin, the thermal budget at the mixing chamber stage is typically a few microwatts. A single copper coaxial cable of conventional dimensions carries several hundred microwatts from 300 Kelvin to 20 millikelvin, which is why dilution refrigerator designs use stainless steel or cupronickel coaxial cable, heavily thermally anchored at each intermediate stage.

Magnetic field requirements add a further packaging constraint. Some topological qubit proposals require a small applied field of a few hundred millitesla to create the vortex lattice in the proximitized superconductor. Others, including semiconductor-topological insulator nanowire architectures, require a field along the nanowire axis of one to two tesla. In either case, a superconducting solenoid wound around the device stage inside the cryostat applies the field. Managing stray fields to avoid saturating adjacent magnetic components or driving nearby superconducting contacts into the normal state requires a combination of superconducting lead shields at millikelvin temperatures and mu-metal shielding at room temperature.

Material Defects, Doping, and Fermi Level Control

The dominant native defect in bismuth selenide is the selenium vacancy, formed preferentially because selenium has a higher vapor pressure than bismuth and tends to re-evaporate from the growing film surface before fully incorporating into the lattice. Each selenium vacancy acts as an n-type donor. The native defect density in as-grown bismuth selenide films is typically 10 to the 18th to 10 to the 19th per cubic centimeter, enough to place the Fermi level firmly in the conduction band and shunt the topological surface state with bulk electrons. Scanning tunneling microscopy has mapped this defect landscape in detail, identifying selenium vacancies and bismuth antisite substitutions as the two dominant n-type defects and providing quantitative estimates of their concentrations as a function of growth conditions.

Diagram 11.6 - Defect Types and Fermi Level Pinning in Bi2Se3

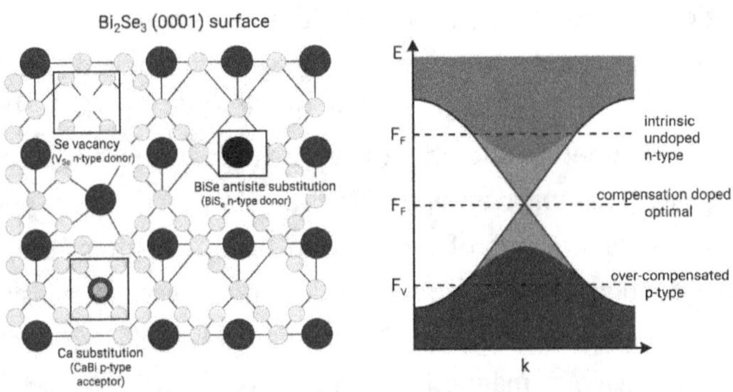

The two primary approaches to Fermi level control are compensation doping and electrostatic gating. Compensation doping adds p-type acceptors such as calcium at a concentration calibrated to cancel the electron contribution from selenium vacancies. The manufacturing challenge is that the optimal calcium concentration depends on the selenium vacancy density, which varies with growth conditions, necessitating tight control of growth parameters or a post-growth ion implantation and annealing step. Electrostatic gating with a top gate electrode insulated by hafnium oxide or aluminum oxide allows the Fermi level to be tuned in real time. Gate tuning to the charge-neutrality point of the topological-surface-state Dirac cone has been demonstrated in research devices, confirming that the surface state can be isolated electrostatically even in films with significant bulk doping. Fermi-level pinning at the gate dielectric interface, a well-known problem in III-V semiconductor technology, reduces gate efficiency and requires passivating the topological insulator surface before dielectric deposition.

Scaling: From Research Nanowires to Wafer-Scale Processes

The research literature is dominated by exfoliated flakes and vapor-liquid-solid-grown nanowires, neither of which is scalable to wafer manufacturing. The path to a manufacturable device requires replacing stochastic, single-crystal processes with deterministic, lithographically defined processes that can be executed with wafer-level uniformity. The wafer diameter progression for topological insulator MBE mirrors that of compound semiconductor MBE in the 1980s and 1990s. In early experiments, films have been grown on substrates as small as 5 by 5 millimeters. Two-inch wafer growth became feasible with rotating substrate holders. Multiple research groups now report the growth of three-inch wafers of bismuth selenide and BSTS. The jump to four-inch and larger substrates requires larger effusion cells or multi-source arrangements to maintain compositional uniformity, which determines the Fermi-level position.

Diagram 11.7 - Topological Insulator Scaling Roadmap

Process maturity roadmap diags, 16:9 landscape

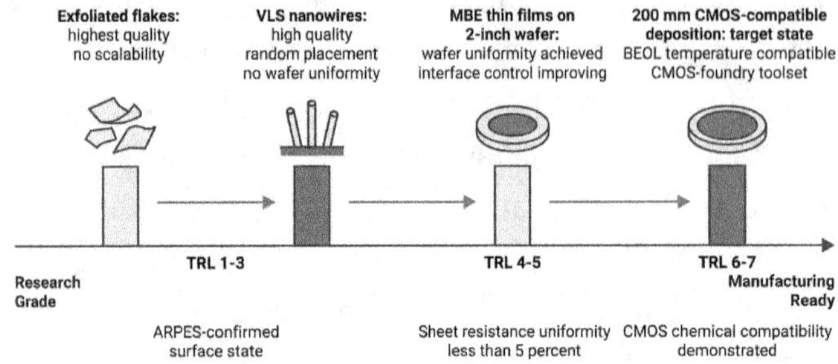

Mininir-style roadmap, 16:9 landscape

Process integration for wafer-scale topological insulator device flow imposes requirements beyond film growth. The film must withstand lithographic patterning, including chemical exposure during photoresist processing, dry etching to define device mesas, and thermal exposure during metal contact deposition and annealing. Bismuth selenide and related chalcogenides are more reactive than silicon or III-V semiconductors: they dissolve in standard wet etchants, are chemically modified by oxygen plasma, and are mechanically fragile because of van der Waals cleavage planes between quintuple layers. Each incompatibility has a known mitigation: a capping layer of aluminum oxide before wet-chemical steps, ultraviolet ozone cleaning instead of oxygen plasma, and bonding to a silicon handle wafer before steps involving mechanical contact with the film. Yield in a complex flow is the product of individual step yields. Improving the interface preparation and gate dielectric deposition steps from their current laboratory yields of approximately 70-80 percent to the 95+ percent needed for manufacturable processes is the near-term engineering target.

Integration with CMOS Control Electronics

The primary CMOS integration constraint is thermal budget. Conventional silicon CMOS back-end-of-line processing has a hard upper limit of approximately 400 degrees Celsius to avoid melting existing copper or aluminum metallization. Topological insulator MBE growth under standard research conditions requires substrate temperatures of 250 to 350 degrees Celsius, which are, in principle, within the BEOL thermal budget. Contamination is the most operationally significant constraint. Bismuth and selenium are both deep-level impurity species in silicon: even parts-per-billion concentrations create energy levels deep within the band gap that degrade minority-carrier lifetime, p-n junction leakage currents, and transistor threshold-voltage stability. Any silicon wafer exposed to bismuth or selenium is effectively disqualified from further CMOS processing in a facility maintaining silicon device specifications.

Diagram 11.8 - CMOS Integration Architecture for Topological Device

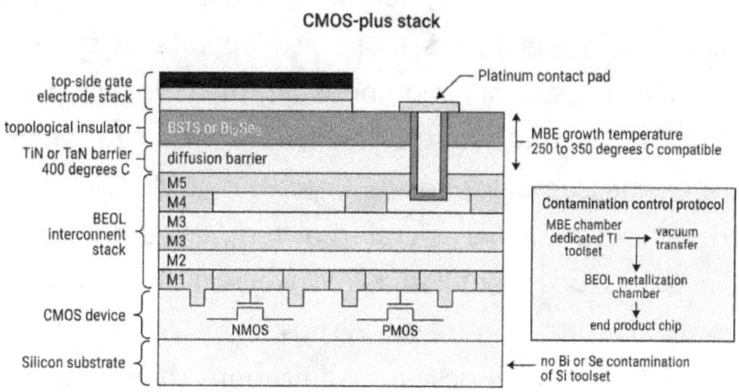

The deposition of topological insulator films on silicon must occur in tooling physically segregated from the main silicon

process flow, with dedicated load ports, transfer arms, and exhaust handling. This is a facility engineering problem solved the same way that III-V-on-silicon integration programs at major semiconductor manufacturers addressed the analogous challenge of integrating gallium arsenide or indium phosphide with silicon CMOS: by designating compound-semiconductor tools as quarantined and implementing rigorous wafer-level contamination-tracking protocols. At the device level, the via-contacted geometry, in which the topological insulator film is deposited on a planarized BEOL stack and contacted through vias that connect to copper metallization below, is essentially identical to the geometry used for thin-film transistors and MEMS devices fabricated monolithically on CMOS substrates. The specific challenge for topological insulators is ensuring that the fluorine-based plasma etch chemistry does not attack the topological insulator film; this is addressed by depositing an etch-stop layer on the topological insulator before oxide deposition.

The cryogenic operating temperature of most current topological devices adds a system-level integration challenge: the CMOS control electronics must also operate at cryogenic temperatures, or the connection between the cryogenic device and room-temperature control must be managed without introducing unacceptable noise. Cryogenic CMOS, meaning standard silicon transistors operated at temperatures from 4 K to 100 mK, has been studied extensively in the context of quantum computing control and shown to be feasible for specific circuit types with design modifications that account for changes in threshold voltage, carrier mobility, and junction leakage at low temperatures. Commercial cryogenic CMOS processes are becoming available from foundries serving the quantum computing market, providing the technology bridge between the topological device layer and the room-temperature system. Marcus's earlier background in cryogenic control systems puts him in exactly the position of having to specify this interface.

Defect Imaging and Material Qualification

The metrology bridging fabrication and device performance in topological insulator manufacturing differs from conventional semiconductor process control. X-ray diffraction and electrical test structures provide useful information but do not directly reveal whether a specific area of the film contains device-quality topological surface states. Scanning tunneling spectroscopy (abbreviated STS) is the most direct probe: it maps the local density of states at atomic resolution. It can detect the presence or absence of the topological surface state in a specific region. An STS measurement requires a cryogenic scanning tunneling microscope operating at or below 4 Kelvin, with the sample in vacuum, and acquiring a complete spatial map across even a millimeter-scale area can take many hours. The role of STS in a manufacturing environment is as a materials qualification tool: a periodic measurement run on representative samples that confirms the growth recipe produces topological surface states of the required quality.

Diagram 11.9 - Scanning Tunneling Spectroscopy of Topological Surface State

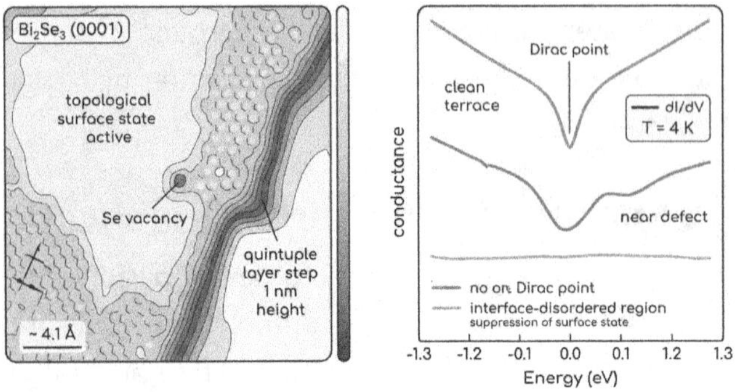

Faster, more scalable proxies for surface state quality use transport measurements. The key signature of topological surface-state transport is weak antilocalization, a quantum-interference correction to low-temperature conductance that has the opposite sign to that of a conventional two-dimensional electron gas. In a conventional metal, disorder-induced backscattering increases the probability of electron scattering, thereby decreasing the conductance at low temperatures. In a topological surface state, where time-reversal symmetry protects against backscattering, the quantum interference contribution has the opposite sign, and the conductance increases as the temperature is lowered below approximately 1 K. This negative magnetoresistance signature disappears when a small perpendicular magnetic field breaks time-reversal symmetry. Weak antilocalization in bismuth selenide thin films on silicon serves as a transport-accessible indicator of topological surface-state activity, measurable on a corner sample from a production wafer within a few hours at 4 Kelvin.

Diagram 11.10 - Process Control Architecture for Topological Insulator MBE

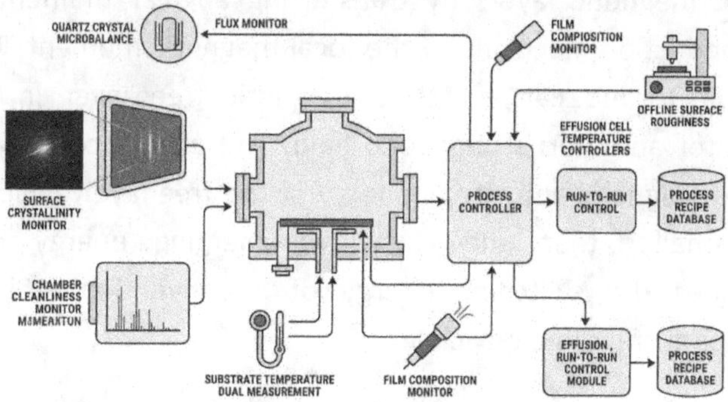

The weak antilocalization measurement, combined with van der Pauw Hall measurements at 77 Kelvin to determine bulk carrier density, provides a two-measurement qualification protocol that can be executed on corner samples from production wafers in less than a day. The weak antilocalization amplitude correlates with the surface-state coherence length: a longer coherence length indicates less disorder and higher surface-state quality. The bulk carrier density indicates how well the Fermi level has been controlled. Together, these two measurements serve as manufacturing accept/reject criteria for topological insulator film runs, replacing slow STS for day-to-day process monitoring while maintaining a direct physical connection to the surface state properties that determine device performance.

What Can We Build With This?

The device category closest to production readiness is spin-orbit torque magnetic random access memory, abbreviated SOT-MRAM. Spintronics uses electron spin, the intrinsic angular momentum of the electron, with only two allowed orientations in a magnetic field, as the information variable, in addition to or instead of charge. Spin-polarized currents exert a torque on adjacent magnetic layers by transferring angular momentum from conduction electrons to the local magnetic moment. This spin-orbit torque can switch a magnetic free layer in the absence of an external magnetic field. The energy cost scales with the magnetic anisotropy energy of the free layer, which is much smaller than the capacitive charging energy that determines the switching energy of a conventional CMOS transistor at the same device area.

Diagram 11.11 - Topological Insulator Spin-Orbit Torque MRAM Device

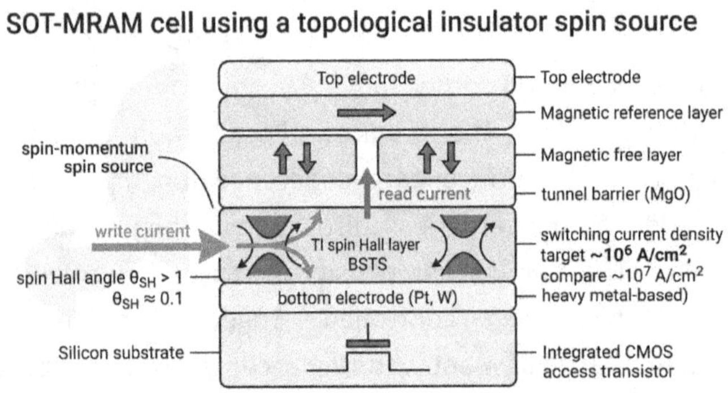

Topological insulator surfaces are attractive spin sources because of spin-momentum locking. In a conventional spin Hall material such as platinum, the spin Hall effect arises from asymmetric scattering of spin-up and spin-down electrons. This bulk effect depends on impurity density and the strength of spin-orbit coupling. The spin Hall angle, defined as the ratio of transverse spin current to longitudinal charge current, is approximately 0.1 to 0.3 for the best heavy metals. In a topological insulator surface, the spin current is not generated by scattering. Still, by the band structure itself, because momentum and spin are locked together, a charge current automatically carries a transverse spin current. The spin Hall angle of topological insulator surfaces has been measured to range from 1 to more than 10 in different experimental configurations, a factor of 10 or more larger than that of platinum. That factor directly reduces the switching current density required to flip a magnetic bit. It directly reduces write energy per bit, the primary figure of merit that makes SOT-MRAM competitive with NAND flash at advanced technology nodes.

Samsung's Advanced Institute of Technology and Intel's components research division have both published results on SOT switching in topological insulators. Samsung's work used bismuth selenide as the spin source in a magnetic tunnel junction stack. It demonstrated switching at current densities significantly below those required by platinum reference devices at the same junction area. The Intel work identified the surface state contribution by comparing switching behavior above and below the temperature at which bulk conductance becomes significant, providing direct experimental evidence that the topological surface state is responsible for the enhanced torque efficiency. Neither result has been translated into a shipping product. Still, both represent process-compatible demonstrations: the topological insulator layer was integrated into a device stack fabricated using equipment and processes compatible with a semiconductor manufacturing flow. The engineering gap is Fermi-level control at scale and room-temperature surface-state dominance, both of which are materials engineering problems with well-defined solution pathways and active development programs.

Diagram 11.12 - Device Readiness and Integration Summary

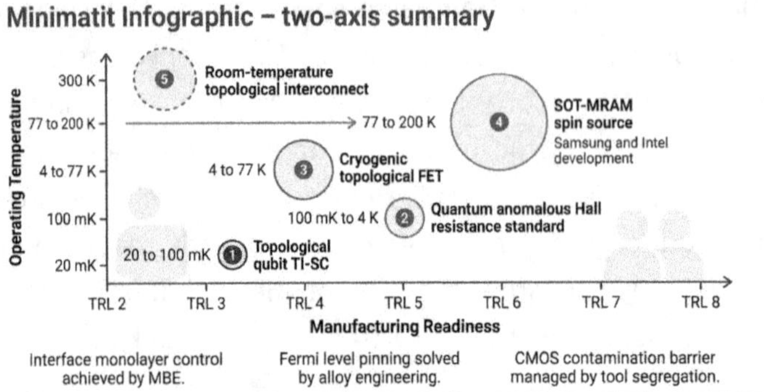

Executive technical tone-axis summary 16:9 (landscoape)

Beyond SOT-MRAM, two additional device categories are transitioning from research to pilot-line fabrication. The topological insulator field-effect transistor for low-power logic exploits the surface state as the channel to suppress backscattering and achieve higher channel mobility than a conventional semiconductor channel of the same thickness. At room temperature in a patterned device, this mobility advantage is degraded by edge disorder, contact resistance, and bulk shunting. Research groups most optimistic about this path are working on ultrathin films with five or fewer quintuple layers, in which the bulk contribution is suppressed by quantum confinement. The quantum anomalous Hall effect resistance standard, in which the integer quantum Hall effect observed in a magnetically gapped topological insulator at zero magnetic field provides a resistance standard traceable to fundamental constants, has been demonstrated by groups at the National Institute of Standards and Technology and several national metrology institutes using chromium-doped bismuth telluride films. This application has lower process uniformity requirements than an active device because it requires a single well-characterized sample rather than a reproducible population.

Takeaway

The engineering distance between a topologically fascinating material and a manufacturable device is real, and it has specific dimensions. Interface quality at the monolayer level is the yield-limiting parameter for device-quality topological surface states. Bulk conductance shunting is the primary operating constraint, addressed by alloy engineering to achieve intrinsically insulating BSTS compositions and by electrostatic gate tuning at the device level. MBE is the current gold-standard deposition technique, scalable to wafer formats and compatible with early manufacturing, but at the cost of substantial investment in process control. CVD is the long-term scalability path, requiring well-defined, precedent-setting precursor chemistry and reactor development work in the history of III-V device development. Cryogenic packaging is a challenge, but not a new one: the quantum computing industry has developed the toolbox and the supply chain. CMOS integration requires contamination segregation, not the discovery of new materials. And the first commercial topological device, the spin-orbit torque magnetic memory cell, is already in process development at major semiconductor companies.

For Priya, standing in that doorway, none of this is news. She has spent twenty years watching the distance between a topological insulator crystal and a manufacturable device. What she knows, and what she is making Marcus understand, is that the distance is finite. It has units. It can be measured. And measured engineering problems can be closed by systematic work. The physics of topological insulators is established. The application in spin-orbit torque memory is commercially compelling. The engineering is happening now. The question is which engineering team closes the gap first.

The next chapter enters the laboratory, where the characterization tools needed to certify whether a topological device is actually topological are used. Understanding how angle-resolved photoemission spectroscopy, scanning tunneling microscopy, and transport measurements together constitute the quality-control toolkit for topological materials is the bridge from fabrication to certification, and it is where everything covered in this chapter comes under the measurement microscope.

12 The Quantum Materials Laboratory

The tour begins before the morning stand-up. Priya Nair badges them through a corridor that runs the length of Axiom's second floor, past the glove boxes and the storage dewars, and stops at the first instrument bay. The machine in the center is roughly the size of a compact car turned on its side: polished stainless steel, a turbomolecular pump humming at the far end, a hemispherical electron analyzer mounted above a sample manipulator cooled to fifteen Kelvin. 'Angle-resolved photoemission spectroscopy,' Priya says. 'We shine a UV laser on the sample surface, measure the kinetic energy and emission angle of every photoelectron that comes off, and reconstruct the full band structure. If the topological surface state is there, you will see a Dirac cone at a momentum value that no bulk band reaches. If you do not see the cone, the material is not topological. Full stop.' Marcus looks at the analyzer. 'How long per run?' 'Three to eight hours per sample orientation. We run it overnight.'

Twenty meters down the hall, behind a polycarbonate partition, sits the scanning tunneling microscope. Sasha is reviewing data outside the enclosure. The STM is a stout cylinder nested inside vibration-isolation springs, with the sample stage cooled to 4 K by a liquid helium cryostat. A tungsten tip sharpened to a single atom scans the material surface at roughly five angstroms, and the quantum tunneling current encodes both topography and local electronic structure at atomic resolution. 'Your spatial data,' Sasha says, pointing at a false-color image of bismuth selenide surface corrugation, 'and the local density of states at each pixel. You can see exactly where the surface state electrons live.' ARPES gives the band structure. STM gives surface uniformity. Transport tells you whether any of it survives when you wire it up,' Priya says. 'Without all three, you do not have a device component. You have a research result.' Marcus writes that down.

The third station is at the far end of the floor: the transport cryostat, a dilution-refrigerator-compatible platform with four-probe contact geometry and a superconducting magnet capable of fourteen Tesla. A lithographically patterned Hall bar sits on the cold stage, connecting a material sample to a lock-in amplifier chain outside the vacuum jacket. Priya hands Marcus a printed characterization report, four pages of curves. 'By the end of this chapter,' she says, 'you will be able to read that without asking me what any of it means.' Marcus flips to the Shubnikov-de Haas oscillation plot on page two. The periodicity in the inverse field is already legible to him as structure, not noise. 'I can see something in there,' he says. 'Good,' Priya says. 'That is where it starts.'

Why It Matters

Every topological material claim that reaches a hardware team arrives as a characterization report: a slide deck from a university collaborator, a datasheet from a vendor, a journal paper, or an internal memo. The report contains measurements, interpretations of those measurements, and an implicit claim that the material is topological and ready for device integration. The hardware engineer who cannot read that report independently is dependent on the materials scientist to interpret the data. They cannot push back when the interpretation is optimistic, identify missing measurements, or ask the right questions during a design review. In the most practical sense, they are a customer who cannot read the invoice.

The importance of that literacy is not hypothetical. The retractions surrounding Majorana zero-mode observations, culminating in the 2021 Microsoft retraction of a Nature paper reporting quantized conductance in InAs nanowires, illustrate the cost of a measurement ecosystem in which the hardest signatures to fake were also the hardest to interpret correctly. Engineers who understood what a zero-bias conductance peak does and does not prove were positioned to flag the ambiguity before program resources were committed. Engineers who could not read that measurement relied on the team that ran it for assurance. The difference in program risk is not small.

This chapter covers the characterization pipeline for topological materials: ARPES for band structure, STM and STS for real-space surface properties, transport measurements for device-relevant electrical behavior, and supporting methods including thermal transport, optical spectroscopy, and synchrotron X-ray characterization. The goal is not to teach the reader to run these experiments, but to read their output and judge whether the evidence supports the proposed device specification. That is characterization literacy, and it is an engineering competence, not a physics elective.

Predicting Topology Before the Experiment

Density functional theory, abbreviated DFT, is the computational workhorse of modern materials physics. Given the atomic composition and crystal structure, DFT solves the quantum-mechanical equations for the energy and spatial distribution of every electron in the unit cell, yielding a band structure and a set of electronic wavefunctions. For topological materials, DFT provides three outputs that matter to the engineer: the locations of band inversions, the values of topological invariants computed from the wavefunction topology across the Brillouin zone, and the predicted dispersion of surface states at the crystal boundary. In practice, DFT introduces approximation errors in the exchange-correlation functional that shift band positions by tens to hundreds of millielectronvolts, which can matter near a band inversion point.

The topological invariants DFT calculates include the Z2 invariants for time-reversal-invariant topological insulators and the Chern number for materials that break time-reversal symmetry. The Z2 invariant, introduced by Kane and Mele in 2005 and extended to three dimensions shortly after, takes one of two values: zero for a trivial insulator and one for a topological insulator. Computing it from a DFT band structure requires evaluating the parity of occupied electronic states at time-reversal-invariant momentum points in the Brillouin zone, a calculation that modern codes perform automatically. A material flagged as Z2 nontrivial is a candidate for experimental topological surface states; a material flagged as trivial is not, and no amount of optimistic measurement interpretation changes that unless the DFT is wrong about the band order, which is possible but documentable. The prediction is testable, and testability is its value.

Diagram 12.1 - DFT Band Structure and Topological Invariant Calculation

DFT-calculated band structure for Bismuth Selenide (Bi_2Se_3)

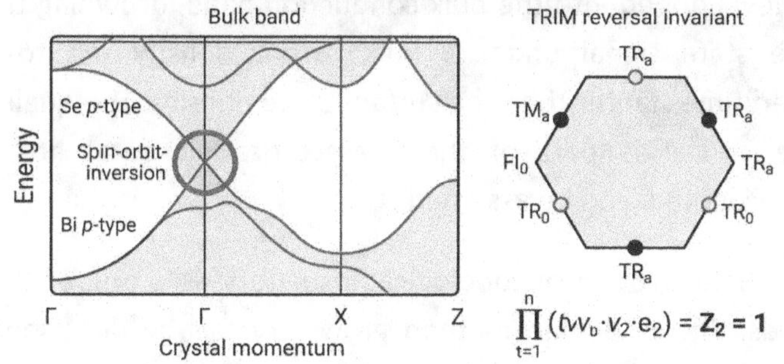

The Materials Project (materialsproject.org) and the Topological Materials Database (topologicalquantumchemistry.com) provide pre-calculated DFT band structures and topological classifications for tens of thousands of inorganic crystals. For the hardware engineer evaluating a material, these databases are the first stop. Searching for Bi2Se3 in the Materials Project returns the DFT band structure, band gap, Z2 topological indices, and predicted surface-state dispersion, benchmarked against experiments. The workflow: look up any candidate material before accepting it for evaluation. If the databases classify it as trivial, ask the proposing team to explain the discrepancy. If topological, note the predicted surface state energy relative to the Fermi level; that determines whether the surface state will dominate transport or be overwhelmed by bulk conduction.

Single Crystal Growth: The Substrate for Characterization

Reliable characterization requires reliable crystals. A material's topological surface state is a boundary phenomenon that depends on the surface being clean, stoichiometric, and structurally ordered at the atomic level. A crystal grown with excess selenium vacancies in Bi_2Se_3, for instance, will show a Fermi level doped into the bulk conduction band, drowning the surface state signal under a bulk carrier density ten to a hundred times larger than the surface state density. The quality of the crystal is part of the characterization data, not a prerequisite that can be assumed.

Single-crystal growth of topological insulators uses one of two methods. The Bridgman method grows crystals by directional solidification: a polycrystalline charge is melted in a sealed quartz ampoule and pulled through a temperature gradient, so that the solid-liquid interface advances through the melt from one end to the other. For layered materials such as Bi_2Se_3 and Bi_2Te_3, this yields centimeter-scale crystals that cleave cleanly along the van der Waals layers, exposing fresh surfaces for ARPES and STM. The residual resistivity ratio of a Bridgman crystal, the room-temperature resistivity divided by the low-temperature residual resistivity, is the primary quality metric: a ratio above 50 indicates low defect density and an adequate mean free path; a ratio below 10 indicates significant disorder that will broaden momentum-space features in ARPES and reduce the coherence length in STM.

Diagram 12.2 - Bridgman Crystal Growth and Quality Metrics

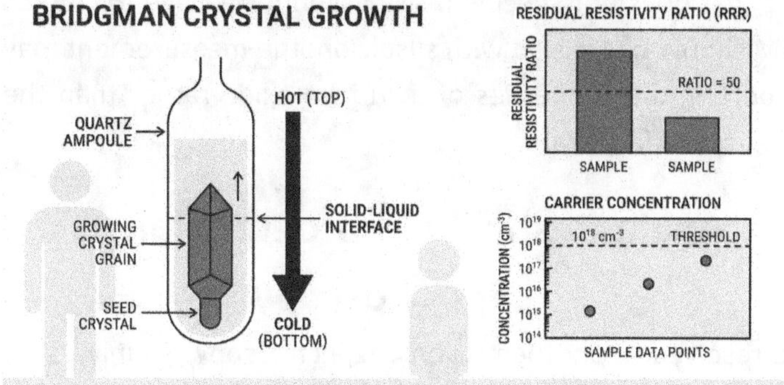

Bridgman crystal growth process and nees 16:9 horizoral layout

Flux growth is an alternative for materials that decompose before melting or require a lower growth temperature. The components are dissolved in a molten flux, and the temperature is slowly reduced while the target compound crystallizes out of solution. Flux growth produces smaller crystals than Bridgman, but can achieve lower defect densities in some systems. For the engineer evaluating a crystal's suitability for characterization, the relevant documentation includes the growth temperature profile, the flux composition and separation method, and, at a minimum, one Hall-effect measurement of carrier concentration at low temperature. A carrier concentration above 10^18 per cubic centimeter in a nominally undoped Bi2Se3 crystal indicates a selenium-vacancy doping level that will require compensation before the crystal is usable for surface-state transport experiments.

Surface preparation before ARPES or STM is as important as crystal quality. Topological insulators like Bi2Se3 cleave along the van der Waals gap between quintuple layers, exposing a fresh Se-terminated surface in ultrahigh vacuum. Air exposure oxidizes the selenium surface layer within minutes, converting the clean topological surface state into a disordered oxide with completely different spectral features. Any characterization report that does not specify in situ vacuum cleavage for ARPES or STM should be treated with suspicion: the measurement may be reporting the properties of a surface oxide rather than the topological surface state.

Angle-Resolved Photoemission Spectroscopy

Angle-resolved photoemission spectroscopy, universally abbreviated as ARPES, is the primary experimental technique for mapping the electronic band structure of a crystalline material. The measurement is based on the photoelectric effect: a photon with sufficient energy strikes the material surface and ejects an electron from an occupied electronic state. The kinetic energy of the emitted photoelectron equals the photon energy minus the binding energy of the state from which it was ejected, minus the work function of the material. ARPES adds the angular dimension: by measuring kinetic energy and emission angle simultaneously, it recovers the electrons' in-plane crystal momentum in the solid, because the parallel component of the photoelectron's momentum is conserved across the surface. The result is a two-dimensional map of electronic spectral weight as a function of binding energy and crystal momentum, which is the band structure.

Modern ARPES instruments use a hemispherical electron analyzer with a two-dimensional CCD detector. The analyzer accepts electrons emitted within a narrow angular cone, disperses them by kinetic energy along one axis, and by emission angle along the other. A single detector image captures a slice through the band structure in the energy-momentum plane. By rotating the sample, the full Brillouin zone is mapped. The photon source for a laboratory setup is typically a helium gas discharge lamp at 21.2 eV or a laser; synchrotron-based ARPES at facilities like the Advanced Light Source uses tunable photon energies from 20 eV to several hundred eV, providing dramatically improved momentum resolution and the ability to probe surface versus bulk states selectively by tuning the photon energy to control photoelectron escape depth.

Diagram 12.3 - ARPES Setup and Photoelectron Emission

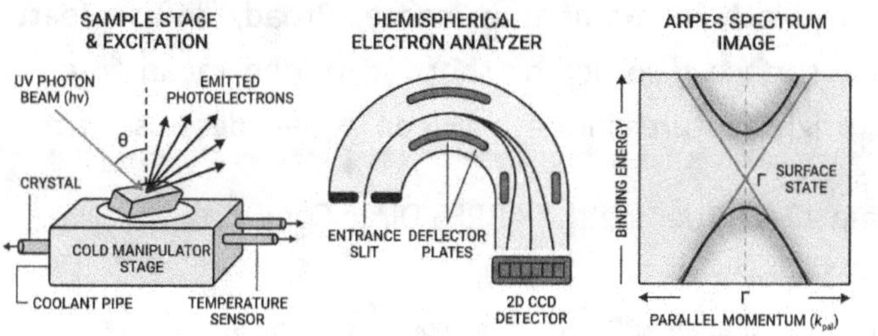

ARPES measurement geometry; illustrating an oftag measurement results

The ARPES signature of a topological surface state is the Dirac cone: two bands of opposite spin that disperse linearly in momentum and cross at a single energy point called the Dirac point. The linearity distinguishes the Dirac cone from conventional parabolic bands, and the crossing at a single point distinguishes it from an accidental crossing in a trivial material. In an ARPES spectrum from a clean Bi2Se3 surface, the Dirac cone appears centered at the Gamma point of the surface Brillouin zone, with the Dirac point roughly 300 millielectronvolts below the Fermi level in undoped crystals. The cone spans approximately plus or minus 0.1 per angstrom in crystal momentum at binding energies accessible with He I radiation, and the Fermi-level crossing shows a circular constant-energy contour rather than the closed elliptical contours of conventional parabolic bands.

Reading an ARPES spectrum for topological evidence requires checking four features. First, confirm the Dirac cone is present at the expected high-symmetry momentum point. Second, confirm that it crosses the Fermi level so the surface state is metallic and contributing to conduction. Third, check whether bulk bands near the Fermi level are also metallic; if so, bulk conduction will dominate the device. Fourth, check the Dirac cone linewidth in momentum space. Broad, diffuse features indicate surface disorder or short scattering mean free path; sharp, bright features indicate a clean, well-ordered surface.

Diagram 12.4 - Reading the ARPES Dirac Cone

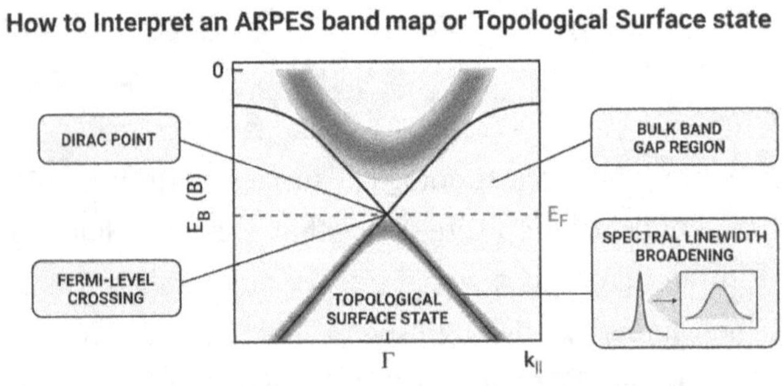

How to inepret an ARPES band map for a topological surface state

A common source of confusion is the difference between topological surface states and Rashba-split surface states in trivial materials. Rashba splitting, arising from spin-orbit coupling at surfaces lacking inversion symmetry, also produces spin-split bands with k-linear dispersion near high-symmetry points. The distinction is topological: a Rashba-split surface state comes from a trivial bulk and disappears on different crystal faces. An ARPES measurement alone cannot always distinguish the two; it must be interpreted in conjunction with the DFT prediction and the surface state's behavior across multiple terminations. A true topological surface state appears on every non-magnetic surface of a topological insulator; a Rashba state is termination-dependent.

Scanning Tunneling Microscopy and Spectroscopy

Scanning tunneling microscopy, abbreviated STM, images the atomic-scale structure and electronic properties of conducting surfaces. An atomically sharp tungsten tip is brought to within a few angstroms of the sample surface while a bias voltage is applied between the tip and the sample. At this distance, quantum mechanical tunneling drives an electrical current across the vacuum gap; the tunneling current falls exponentially with increasing tip-sample distance, roughly one order of magnitude per angstrom. By scanning the tip across the surface while a feedback loop adjusts the tip height to maintain constant current, the instrument traces a map of constant local density of states that closely tracks the physical surface topography at atomic resolution. The output is a real-space image of the surface with sub-angstrom height sensitivity.

Scanning tunneling spectroscopy (abbreviated STS) extends STM from topographic imaging to local electronic-structure measurement. The technique freezes the tip-sample distance and sweeps the bias voltage, recording the current as a function of voltage. The differential conductance dI/dV is proportional to the local density of states at each energy. On a topological insulator surface, the STS spectrum shows a finite density of states spanning the bulk gap, arising from the topological surface state. In a nanowire in the topological phase, the spectrum at the wire end shows a zero-bias conductance peak, signaling the presence of a zero-energy mode that may be a Majorana bound state.

Diagram 12.5 - STM Tip on Crystal Surface with Tunneling Current

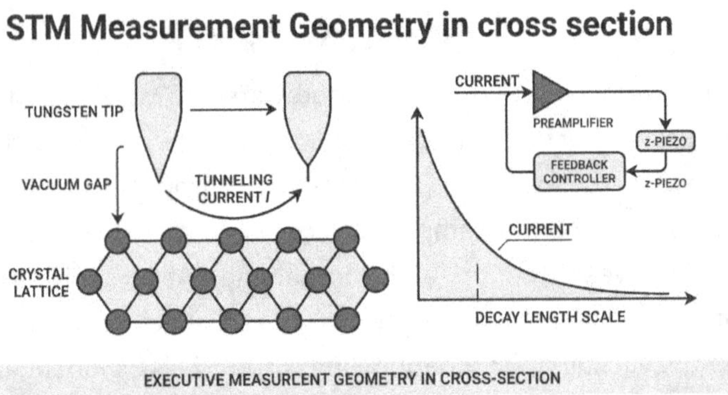

The STS measurement is most powerful when combined with topographic imaging at the same location. A region that shows a sharp, clean surface in STM topography but a suppressed or absent surface state signal in STS spectroscopy indicates a local electronic perturbation, such as a subsurface defect or a buried adsorbate, that disrupts the surface state without visibly roughening the topography. This kind of spatial correlation between topographic and spectroscopic data is only accessible with STM and has no analog in momentum-averaged techniques.

The zero-bias conductance peak in STS spectroscopy has been the most contested signature in the characterization of topological materials over the past decade. A Majorana bound state at the end of a one-dimensional topological superconductor should produce a peak in differential conductance at exactly zero bias, spatially localized at the wire ends and absent in the bulk. The 2012 reports from the Kouwenhoven group at Delft reported such peaks in InAs nanowires proximitized to superconductor contacts. The problem, as the subsequent decade established, is that trivial Andreev bound states at the nanowire ends can produce peaks at or near zero bias nearly indistinguishable from Majorana peaks in conductance alone. The 2021 retraction of the Microsoft-affiliated Nature paper acknowledged that what appeared to be a quantized plateau was, in the reanalyzed data, consistent with a trivial Andreev state.

Diagram 12.6 - STS Spectrum at Nanowire End: Topological vs. Trivial

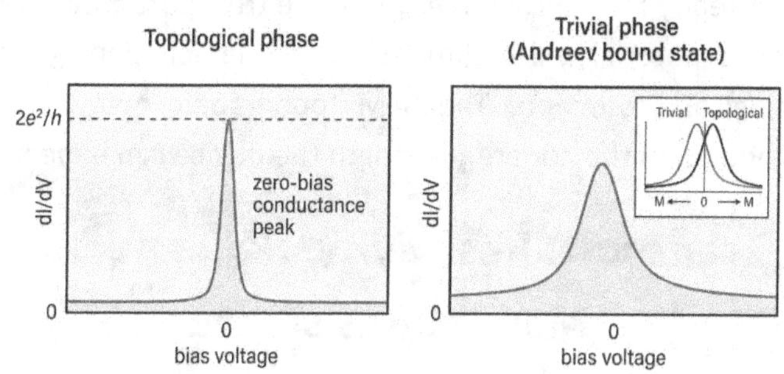

Beyond nanowire spectroscopy, STM and STS provide two additional outputs relevant to the integration of topological insulator devices. The first is quasiparticle interference imaging, QPI: when a surface state electron scatters off an impurity, it produces standing-wave oscillations in the local density of states. The Fourier transform of a QPI image gives the momentum-space structure of allowed scattering vectors. For a topological surface state with spin-momentum locking, backscattering is forbidden by time-reversal symmetry, so the Fourier-transformed QPI image shows an absence of intensity at momentum transfer 2k. This absence provides direct spatial confirmation of spin-momentum locking, which distinguishes a topological surface state from a Rashba state.

The second output is atomic-resolution mapping of surface uniformity. A topological surface state that looks beautiful in ARPES momentum space may coexist with significant surface disorder that destroys phase coherence on device-relevant length scales. STM topographic images at atomic resolution reveal terraces, step edges, adatoms, substitutional defects, and vacancy clusters that are invisible to momentum-averaged spectroscopic techniques. A material with a sharp Dirac cone in ARPES but a high density of nanometer-scale vacancy clusters in STM is not ready for device integration: the transport mean free path in that material will be limited by the defect spacing, not by topological protection. The STM topographic map sets a realistic bound on the coherence length the device can expect.

Transport: Resistivity, Hall, and Magnetoresistance

Electronic transport measurements assess the material's electronic behavior under conditions closer to the device environment: lithographically patterned contacts, applied magnetic fields, and temperatures from millikelvin to room temperature. The three primary transport measurements for topological material characterization are longitudinal resistivity, Hall resistivity, and magnetoresistance. Each provides a different piece of the electronic picture, and each has a specific signature in topological materials.

Longitudinal resistivity is the fundamental measure of resistance to current flow. The standard geometry for the four-probe measurement is to inject current through two outer contacts and measure the voltage between two inner contacts, eliminating contact resistance. The temperature dependence of resistivity is the first diagnostic for topological behavior. A true topological insulator has an insulating bulk, so the bulk resistivity increases as temperature decreases while the surface-state conductance remains approximately constant. A film showing monotonically increasing conductance as temperature falls is typically a metal or heavily doped semiconductor, not a surface-state-dominated material. A film showing a resistance minimum at intermediate temperature before decreasing further is a signature of weak antilocalization, discussed in the next section.

Diagram 12.7 - Hall Bar Transport Measurement Geometry

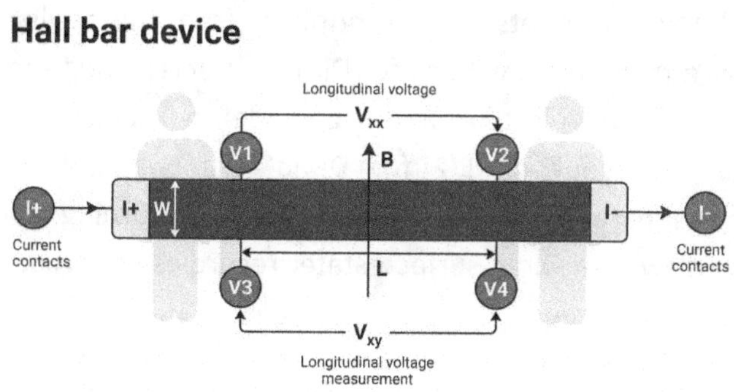

The Hall effect provides carrier density and carrier type. When a magnetic field is applied perpendicular to the current flow, the Lorentz force deflects charge carriers toward one edge, building a transverse electric field. The Hall coefficient equals one over the product of carrier density and charge. For a topological insulator, Hall measurements distinguish surface-state-dominated from bulk-dominated transport: the surface state in bismuth selenide has a carrier density of roughly 10^13 per square centimeter in a well-optimized film, while bulk n-type doping from selenium vacancies can add 10^13 to 10^15 per square centimeter of bulk electrons, dominating the Hall signal. A Hall measurement on a material claiming surface-state dominance that returns a carrier density consistent with heavily doped bulk transport is not a material whose surface state is performing the claimed function.

Shubnikov-de Haas oscillations, abbreviated SdH, are periodic oscillations in longitudinal resistivity as a function of the inverse of the applied magnetic field, arising from Landau level quantization. The oscillation period is proportional to the cross-sectional area of the Fermi surface via the Onsager relation. For a topological surface-state Dirac cone, the oscillation period determines the surface-state carrier density, comparable to that from Hall measurements. The Berry phase from the oscillation analysis is a transport-level test for Dirac character: the Landau-level fan diagram, plotting oscillation index n against 1/B(n), yields a y-intercept of 1/2 for Dirac fermions and 0 for conventional parabolic bands. An SdH analysis returning zero is inconsistent with a Dirac surface state, regardless of what the ARPES spectrum shows.

Diagram 12.8 - Shubnikov-de Haas Oscillations in Longitudinal Resistivity

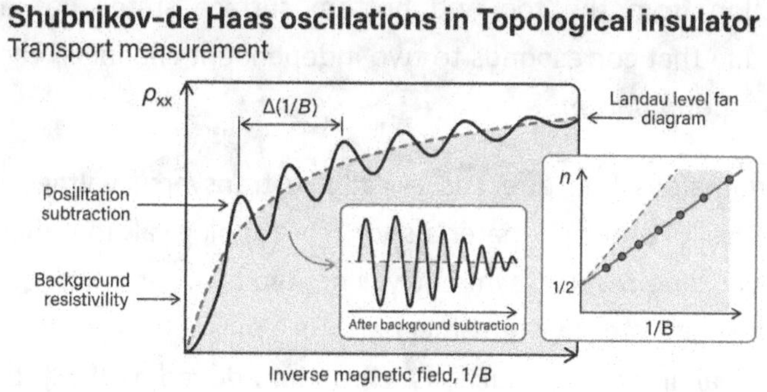

Shubnikov-de Haas oscillations in a topological insilator transport measurement

Magnetotransport Signatures of Topological Phases

Magnetoresistance is the change in a material's resistance upon application of a magnetic field. In a conventional conductor, magnetic fields generally increase resistivity by curving electron trajectories. In topological materials, two quantum interference phenomena produce characteristic signatures diagnostic for topological surface states: weak antilocalization and the anomalous Hall effect.

Weak antilocalization, abbreviated WAL, arises from quantum interference of an electron wavefunction with itself as it traverses a closed trajectory by scattering off disorder. In a material with spin-orbit coupling, the two time-reversed paths around a closed loop accumulate a phase of pi, causing destructive interference that reduces backscattering below the classical value, producing conductance higher than the classical prediction at zero field. A small magnetic field breaks the time-reversal condition, reducing the correction: the WAL signature is a sharp positive magnetoresistance peak at zero field, meaning resistance is at a local minimum at zero field and increases as a small field is applied. For a topological insulator, the WAL correction from the top and bottom surface states has an amplitude that corresponds to two independent channels, each with a π Berry phase.

The anomalous Hall effect is a Hall-like transverse voltage in magnetically ordered materials or, in topological materials, wherever time-reversal symmetry is broken by magnetic doping or proximity to a ferromagnet. In magnetically doped topological insulators, such as chromium-doped Bi2Se3, the Berry curvature of the surface-state bands contributes to the Hall conductance in the absence of an external magnetic field. The quantum anomalous Hall effect, first observed by Chang and coworkers in 2013 in Cr-doped Bi2Te3 films at millikelvin temperatures, is the quantized version: a Hall conductance of exactly one conductance quantum per surface, with zero longitudinal resistance, arising from a single chiral edge channel when the Fermi level is inside the magnetically opened gap. Its observation confirms both the topological surface state and the magnetic exchange gap.

Diagram 12.9 - Weak Antilocalization Magnetoresistance Curve

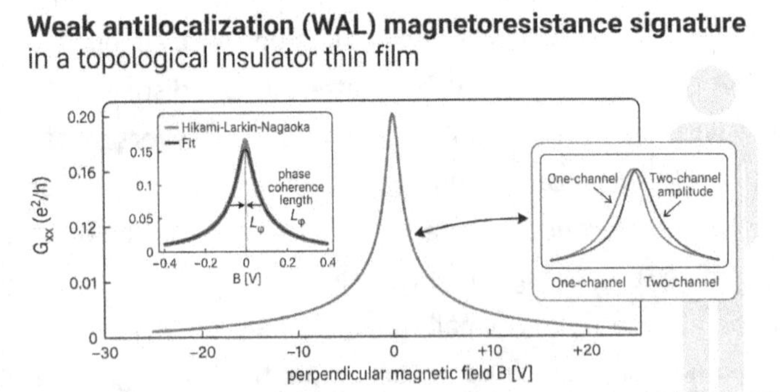

Weak antilocalization (WAL) magnetoresistance signature in a topological insulator thin film

The thermal Hall effect and the Nernst effect provide complementary information on magnetotransport. The thermal Hall effect measures the transverse temperature gradient that develops when heat current flows through a material in a perpendicular field. In Dirac surface states, the linear band dispersion yields a characteristic temperature dependence of the thermal Hall signal that differs from that of a parabolic band. The Nernst effect measures the transverse electric field that develops when both a temperature gradient and a magnetic field are applied. In Weyl semimetals, whose band structure features linearly touching Weyl nodes carrying a quantized Berry phase, the Nernst coefficient is anomalously large due to Berry curvature concentrated near those nodes. The anomalous Nernst effect in Weyl semimetals such as Co3Sn2S2 yields Nernst coefficients that are orders of magnitude larger than those in conventional metals, providing direct evidence for the topological phase.

Optical, Neutron, and Synchrotron Spectroscopy

Optical spectroscopy methods, including terahertz and mid-infrared spectroscopy, measure a material's optical conductivity as a function of photon frequency. A topological surface state with Dirac dispersion produces a modified optical conductivity: an inter-band transition from the lower to the upper Dirac cone that is linear in frequency with a minimum photon energy set by twice the Fermi energy from the Dirac point. This linear optical conductivity differs from the quadratic onset of a parabolic band and from the constant conductivity of massive Dirac fermions, providing a bulk-averaged fingerprint of the surface state that complements momentum-resolved ARPES data. Terahertz time-domain spectroscopy spans the 1-100 meV range relevant to topological gap energies and surface-state scattering rates.

Diagram 12.10 - Optical Conductivity of Dirac Surface States vs. Conventional Metal

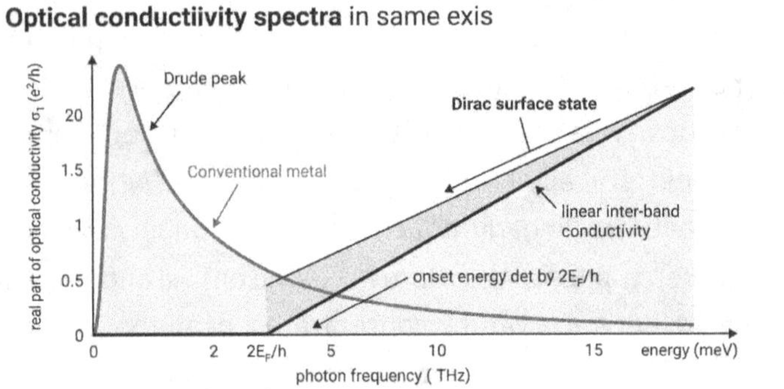

Caption: Optical conductivity spectra translati to minimised and energy (meV)

Neutron scattering is the primary tool for studying magnetic structure and spin dynamics in magnetically ordered topological materials. Unlike X-ray diffraction, which scatters from electron density, neutrons scatter from both nuclear density and electron spin orientation. Elastic neutron scattering measures magnetic order: the arrangement and magnitude of ordered moments in materials like MnBi2Te4, which is intrinsically magnetic and hosts the quantum anomalous Hall effect without extrinsic doping. Inelastic neutron scattering measures spin waves, whose dispersion encodes exchange interactions and magnetic anisotropy. For magnetic topological insulators, the combination of neutron-determined magnetic structure, ARPES-measured surface-state dispersion, and transport-measured Hall conductance constitutes the full characterization suite to confirm the quantum anomalous Hall phase.

Synchrotron X-ray methods provide structural characterization at resolutions not accessible to laboratory diffractometers. High-resolution X-ray diffraction at a synchrotron beamline measures lattice constants and strain fields in epitaxial thin films with sub-picometer precision. For a topological insulator film grown on a lattice-mismatched substrate, the film lattice constants are strained relative to the bulk; the magnitude and distribution of that strain determine whether the topological phase is preserved or driven trivial. X-ray absorption spectroscopy at the L-edges of heavy atoms provides element-specific information about oxidation states and local coordination environments relevant to interface chemistry. Extended X-ray absorption fine structure analysis extracts nearest-neighbor distances and coordination numbers, providing a local structural probe that complements the long-range order information of diffraction.

Diagram 12.11 - Synchrotron X-Ray Diffraction of Topological Insulator Thin Film

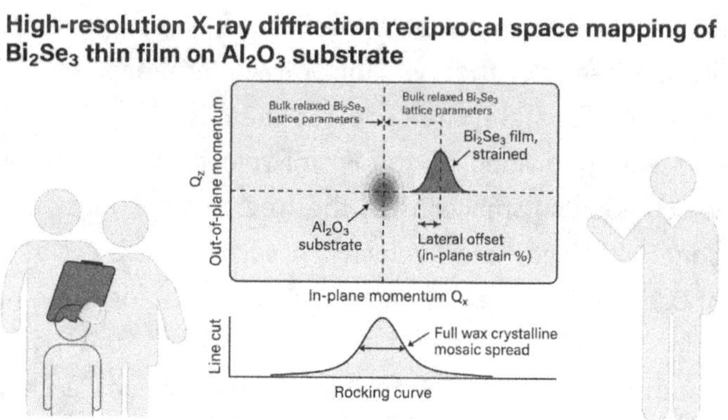

Quantum Oscillations and Fermi Surface Mapping

Quantum oscillations in magnetization, the de Haas-van Alphen effect, and in electrical resistance, the Shubnikov-de Haas effect, already introduced, are among the most precise tools for mapping the Fermi surface of a conducting material. Both effects are periodic in the inverse field with a frequency proportional to the extremal cross-sectional area of the Fermi surface. For a topological insulator where the Fermi level intersects only the Dirac cone surface state, the Fermi surface is a single circle whose area gives one SdH frequency. For a material in which the Fermi level intersects both the surface Dirac cone and bulk electron pockets from n-type doping, the SdH spectrum shows multiple frequencies, and decomposing the oscillation spectrum via a fast Fourier transform is necessary to identify the surface-state contribution.

The cyclotron effective mass of quasiparticles on the Fermi surface can be extracted from the temperature dependence of the oscillation amplitude through the thermal damping factor in the Lifshitz-Kosevich theory. For Dirac fermions on the topological surface state, the cyclotron mass is proportional to the Fermi energy divided by the Fermi velocity squared times hbar, which is much smaller than the free electron mass for a Dirac cone with high Fermi velocity. A surface state cyclotron mass of 0.1 to 0.2 free electron masses is typical for Bi2Se3 at accessible Fermi energies, and extracting this from temperature-dependent SdH measurements provides a check against the ARPES-derived Fermi velocity. The agreement between the SdH-extracted carrier density, the Hall carrier density, and the DFT-predicted surface-state Fermi-surface area is strong confirmatory evidence that the surface state is the dominant conducting channel.

Angle-dependent quantum oscillation measurements, in which the applied field is rotated relative to the sample plane. In contrast, the oscillation frequency is tracked, providing the dimensionality signature of each Fermi surface sheet. A two-dimensional Fermi surface, such as the topological surface state Dirac cone, has an oscillation frequency that diverges as the field is tilted away from the surface normal, because the projection of the field perpendicular to the 2D surface decreases as cos theta. Bulk three-dimensional Fermi surfaces exhibit oscillation frequencies that vary less dramatically with angle, reflecting the full three-dimensional geometry of the Fermi surface. The angular dependence of SdH frequencies is therefore a direct diagnostic for the dimensionality of each conducting channel. This is particularly useful in thick films, where bulk conduction competes with surface conduction, and proving that the surface state contributes distinctly requires demonstrating its 2D Fermi-surface geometry.

Diagram 12.12 - Quantum Oscillation Fermi Surface Mapping: 2D vs. 3D Channels

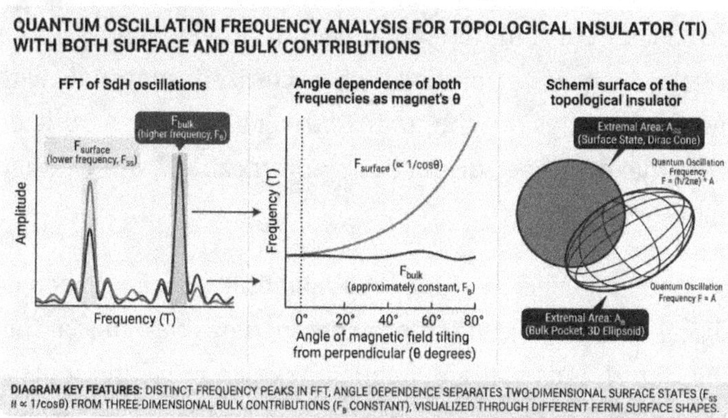

What Can We Build With This?

Characterization literacy is risk management. That is not a metaphor. An engineer who can read an ARPES band map, interpret a transport magnetoresistance curve, and evaluate an STM spectrum is identifying and quantifying the risks that a material does not perform as claimed. The engineer who cannot perform that reading transfers the risk assessment function to the materials scientist, the vendor, or the collaborator who produced the report. In a field where characterization methods have been misapplied, signatures overinterpreted, and at least one retracted Nature paper reflects a systematic failure of independent review, that transfer is not a costless delegation. It is a program vulnerability.

The first thing an engineer can build with characterization literacy is a material acceptance protocol: a written specification for the evidence required before a topological material enters device integration. At minimum: ARPES confirmation of surface state dispersion, STM confirmation of surface uniformity with defect density quantified, transport confirmation of WAL behavior with phase coherence length extracted, SdH confirmation of surface state carrier density with Berry phase analysis, and Hall measurement with surface-state fraction calculated. A material that cannot provide all five is not characterized. It is a partially characterized material with unknown properties in the untested dimensions. A written protocol makes that distinction enforceable rather than negotiable.

The second thing is a vendor evaluation rubric. When a topological materials vendor provides a datasheet for a thin film, the datasheet's value depends on which measurements it reports and how those measurements were made. A datasheet that reports ARPES data without specifying the photon source, measurement temperature, surface preparation method, and sample orientation relative to the Brillouin zone is a marketing document, not a datasheet. A datasheet that reports Hall carrier density without specifying measurement temperature, contact geometry, and film thickness needed to convert sheet resistance to bulk resistivity is underspecified. The engineer with characterization literacy identifies which measurements are complete and which are missing, and whether the reported values are internally consistent. That is the engineering equivalent of reading a circuit datasheet and distinguishing worst-case guaranteed parameters from typical-value optimistic ones.

The third is the capacity to participate in design reviews as a peer of the materials scientist. The engineer who cannot evaluate characterization evidence independently defers to the materials scientist in every case, creating a single point of failure. The engineer who can read the ARPES data, check whether the Dirac cone linewidth is consistent with the coherence length assumed in the device simulation, and compare the transport-carrier density with the Hall-measured surface-state density provides independent verification. Design reviews with that capacity catch inconsistencies before they propagate into fabricated devices.

The broader principle is that characterization literacy transfers power from the specialist to the system. Team members who read across disciplinary boundaries are the nodes through which information flows between specializations. An electrical engineer who can evaluate a materials characterization report translates that evaluation into device design constraints, identifies mismatches between what the materials team is delivering and what the device team expects, and catches failure modes that propagate silently when no one speaks both languages. In topological materials, where the field is young and overinterpreted results are documented, fluency is a job requirement.

There is a precedent in semiconductor engineering. The engineers who learned to read secondary ion mass spectrometry depth profiles and identify dopant out-diffusion before it appeared as a yield failure, who insisted on TEM cross-sections of gate oxide interfaces before accepting a new process node, were doing risk management using characterization as the instrument, not materials science. The field of topological materials is at an earlier stage of the same curve. The characterization tools exist. The signatures are identified. The failure modes from misinterpreting those signatures are documented in retracted papers and abandoned programs. The programs that built characterization literacy in semiconductors won the yield race. The programs in topological materials that did not pay for it are still paying for it now.

Takeaway

Five characterization techniques form the complete evidence base for a topological material: ARPES for band structure and Dirac cone dispersion, STM and STS for real-space surface uniformity and local density of states, transport measurements for carrier density and WAL signature, SdH oscillations for Fermi surface geometry and Berry phase, and Hall effect for surface-state-to-bulk carrier ratio. A material supported by all five, with internally consistent measurements and agreement with DFT predictions, is a characterized topological material. A material supported by fewer than all five, or with unexplained inconsistencies between measurements, is a research result with an open characterization checklist. The engineer's role is to know which box is which.

The DFT databases are the starting point for any crystal growth. The ARPES data confirm the band structure. The STM data are used to check spatial uniformity. The transport data is the device-relevant operating confirmation. The SdH data are used for the Fermi-surface consistency test. Reading all five together, knowing what agreement and disagreement mean, is characterization literacy. It is the difference between a program that accepts a material because the ARPES images look impressive and one that accepts it because the evidence is complete. The history of the field tells you which kind of program reaches device integration.

The next and final chapter of this book asks where the field goes from here. The characterization tools covered in this chapter are already producing results at leading research groups and national laboratories, but they are not yet in journal papers. The fabrication techniques from the previous chapter are advancing toward the interface control tolerances required by topological qubit architectures. The theoretical predictions from earlier chapters are being confirmed experimentally across an increasing number of material classes. The road ahead is not a prediction. It is an extrapolation from a trajectory that is already clearly visible to the engineer who knows how to read the characterization data.

13 The Road Ahead

Friday afternoon at Axiom Quantum. The whiteboard in the main conference room held a single slide: "Three Years." Priya stood at one end with a marker; Marcus, Sasha, and Yuki had pulled chairs up close enough to read every milestone box. The slide was a roadmap of territory none of them had crossed yet, drawn from data and conviction in roughly equal parts.

Priya walked the columns left to right. Year one: topological qubit demonstration at the device level, non-Abelian statistics confirmed, ten milliseconds of coherence. Year two: navigation-grade magnetometer packaged and deliverable. Year three: manufacturable thin-film process at sixty-percent yield on six-inch wafers. "Every milestone here," she said, setting the marker down, "depends on a materials engineering problem that has not been fully solved. That is not a risk slide. That is why we exist. So let's be honest about where the field is going."

Marcus looked at the slide, then at the river outside. He had spent fourteen years in semiconductor manufacturing, a world where the next process node was in the fab before the current one was released. This was different. The rail did not yet exist. "Not the optimistic version," he said. "The accurate version." Sasha picked up the marker. Yuki pulled her chair closer.

Why It Matters

Twelve chapters have built a foundation. You understand what makes a material topological, what a Chern number counts, and why ordinary perturbations cannot gap the Dirac cone on the surface of a topological insulator. You understand Majorana fermions, topological superconductors, the quantum anomalous Hall effect, and the moiré systems that emerged in twisted bilayer graphene and have rewritten the textbooks on strongly correlated phases. You have earned the right to ask the practical question: what happens next?

This chapter is organized not as a prediction but as a map. The engineering problems that separate current laboratory demonstrations from commercial topological hardware are clear and well-defined, rooted in physics rather than in funding cycles. Near-term opportunities are real and close to manufacturing. Medium-term opportunities are in active development in the laboratory. Long-term opportunities represent the kind of step-change that redefines an entire hardware sector, comparable to the transistor replacing the vacuum tube.

More importantly, this chapter is about you. The field is short on engineers who can move between crystal physics and device engineering without losing resolution at either end. It needs people who can read an ARPES spectrum, specify an MBE growth recipe, and explain both to a systems architect. The twelve preceding chapters have given you the vocabulary. This chapter maps the territory where that expertise is most needed, where the roles are opening, and how to keep learning after you close this book.

Near-Term: What Is Genuinely Close to Manufacturing

Sasha drew a horizontal line across the top of the whiteboard and labeled three zones: close, developing, and transformational. "Everything feels close from inside the lab," he said. "The question is what close means from the perspective of a manufacturing line." Under scrutiny, he wrote three items without hesitation: NV-center magnetometers, topological-insulator-based interconnects, and the first commercial topological qubit prototypes.

Nitrogen-vacancy (NV) center magnetometers represent the clearest near-term win in quantum sensing. An NV center is a defect in a diamond lattice in which a nitrogen atom replaces a carbon atom adjacent to a vacancy, creating a spin-two-level system that can be initialized, read out, and operated at room temperature using visible light and microwaves. The spin resonance frequency shifts in proportion to local magnetic fields, yielding sensitivities approaching 1 pT/Hz in miniaturized form factors, without cryogenic cooling. Companies, including Quantum Diamond Technologies and several defense contractors, have been shipping or qualifying sensor modules since the early 2020s. The remaining engineering challenge is photonic and RF integration at the package level, not diamond synthesis.

Topological-insulator-based interconnects sit further along the timeline but represent a genuine near-term opportunity at the semiconductor node boundary. Conventional copper interconnects suffer severe grain-boundary scattering at the nanometer scale, thereby increasing resistivity and reducing electromigration failure rates. The topologically protected surface states of bismuth selenide (Bi2Se3), a three-dimensional topological insulator whose surface Dirac cone forbids backscattering without a spin flip, conduct along surfaces without grain-boundary losses. The engineering challenge is depositing device-quality Bi2Se3 within the back-end-of-line thermal budget of under 400 degrees Celsius. Sputtering and atomic layer deposition approaches are showing promise at the research level.

Diagram 13.1 - Near-Term Quantum Technologies Timeline

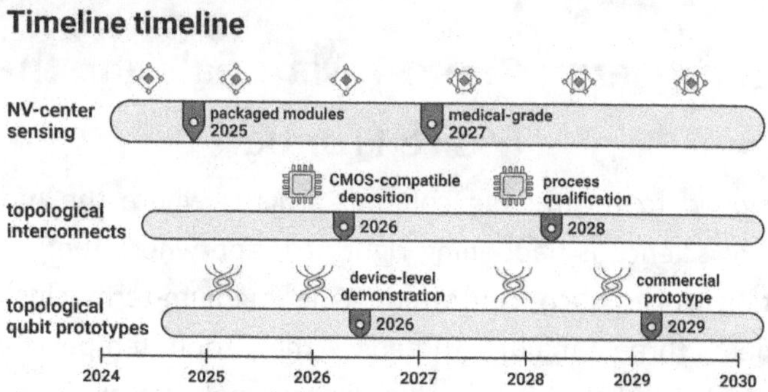

Topological qubit prototypes main: timeline an executive technical tax

First commercial topological qubit prototypes define the most demanding near-term milestone and the one directly on Axiom's roadmap. Microsoft's 2023 topological gap protocol, using indium arsenide (InAs) nanowires proximitized with aluminum, provided evidence for Majorana modes via a transport signature: a zero-bias conductance peak that survived rotation of the applied magnetic field in ways that trivial Andreev bound states would not. The engineering path forward requires three advances to operate simultaneously: coherence times in the Majorana modes long enough to perform gate operations, braiding protocols that physically move the modes to execute those gates, and millikelvin-scale cryogenic packaging. None of these is physics-limited. All are engineering problems with clear experimental benchmarks.

Yuki connected her sensor roadmap to the NV platform. "We are going to benefit from everything those companies learn about optical integration and microwave control. The materials are different, but the integration problem is structurally similar." Marcus recognized the pattern: solve the integration problem once, apply it across device families. The quantum materials field was young, but it was learning that discipline.

Medium-Term: Room-T Materials and the Moire Frontier

Priya moved to the middle column. "This is where the most important science is happening right now and where the most marketing noise is concentrated." The medium-term cluster contained three major threads: the room-temperature topological insulator hunt, two-dimensional materials and twisted bilayer systems, and fractional Chern insulators as a route to non-Abelian anyons beyond the Majorana framework. For each, the physics was established in the laboratory, but the engineering path to a manufacturable device was five to fifteen years away.

The room-temperature topological surface state problem is one of the central open challenges in the field. Bi2Se3 has a bulk bandgap of approximately 0.3 electronvolts; at room temperature, thermally excited bulk carriers outnumber surface-state carriers by a large margin, obscuring topological transport signatures. The engineering requirement is a topological insulator with a bulk gap above 0.5 electronvolts and surface Dirac states that remain stable under ambient conditions without cryogenics. The Topological Materials Database lists over 5,000 candidate compounds with symmetry-protected topological band structures. Still, most are air-sensitive, difficult to cleave for characterization, or contain rare-earth elements impractical for large-scale production.

Diagram 13.2 - AI-Driven Materials Discovery Flow

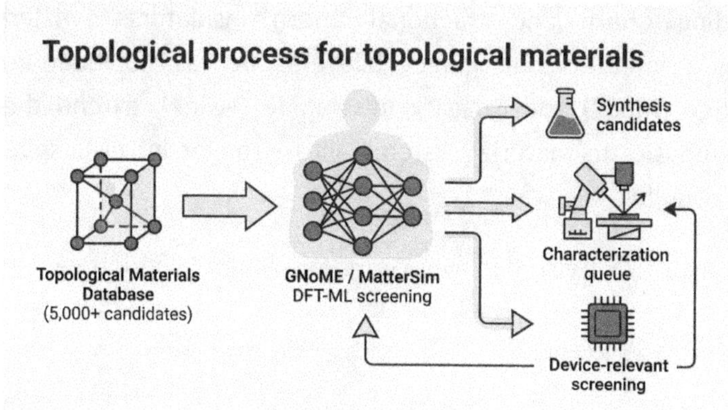

Active research directions include chalcogenide-halide compounds such as bismuth oxyhalides, which have larger bulk gaps and better ambient stability than binary chalcogenides; heavy-element oxides, including iridium and osmium compounds, where strong 5d spin-orbit coupling drives topological band inversion; and organic topological insulator candidates that are manufacturable via solution-phase deposition. None has yet demonstrated the clean-room-temperature Dirac surface states required for device applications. AI-driven computational screening is accelerating the candidate pipeline beyond what laboratory synthesis can evaluate.

Twisted bilayer graphene systems represent the most rapidly evolving frontier as of the mid-2020s. Pablo Jarillo-Herrero's 2018 MIT discovery that graphene bilayers twisted to the magic angle of approximately 1.1 degrees exhibit superconductivity and correlated insulating phases at temperatures accessible in a standard helium-4 cryostat opened a branch of topological physics that had not previously existed. At the magic angle, the moiré superlattice produces nearly flat electronic bands in which electron-electron interactions dominate over kinetic energy, driving the system into strongly correlated phases, including Chern and fractional Chern insulators. Twisted transition-metal dichalcogenide bilayers, such as molybdenum disulfide (MoS2) and tungsten diselenide (WSe2), extend the same physics to material systems with stronger intrinsic spin-orbit coupling.

Diagram 13.3 - Twisted Bilayer Graphene Moire Superlattice

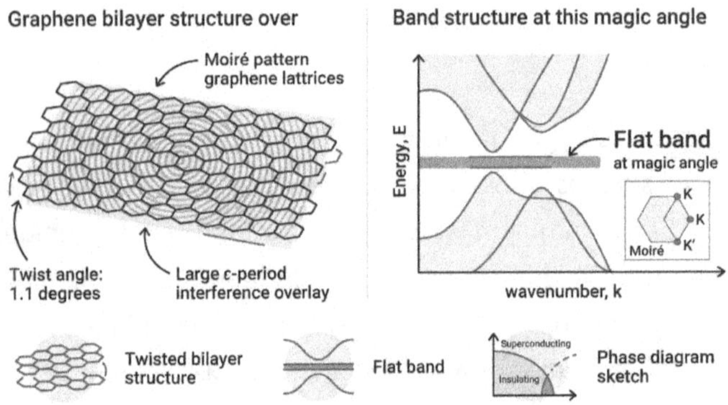

The engineering significance of the moiré frontier is that it provides a route to strongly correlated topological phases using 2D materials fabrication infrastructure already in place at leading semiconductor laboratories. Graphene and transition-metal dichalcogenides are well characterized and compatible with electron-beam lithography and gate electrode deposition. Controlling the twist angle to within a few hundredths of a degree is the primary manufacturing challenge; several groups have demonstrated robotic assembly systems that routinely achieve this precision.

Fractional Chern insulators (FCIs) are the moiré analog of fractional quantum Hall states and represent the most promising route to non-Abelian anyons outside the Majorana framework. A Chern insulator with a lowest-occupied band carrying a nonzero Chern number exhibits a quantized Hall conductivity. When interaction strength exceeds the band's kinetic energy, fractional filling states appear, hosting quasiparticles with fractional charge and, at certain filling fractions, non-Abelian exchange statistics. FCI states in twisted bilayer graphene were confirmed in the early 2020s, the first fractional topological phases realized without a large external magnetic field. The engineering path to a working non-Abelian qubit platform requires identifying material systems where FCI states survive realistic disorder.

Diagram 13.4 - Fractional Chern Insulator Phase Diagram

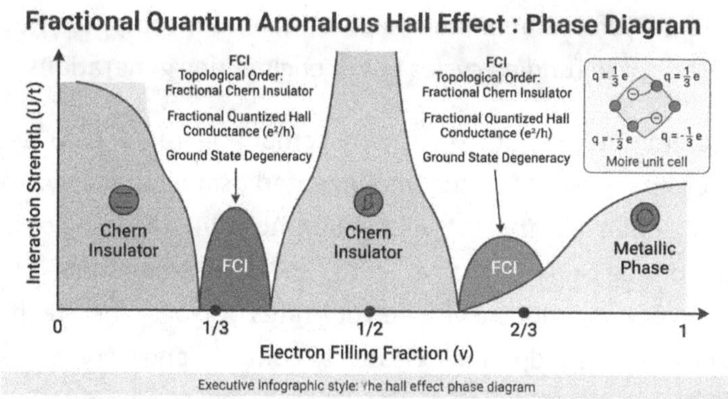

Marcus asked Sasha whether the FCI path and the Majorana path were competing or complementary for fault-tolerant computing. "Same goal, different engineering bets," Sasha said. "Majorana platforms store quantum information in non-locally encoded zero modes protected from local perturbations. FCI platforms do the same using the non-Abelian anyons of the fractional topological phase. The physical protection mechanism is topological in both cases. The tradeoff is operating conditions and fabrication requirements. Majorana platforms are further along experimentally, but require very precise semiconductor-superconductor interfaces. FCI platforms are earlier but may be more manufacturable at scale once the moiré materials are characterized at the device level."

Long-Term: Fault-Tolerant Topological Computing

Yuki read the third column heading aloud: transformational. "Meaning: if this happens, it changes the entire hardware landscape in a way that makes everything else look like a warm-up." The honest timeline for room-temperature topological quantum computing? None of them pretended to know. The physics was real. The materials were in the laboratories. The gap to a manufacturable fault-tolerant quantum computer was measured not in funding cycles but in engineering generations.

Fault-tolerant topological quantum computing requires three engineering layers to be implemented simultaneously: a physical qubit platform with non-Abelian, topologically protected logical qubits; a gate set implementable via topological operations with error rates below the fault-tolerance threshold; and classical control and cryogenic infrastructure that sustain the device over computation timescales. The canonical surface code fault-tolerance threshold is approximately one percent per gate operation. Topological qubits, if they perform as theory predicts, should achieve physical error rates orders of magnitude below this through the intrinsic protection of the non-Abelian state. The engineering challenge is to demonstrate protection in a real, fabricated device with real disorder, not in a theoretical model with perfect interfaces.

Diagram 13.5 - Fault-Tolerant Topological Computing Architecture Stack

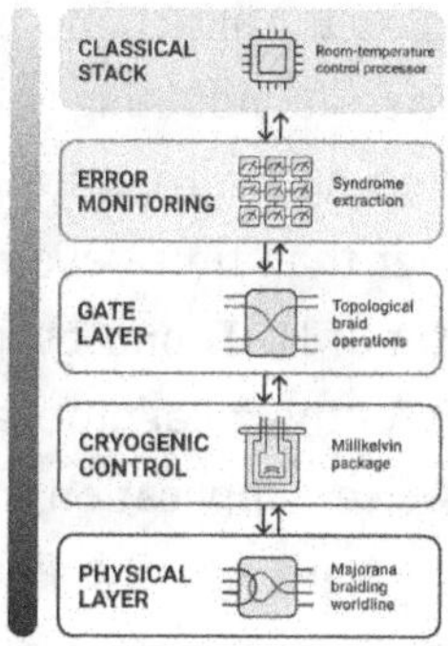

Room-temperature superconductivity represents a separate transformational possibility. Niobium, the workhorse of superconducting qubits, has a critical temperature of approximately nine kelvin. High-temperature cuprate superconductors, such as yttrium barium copper oxide (YBCO), operate up to approximately 138 kelvin. The 1986 discovery by Johannes Bednorz and Karl Müller of superconductivity in lanthanum barium copper oxide at 35 kelvin, which earned them the 1987 Nobel Prize, launched a four-decade search for ambient-condition superconductivity. Recent claims involving hydrogen-rich materials at high pressures and synthesized compounds at ambient pressure have not survived independent replication as of the mid-2020s. A confirmed room-temperature superconductor would be transformational: the dilution refrigerator, currently the dominant driver of cost and complexity in superconducting quantum hardware, would no longer be required for operation.

Higher-order topological insulators (HOTIs) extend topological protection to geometries that are more accessible than room-temperature superconductors. A first-order topological insulator conducts on its two-dimensional surfaces. A second-order HOTI has insulating surfaces but conducting one-dimensional hinge states at the junctions between surfaces. A third-order HOTI confines conducting states to its zero-dimensional corners. Hinge and corner states are protected by crystalline symmetry rather than time-reversal invariance alone. Experimental confirmation of HOTI phases in bismuth, tungsten ditelluride (WTe2), and breathing kagome lattice materials was reported by 2020. Device applications include nanoscale topological waveguides, where current flows along protected hinge channels, and corner states offer quantum-dot analogs with topological protection that could extend coherence lifetimes beyond those of conventional quantum dots.

Diagram 13.6 - Higher-Order Topological Insulator Geometry

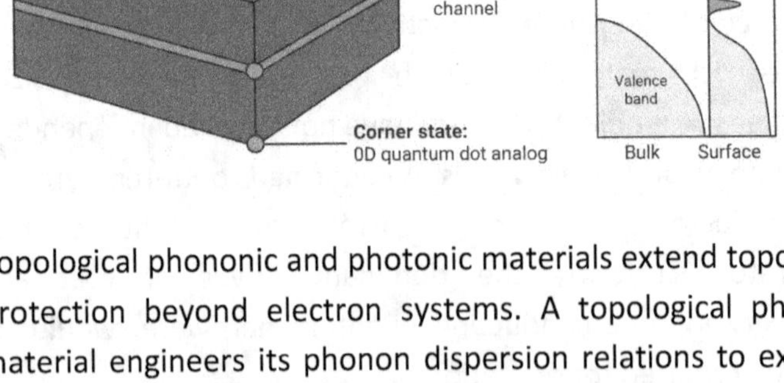

Topological phononic and photonic materials extend topological protection beyond electron systems. A topological phononic material engineers its phonon dispersion relations to exhibit a topology analogous to electronic band topology, producing phonon edge states that guide mechanical vibrations along protected channels immune to defect scattering. Topological photonic crystals do the same for light, using periodic dielectric structures to create topological photon modes that propagate regardless of defect placement. Both offer device opportunities without cryogenic requirements: topologically protected acoustic channels for vibration-isolated signal pathways in MEMS devices and topological photonic interconnects for defect-tolerant light routing in data-center optical circuits. The engineering timeline is shorter than for quantum computing because the energy scales are classical and operation is at ambient temperature.

Adjacent Fields: AI Discovery and Automated Synthesis

Priya saved the most practically consequential section for last. "The tools for finding and making these materials are changing faster than the materials themselves. When I started my PhD, identifying a single topological insulator candidate meant years of DFT calculations followed by months of synthesis. The computational tools available now can screen tens of thousands of candidates in the time it used to take us to evaluate one."

Google DeepMind's GNoME system, described in a 2023 Nature paper, screened 2.2 million candidate crystal structures using a graph neural network trained on density functional theory (DFT) data, thereby identifying approximately 380,000 novel, stable compounds. DFT is a quantum-mechanical method that calculates a material's electronic structure from atomic positions without empirical fitting parameters; GNoME predicts formation energy, stability, and electronic properties orders of magnitude faster than full DFT calculations. Microsoft Research's MatterSim applies similar machine-learning force-field methods to predict materials' behavior at finite temperatures, bridging zero-kelvin DFT outputs and the room-temperature performance required by device engineering. The bottleneck has shifted from computational screening to experimental synthesis and characterization: the AI pipeline generates validated candidates faster than the laboratory can test them.

Diagram 13.7 - GNoME and MatterSim Materials Discovery Pipeline

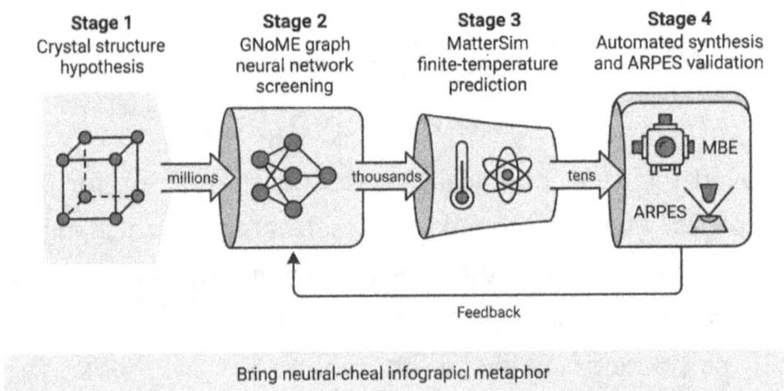

Automated synthesis platforms are beginning to close the gap on the laboratory side. Self-driving laboratories combine robotic synthesis, deposition, and characterization into closed-loop workflows guided by machine learning. In topological insulator thin-film growth, a self-driving MBE system would autonomously vary growth parameters, measure the resulting film in situ using reflection high-energy electron diffraction (RHEED) and ellipsometry, and automatically update the deposition parameter search, compressing months of manual optimization into days. Multiple groups have published partial demonstrations for topological insulator films as of 2024.

In-situ ARPES closes the loop on characterization. ARPES directly maps the electronic band structure by measuring the kinetic energy and emission angle of electrons ejected by ultraviolet photons, thereby reconstructing the E(k) dispersion and imaging the Dirac cone of a topological surface state. Conventional ARPES requires transferring the sample from the growth chamber, thereby introducing contamination. In-situ systems connect MBE growth and ARPES analysis via an ultra-high-vacuum transfer line, enabling band-structure measurements immediately after growth. Combined with automated synthesis, in situ ARPES makes the iteration cycle as fast as the equipment allows, rather than as fast as manual sample preparation permits.

Diagram 13.8 - In-Situ ARPES and Automated MBE System

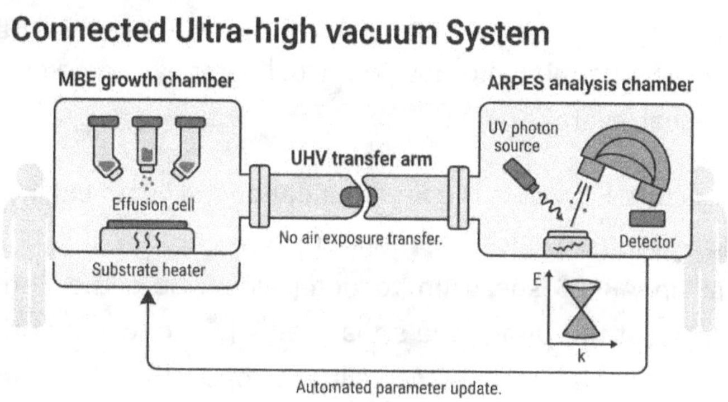

Marcus looked at this section and recognized a new kind of engineer in its implications. In conventional semiconductor development, the handoff from materials researcher to process engineer to device engineer was clear and sequential. The AI-accelerated pipeline was compressing the front end so fast that the handoff boundaries were blurring: materials science roles were becoming partly computational, process engineering required enough understanding of screening results to evaluate which candidates were worth synthesizing, and the device engineer's core role was unchanged but would face a pace of incoming material candidates faster than any prior transition. "We're going to need people who can read a graph neural network prediction and then go put the sample in the MBE," Marcus said. "That's a new kind of engineer."

The Skills the Next-Generation Engineer Needs

Yuki had seen the same problem at NIST before joining Axiom: programs staffed by physicists who were exceptional at characterization but uncomfortable with device integration, and engineers who were excellent at integration but could not read band structures. "The gap isn't going to close by itself," she said. "The universities are not producing the hybrid profile in large numbers. The people who develop it deliberately are going to have unusual leverage."

Band structure literacy is the first foundational skill. An engineer working with topological materials in any capacity needs to examine an ARPES spectrum to determine where the Fermi level lies, what the Dirac cone signature looks like, whether the bulk gap is large enough to keep surface conduction dominant, and what impurity bands or surface reconstructions mean for device performance. This does not require deep knowledge of the derivations of the Bloch theorem; it requires pattern recognition in E(k) space and physical intuition about which features matter. Building that pattern recognition requires reading the characterization sections of actual materials papers and asking, for every proposed material, what the band structure looks like and whether it has been measured.

Diagram 13.9 - Next-Decade Engineer Skill Stack

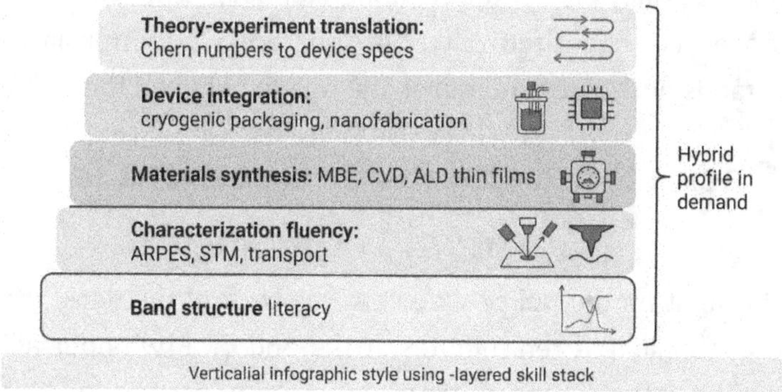

Characterization fluency extends beyond ARPES to scanning tunneling microscopy (STM) and transport measurements. STM measures the local density of states at atomic spatial resolution, resolving Landau levels, Friedel oscillations, and surface-state distributions that ARPES, which averages over the illuminated area, cannot resolve. Transport fluency means understanding what longitudinal and Hall resistance measurements reveal about a quantum Hall state, what a zero-bias peak in differential conductance implies for Majorana physics, and what the transport signatures of a topological phase transition look like versus a trivial gap closing. Engineers fluent in all three methods can design measurement sequences that efficiently answer device-relevant questions.

Theory-experiment translation is the rarest skill and the most consequential. It means moving from a Chern number, a topological invariant calculated from the Berry curvature integrated over the Brillouin zone, to a device specification: what geometry, interface quality, operating temperature, and magnetic-field tolerance the topological protection requires. A theoretical physicist can compute a Chern number of one and a topological gap of 0.15 electronvolts without specifying what that means for contact resistance in a Hall bar. An engineer can measure a Hall bar without understanding why the Hall resistance is quantized at h/e-squared. The translator understands both sides and builds the bridge between them.

Open Ethical and Policy Questions in Quantum Technology

Priya brought up the policy slide near the back of the deck, the one that usually got ten minutes at the end of a two-hour all-hands. She gave it more time. "There's a version of this conversation where we discuss only what's physically possible and treat ethics and policy as someone else's problem. I don't want that version. The hardware we're building has consequences that extend well beyond the lab."

Cryptographic implications are the most immediate policy question in this space. A sufficiently capable quantum computer running Shor's algorithm can factor large integers in polynomial time, thereby breaking RSA and elliptic-curve cryptography, which secure current internet communications and financial transactions. NIST's post-quantum cryptography standardization process selected lattice-based schemes, including CRYSTALS-Kyber, in its 2022 first round. The timeline for a cryptographically relevant quantum computer is uncertain, but most analyses estimate it will take 10 to 20 years, starting in the mid-2020s. Systems with 40-year operational lifetimes that store sensitive data today are potentially vulnerable to harvest-now, decrypt-later attacks. Engineers building quantum hardware are part of the supply chain for this capability.

Diagram 13.10 - Quantum Technology Policy Landscape

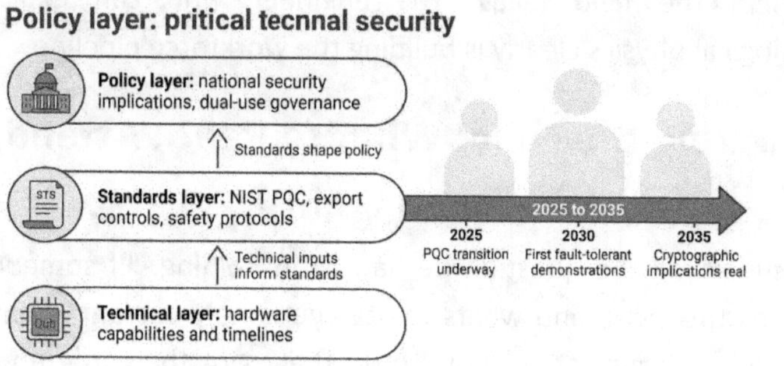

Technical layer: hardware capabilities and timelines

Export control frameworks extend to advanced quantum computing hardware and the materials used to build it. The Commerce Department's Entity List and Export Administration Regulations affect which components can be exported, to whom, and under what conditions. Topological materials grown at U.S. institutions for quantum computing applications are subject to these frameworks in ways that shape research collaboration design, technology transfer agreements, and supply chains. Engineers who understand the regulatory landscape flag risks during the design phase rather than at the shipping dock.

Equity and access in the quantum workforce form a third dimension. The current talent pipeline draws predominantly from a small set of research universities with active condensed matter physics programs near national laboratories or quantum hardware companies. National quantum initiatives in the United States, the European Union, and the United Kingdom have made it an explicit priority to broaden this pipeline. The practical implication for working engineers is that mentoring, knowledge sharing, and the development of accessible educational resources directly help address the infrastructure problem the field faces. The engineer who can explain topological physics clearly is building the workforce pipeline.

Tracking the Field: What to Read, Attend, and Ignore

Marcus asked the question he had been holding. "If someone finishes this book and wants to stay genuinely current, what's the actual answer about how to do that? Not the conference-brochure answer." Priya, Sasha, and Yuki exchanged a brief look. "You follow five to eight research groups whose work is directly relevant to what you're building," Priya said. "You read their preprints on arXiv when they appear. And you ignore approximately ninety percent of conference abstracts and press releases."

The arXiv condensed matter preprint server is the primary real-time channel for the field. Papers appear months before journal publication, and arXiv is where genuinely new results are first visible. The relevant subcategories are cond-mat. mes-hall for mesoscale and nanoscale physics covering topological insulators, quantum Hall effects, and nanowire devices; cond-mat. supr-con for superconductor research; and cond-mat. str-el for strongly correlated electrons, covering Mott insulators, fractional quantum Hall states, and moiré systems. A practical workflow is a 15-minute daily discipline: set up author and subcategory alerts, read abstracts, and read full papers only when the results are directly relevant to your work or present genuinely new experimental findings.

Key journals include Physical Review Letters, Physical Review X, Nature Materials, Nature Physics, and npj Quantum Materials. The prestige hierarchy matters less than content: PRL publishes results too technical for Nature, and npj Quantum Materials focuses on synthesis and characterization directly relevant to engineering applications. Reviews of Modern Physics is the place for comprehensive tutorial reviews of mature subfields. The Hasan-Kane 2010 review of three-dimensional topological insulators remains the standard reference for that subfield. Reading one comprehensive review per subfield at the beginning of your engagement with it is more efficient than reconstructing the field from primary papers alone.

Diagram 13.11 - Field Navigation Map for the Practicing Engineer

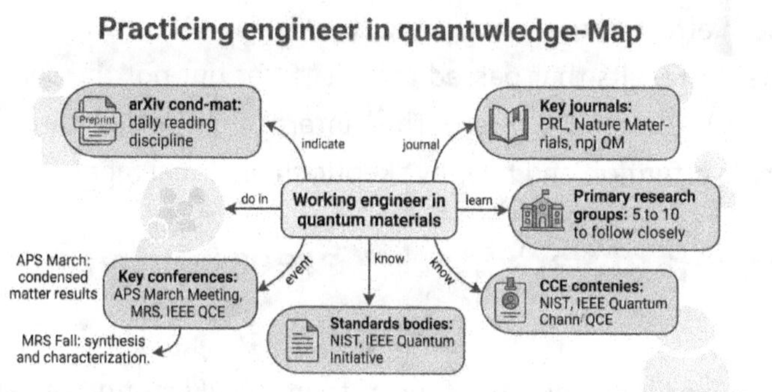

A knowledge-map, trica infographic for the practicing engineer in quantum.

Conference strategy requires selectivity. The American Physical Society March Meeting, attended by approximately 12,000 physicists, is the primary venue for condensed matter results, including topological materials. The Materials Research Society Fall Meeting in Boston focuses on synthesis and characterization, which are most relevant to engineers on the materials growth side. IEEE Quantum Week, launched in 2019, is the most systems-oriented quantum technology conference and the best venue for hardware engineering discussions crossing materials, devices, and systems architecture. One condensed matter physics meeting and one quantum engineering meeting per year, combined with systematic arXiv reading, cover more ground than scattered attendance at every event with "quantum" in its name.

What to ignore is as important as what to read. Press releases announcing quantum supremacy milestones, room-temperature superconductivity breakthroughs, or revolutionary coherence times without peer-reviewed papers require skepticism proportional to the claim. The checklist is straightforward: Is there a paper with full methods? Have the key measurements been reproduced by an independent group? Are the operating conditions reported completely? Is the claimed effect large enough to be device-relevant? Sasha's phrase for results that passed the first filter but not the second was 'interesting if true.' The interesting-if-true category deserves attention and healthy skepticism in equal measure.

2035 Hardware Stack: Careers, Programs, Companies

The sun was low when the four of them finally stopped talking and started packing up. Priya looked at the map from the side of the room. "The question I get from every early-career engineer who comes through here is simple: where do I actually go?" Not which university was most prestigious, but where the engineering problems were real, the materials were being grown, characterized, and turned into devices. The work would matter a decade out.

Process engineering roles for the growth of topological materials are concentrated at organizations actively building quantum hardware. Microsoft's quantum hardware division, operating from Redmond and Copenhagen, is the largest employer of topological qubit process engineers. National laboratories, including Sandia, Lawrence Berkeley, and NIST, have programs focused explicitly on the science-to-engineering transition and hire process engineers at both the postdoctoral and permanent staff levels. Key university groups include those of Nitin Samarth at Penn State and the hexagonal boron nitride growth program of Koichi Watanabe and Takashi Taniguchi at NIMS in Japan, whose substrate material supplies essentially all moiré-system research worldwide.

Characterization engineering roles for ARPES analysis, STM operation, and transport measurement development are distributed across national laboratories with synchrotron light sources: the Advanced Photon Source at Argonne, the National Synchrotron Light Source II at Brookhaven, and the Advanced Light Source at Berkeley, all of which operate ARPES beamlines serving research groups globally. These facilities hire staff scientists and beamline engineers who maintain instrumentation and collaborate with visiting teams. The required skill profile combines expertise in optical engineering and vacuum systems with literacy in condensed matter physics. As laboratory ARPES systems based on ultrafast laser sources become more affordable, characterization engineering expertise is increasingly in demand at company and university laboratories outside synchrotron facilities.

Diagram 13.12 - Quantum Materials Career and Company Ecosystem Map

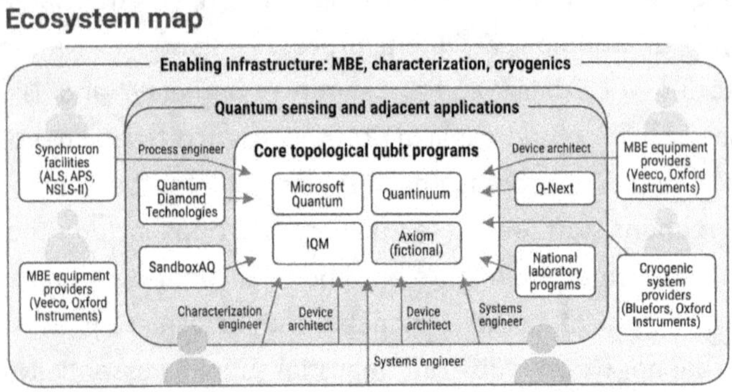

Device architecture and quantum hardware systems engineering are the most cross-disciplinary positions in the ecosystem. A device architect translates topological qubit physics into a manufacturable geometry: specifying the dimensions and composition of semiconductor-superconductor interfaces, gate electrode materials and layouts, contact resistance requirements, and cryogenic package operating conditions. This role requires simultaneous fluency in condensed matter physics, nanofabrication, and systems engineering, and is the one this book has most directly prepared its readers for. Quantum hardware systems engineers work at the integration level, designing cryogenic infrastructure, classical control electronics, microwave wiring, and thermal management for operation at millikelvin temperatures. Both roles are currently undersupplied relative to demand from quantum hardware companies and national laboratory programs, and both carry compensation premiums reflecting that scarcity.

The landscape of graduate and postdoctoral training is concentrated yet internationally distributed. In the United States: MIT's Research Laboratory of Electronics, the Harvard Quantum Initiative, Station Q at UC Santa Barbara, and programs at Caltech, Penn State, Stanford, and Columbia. In Europe, Delft University, the Niels Bohr Institute in Copenhagen, and ETH Zurich's quantum device laboratory have produced a large fraction of the current generation of topological qubit engineers. In Asia, the Beijing National Laboratory for Condensed Matter Physics runs one of the most productive programs in topological insulators globally. An engineer choosing a graduate program here is betting on an advisor network and experimental capabilities, not just a topic.

What Can We Build With This?

The question Marcus wrote at the top of his notebook on his first day at Axiom is the same question this book has been answering since page one. Twelve chapters and a Friday afternoon roadmap discussion later, the answer is more specific than any popular account of the field provides and more honest about timelines than any funding pitch allows.

In the near term, within the capital and workforce already deployed, the buildable products are: NV-center magnetometers at navigation and medical grade in portable packaging without cryogenics, using diamond synthesis that is already manufacturable; topological interconnect test structures in back-end-of-line CMOS process flows, not yet in production but in process qualification at multiple semiconductor research programs; and first-generation topological qubit devices at the single-qubit demonstration level, showing non-Abelian statistics and sufficient coherence for single logical operations. None of this is science fiction. The main things separating laboratory demonstration from a manufacturable product are process engineering, yield optimization, and packaging integration.

In the medium term, five to fifteen years out and requiring materials engineering advances currently in active development, the buildable products include: room-temperature topological interconnects in commercial semiconductor processes, once a topological insulator with sufficient bulk gap and CMOS-compatible deposition chemistry is identified and process-qualified; multi-qubit topological quantum processors performing error-protected logical operations, if Majorana-based or FCI-based coherence and braiding fidelity match theoretical predictions at the device level; and topological photonic circuits providing defect-tolerant light routing in data center optical interconnects, where the physics operates at room temperature and the gap is integration scale rather than fundamental physics.

In the long term, fifteen to thirty years out and requiring both materials advances and fundamental engineering breakthroughs, the buildable products are: fault-tolerant topological quantum computers with enough logical qubits to run Shor's algorithm at cryptographically relevant scale; room-temperature superconducting electronic systems, if ambient-condition superconductivity is confirmed and proven, which would eliminate cryogenic overhead from the quantum hardware stack entirely; and materials-by-design workflows in which AI-driven screening, automated synthesis, and in-situ characterization are fully integrated, compressing the discovery-to-device timeline from decades to years. This last item is an accelerant for all the others: a mature AI-driven materials discovery capability would change the rate at which every other item on this list becomes manufacturable.

In every case, the transition from laboratory demonstration to manufacturable device is an engineering problem, not a physics problem. The physics of topological protection is established. The materials that exhibit it are cataloged. What stands between the current state of the field and the hardware stack of 2035 is process tolerance, interface quality, yield, packaging, cryogenic integration, and the work that translates a topological invariant into a fabrication specification. The transistor was not built by the physicists who discovered quantum tunneling. It was built by engineers who understood the physics well enough to make it manufacturable. The same transition is underway in topological and quantum materials, and the engineers who join now will define the architecture of what comes next.

Takeaway

The whiteboard map was still up when the four of them left the conference room on Friday evening. Marcus photographed it as he always did with whiteboards that represented conversations worth keeping. In the photo: Sasha's three-column taxonomy, Yuki's annotations, Marcus's unanswered questions, and a structure beneath it all that he recognized from years of watching technology transitions. A field that had crossed the boundary from physics to engineering without everyone in it fully realizing the crossing had happened. The physics was known. The materials were in the laboratory. The devices were being built. The boundary had moved.

This book has been a field manual for engineers working at that boundary. It began with the engineering question, the silicon scaling wall, and the need for a new class of materials. It answered that question through twelve chapters: band topology and Chern numbers, the quantum Hall effect, topological insulators from three dimensions to two, Weyl semimetals, topological superconductors and Majorana fermions, quantum sensing, twisted bilayer graphene, and the moiré frontier. Each concept was grounded in a device context. Priya anchored the materials strategy. Sasha translated the theory. Yuki built the sensing applications. Marcus asked the question every reader needs to ask. The book ends where it began: the materials are ready, and the engineers are needed.

The field will have moved by the time you finish reading. New results will have appeared on arXiv, new milestones will have been reached, and some of what this chapter predicts will have been overtaken by experiment, as it should be in a living field. What will not have changed is the structure of the opportunity: the gap between materials physics and manufacturable devices, the shortage of engineers who can close it, and the scale of what closing the gap enables. That gap is yours to work on. The materials exist. The physics is understood. The road ahead is an engineering problem, and you are now equipped to work on it.

14 Closing

It was a Friday in late November, and the Axiom Quantum building had gone quiet. The fabrication lab was locked down for the weekend. The dilution refrigerators were holding temperature without supervision. In the common area on the third floor, Priya stood at the whiteboard with a Sharpie, looking at the band structure diagram she had been annotating since Tuesday. Marcus was in the corner chair, notebook open on his knee, reading back through several months of entries. The notebook was almost full.

Sasha came in with two cups of coffee and dropped into the chair across from Marcus. Yuki arrived a few minutes later, still wearing her cleanroom badge, and pulled up a stool. Outside, the Cambridge sky was the flat grey of a New England November, and the streetlights on Massachusetts Avenue were coming on.

Marcus turned to the last page of his notebook and drew a line under the most recent entry. He thought about a question Priya had asked him during his first week at Axiom: whether he understood why the surface state of a topological insulator could not be removed. He had not understood it then. He understood it now, precisely enough to use the answer in a decision about fabrication. He looked at Priya. She caught his eye and gave a small nod. Then she picked up the Sharpie and added one more annotation to the whiteboard.

The Arc We Traveled

This book began with a provocation: silicon is approaching its physical limits, and the next generation of computing and sensing hardware will be built from materials that exploit quantum mechanics at the level of their crystal structure. The materials exist. The devices are being designed right now by people at companies, national laboratories, and university cleanrooms who need to think simultaneously in terms of crystal physics, device engineering, and system architecture.

Chapters one and two established the historical and engineering context, placing topological materials within the semiconductor transition from germanium to silicon and showing that careful historical reading is a form of risk assessment. Chapters three and four laid the quantum-mechanical and solid-state foundations: quantization, coherence, Bloch's theorem, band gaps, and the effective-mass picture, as the minimum physics vocabulary on which everything else depends. Chapters five and six introduced topology as a physical concept: the Berry phase as a geometric quantity that accumulates when a quantum state traverses a closed loop, the Chern number as the topological invariant that classifies a band structure, and Klaus von Klitzing's 1980 quantum Hall experiment as the first laboratory measurement of a topological invariant.

Chapters seven and eight brought topology into three dimensions through topological insulators: materials that are insulating in the bulk and conducting only at their surfaces, with those surface states mandated by topology and impossible to remove through material imperfections. Bismuth selenide became the model system, and band inversion through spin-orbit coupling became the conceptual core. Weyl semimetals and Dirac semimetals extended the picture to topologically protected bulk band crossings. Chapters nine and ten turned to superconductivity: Cooper pairs and the BCS gap as the mechanism behind zero resistance, and the topologically nontrivial superconductors whose surfaces host Majorana fermions, quasiparticles that are their own antiparticles, and whose nonlocal quantum information is the physical basis for the topological qubit. Chapters eleven and twelve covered the devices, from transmon and topological qubits to quantum magnetometers and gyroscopes. Chapter thirteen grounded all of it in characterization: ARPES, scanning tunneling microscopy, transport in magnetic fields, and molecular beam epitaxy as the techniques that make topological physics measurable and manufacturable.

Diagram C.1 - The Book's Arc: From Engineering Provocation to Quantum Hardware

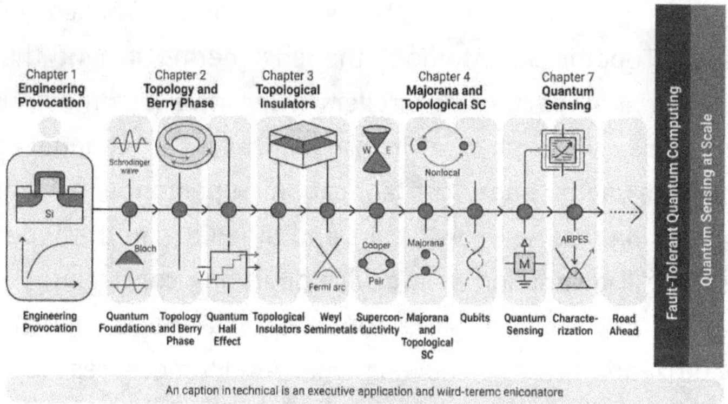

The arc is not a line from ignorance to mastery. It is a map of connected territory where the connections matter as much as the stations. Topology is not a detour from band theory; it is a reinterpretation that reveals the structure that is always present. Superconductivity is the mechanism that makes Majorana modes experimentally accessible. Quantum sensing is the near-term commercial application of the same physics, and the domain where fabrication and characterization skills will first be refined at scale.

The Promise, Restated

The promise this book made was specific: by the last page, the reader would be able to read a quantum materials paper, evaluate a hardware claim, and engage as a peer rather than a tourist. That promise was not about mastering condensed matter physics. It was about the precise subset of that curriculum that a working engineer needs to make real hardware decisions in a field where the materials are already leaving the laboratory.

That subset has a shape. Band structure literacy: reading an E-versus-k diagram, identifying a band gap and a band inversion, understanding what the Fermi level position implies for transport. Topological intuition: the engineering insight that some material properties are integers, insensitive to continuous deformations, with physical consequences that cannot be negotiated away by imperfect fabrication. Superconductivity as an engineering reality: Cooper pairs and the BCS gap; the Type I versus Type II distinction as a device-operating constraint; the topological gap as the basis for Majorana mode stability. Characterization fluency: knowing what ARPES measures, what scanning tunneling microscopy reveals about surface states, and what transport signatures like the anomalous Hall effect mean in a measurement.

The practical test is not the ability to reproduce a derivation. It is the ability to open a preprint in the cond-mat archive. mes-hall and determine whether the claimed result is significant and whether the evidence supports it. It is the ability to follow an APS March Meeting session on topological materials and know which results deserve a follow-up conversation. It is the ability to ask the questions that matter when a company announces a topological qubit: what is the materials platform, what is the

Majorana gap, what is the coherence time, and how many devices were the result measured on.

What to Do Next

The graduate textbooks are now accessible. Bernevig and Hughes's Topological Insulators and Topological Superconductors is the clearest systematic treatment of the mathematical framework, deriving the Fu-Kane model and working through the full topological classification table. Shun-Qing Shen's Topological Insulators builds on the Dirac equation and covers both two- and three-dimensional cases, with an emphasis on physical intuition. Neither requires more mathematical background than this book has built; they require patience with notation and a willingness to work through derivations. The language will be familiar, the physical stakes will be clear, and the steps will be motivated rather than mysterious.

To stay current, Nature Reviews Materials publishes substantive review articles that establish what is understood, what is contested, and the open engineering questions. Reviews of Modern Physics publishes longer treatments, closer to textbook chapters; the topology reviews from the past decade represent the community's settled understanding at a level of rigor the primary literature assumes without stating. For primary research, the practical entry points are arXiv: cond-mat.mes-hall for topological materials, cond-mat. supr-con for superconducting systems, and cond-mat. mtrl-sci for materials predictions. The Materials Project database contains topological characterization for thousands of predicted and confirmed materials, including band structures and topological invariants. ARPES data repositories from major synchrotron facilities let you read experimental data alongside the papers that produced it, building intuition faster than any schematic.

Conferences: the APS March Meeting covers the full spectrum from theoretical classification to device integration. The MRS meetings emphasize synthesis, characterization, and processing. IEEE Quantum Week is the best venue for the intersection of quantum hardware engineering and materials science. Skills with the most leverage: band structure literacy from first-principles calculations, characterization fluency across ARPES and transport and STM, and cryogenic engineering at millikelvin temperatures. The last of these is in short supply relative to demand in the current quantum hardware market.

What We Still Don't Know

Room-temperature topology is the most consequential open question. The topological surface states of three-dimensional topological insulators are observable at room temperature in principle, but in practice, surface transport is dominated by bulk conduction from thermally excited carriers. Topological superconductivity requires millikelvin temperatures. Whether materials can be synthesized with sufficiently large topological gaps and sufficiently clean carrier densities to support room-temperature operation of topological devices remains an open question. There are theoretical predictions of room-temperature quantum anomalous Hall effects in thin films of magnetic topological insulators, and experimental reports of anomalous Hall signatures at elevated temperatures. Still, none have been confirmed to a standard sufficient to support an engineering design decision.

Scalable Majorana-based qubits remain an open engineering problem. The physics is well understood theoretically, and the experimental evidence for Majorana signatures has improved substantially since the first reports in InSb nanowires around 2012. Microsoft's 2023 announcement of a topological qubit marked a meaningful step. But coherence times in current Majorana devices remain shorter than those of the best transmon qubits, and fabrication yield in hybrid semiconductor-superconductor nanowire systems is not yet at the level required for large-scale integration. Materials by design at scale presents a third open challenge: the gap between a computationally predicted topological material and a device-quality sample with controlled interfaces and low disorder is substantial, and the feedback loop between prediction, synthesis, and characterization, though improving, is not yet fast enough to make materials discovery a bottleneck-free process.

These open questions are the conditions that make the field interesting and consequential. The engineers who make progress on room-temperature topologies and scalable Majorana devices are the ones who understand the current state well enough to identify the leverage points.

Diagram C.2 - Friday Evening at Axiom Quantum

Where to Go From Here

Marcus closed his notebook. Not with finality, the way you close something that is finished, but with the ordinary action of someone who has reached the end of a section and will open a new one tomorrow. Priya was still at the whiteboard, adding a new phase diagram in the upper left corner. Sasha was reading one of her printouts with the focused expression of someone working out why something is slightly wrong. Yuki had sat down on the stool and was scrolling through a preprint on her tablet.

The room had the texture of continuing work. Not deadline-driven, but slower and more exploratory: the work of people who have established enough foundation to form the next set of questions. That is the condition this book has been trying to produce. Not the completion of a curriculum, but a foundation from which the next questions can be formed and pursued.

The hardware engineer who has worked through this book can read Bernevig and Hughes with comprehension rather than confusion. They can open a Nature Reviews Materials article on Weyl semimetal device physics and identify which parts are established and which are active areas of research. They can attend an APS March Meeting session and recognize which experimental results are incremental and which are genuine advances. They can evaluate a topological qubit announcement by asking the right questions about the materials platform, the Majorana gap, the coherence measurement protocol, and the reproducibility. They can speak with a condensed matter physicist as a peer, with a shared technical vocabulary and an engineering-grounded set of constraints.

That vocabulary is not a certificate of completion. The field is moving, the open questions are real, and the engineering challenges ahead of room-temperature topological devices and scalable Majorana qubits are substantial. But the engineer who understands the challenges, who can read the primary literature and follow the progress, and who has the conceptual framework to evaluate claims as they arise is the engineer who will be in a position to help solve them. The materials are leaving the laboratory. The devices are being designed. This is the moment when having this foundation matters.

Priya capped the Sharpie and stepped back from the whiteboard. She looked at the phase diagram she had drawn, the boundary between the trivial and the topological, and the invariants on either side. Then she turned around.

"Same question tomorrow," she said. "Different materials."

Marcus opened his notebook to a new page.

15 Glossary

Glossary of Terms for Topological and Quantum Materials Explained

A

Abelian Anyon — A quasiparticle in two-dimensional systems whose exchange only adds a phase to the wavefunction. Contrasts with non-Abelian anyons used for topological quantum computing. *(CH9)*

Angle-Resolved Photoemission Spectroscopy (ARPES) — An experimental technique that measures a material's electronic band structure by ejecting electrons with photons and analyzing their momentum and energy. *(CH4, CH6, CH12)*

Anomalous Hall Effect — A Hall voltage arising without an external magnetic field, often due to Berry curvature or magnetic order. *(CH7)*

B

Band Gap — The energy difference between the valence and conduction bands; determines whether a material is a metal, semiconductor, or insulator. *(CH3, CH4)*

Band Inversion — A reversal of the ordering of conduction and valence bands, typically driven by strong spin-orbit coupling; the defining mechanism behind many topological insulators. *(CH4, CH6)*

Berry Curvature — A geometric property of electronic states in momentum space that acts like a magnetic field in k-space. *(CH5)*

Berry Phase — A geometric phase acquired by a quantum state when it undergoes adiabatic evolution around a closed loop in parameter space. *(CH5)*

Bloch Wave — A wavefunction describing electrons in a periodic lattice, foundational to band theory. *(CH3)*

C

Chern Number — A topological invariant that counts the winding of Berry curvature over the Brillouin zone; central to the quantum Hall effect. *(CH5)*

Cooper Pair — A bound pair of electrons with opposite momentum and spin that forms the basis of superconductivity. *(CH8)*

Cryogenic Packaging — Engineering techniques for wiring, mounting, and thermally anchoring devices operating at millikelvin temperatures. *(CH11)*

D

Density of States (DOS) — The number of available electronic states at each energy level; influences conductivity and optical properties. *(CH4)*

Dirac Semimetal — A material where conduction and valence bands touch at discrete Dirac points with linear dispersion. *(CH7)*

Donut–Coffee Cup Analogy — A visualization of topology: objects with the same number of holes are topologically equivalent. *(CH1, CH5)*

E

Effective Mass — A parameter describing how electrons respond to forces inside a crystal, derived from band curvature. *(CH4)*

Eigenstate / Eigenvalue — Solutions to quantum mechanical operators representing measurable physical quantities. *(CH3)*

F

Fermi Level — The highest occupied energy level at zero temperature; determines carrier type and density. *(CH4)*

Fermi Arc — Open-ended surface states characteristic of Weyl semimetals. *(CH7)*

Fu–Kane Model — A theoretical proposal for inducing topological superconductivity on the surface of a topological insulator via proximity to an s-wave superconductor. *(CH8)*

G

Geometric Phase — A phase acquired due to the geometry of the parameter space, not dynamical evolution; includes Berry phase. *(CH5)*

Gyroscope (Quantum) — A rotation sensor leveraging quantum interference or topological protection for extreme precision. *(CH10)*

H

Hall Conductance — Quantized transverse conductance in the quantum Hall effect, proportional to a topological invariant. *(CH2, CH7)*

Heterostructure — A layered material system combining different semiconductors, superconductors, or topological materials. *(CH6, CH11)*

Higher-Order Topological Insulator (HOTI) — A material whose topology produces hinge or corner states rather than surface states. *(CH7)*

I

Interface Engineering — The design of atomic-scale interfaces to preserve or induce topological or superconducting properties. *(CH11)*

Inversion Symmetry — A spatial symmetry whose presence or absence affects band topology and degeneracies. *(CH3, CH5)*

K

Kramers Degeneracy — A twofold degeneracy of electronic states protected by time-reversal symmetry in systems with spin-orbit coupling. *(CH3)*

Kosterlitz–Thouless Transition — A topological phase transition involving vortex–antivortex unbinding in 2D systems. *(CH2)*

L

Lattice Mismatch — The difference in lattice constants between a film and substrate, influencing strain and defect formation. *(CH11)*

Localization — The suppression of electron transport due to disorder; topological states are protected against localization. *(CH6)*

M

Majorana Zero Mode (MZM) — A quasiparticle that is its own antiparticle, appearing at zero energy in topological superconductors; candidate for topological qubits. *(CH8, CH9)*

Meissner Effect — The expulsion of magnetic fields from a superconductor below its critical temperature. *(CH8)*

Moiré Material — A layered structure with a twist angle that creates long-wavelength interference patterns and emergent topological phases. *(CH13)*

N

Nodal-Line Semimetal — A material where conduction and valence bands touch along a continuous line rather than discrete points. *(CH7)*

Non-Abelian Anyon — A quasiparticle whose exchange transforms the quantum state via matrix operations, enabling topological quantum computation. *(CH9)*

P

Pauli Exclusion Principle — The rule that no two fermions can occupy the same quantum state; it governs band filling. *(CH3)*

Proximity Effect — The induction of superconductivity or magnetism in a material due to contact with another material. *(CH6, CH8)*

Q

Quantum Anomalous Hall Effect (QAHE) — A quantized Hall effect occurring without external magnetic fields, driven by intrinsic magnetism and topology. *(CH7)*

Quantum Oscillations — Periodic variations in magnetoresistance or magnetization revealing Fermi surface geometry. *(CH12)*

R

Relativistic Correction — Adjustments to electronic structure due to relativistic effects, especially important in heavy elements with strong spin-orbit coupling. *(CH3)*

Robustness (Topological) — The immunity of surface or edge states to disorder, defects, or perturbations due to topological invariants. *(CH5, CH6)*

S

Scanning Tunneling Microscopy (STM) — A technique that images electronic states with atomic resolution using quantum tunneling. *(CH12)*

Spin-Momentum Locking — A property of topological surface states where electron spin is locked perpendicular to momentum. *(CH6)*

Spin-Orbit Coupling (SOC) — An interaction between an electron's spin and its motion; essential for band inversion and topological phases. *(CH3, CH4)*

T

Tenfold Way — A classification scheme for topological phases based on symmetries. *(CH7)*

Tight-Binding Model — A method for calculating band structure using atomic orbitals as basis states. *(CH4)*

Topological Invariant — A quantized value (e.g., Chern number, Z_2 index) that classifies a material's topological phase. *(CH5)*

U

Unconventional Superconductor — A superconductor whose pairing symmetry differs from conventional s-wave pairing, often hosting topological phases. *(CH8)*

V

Valence Band — The highest energy band fully occupied by electrons at zero temperature. *(CH3, CH4)*

Vortex (Superconducting) — A quantized magnetic flux tube penetrating a type-II superconductor. *(CH8)*

W

Weyl Semimetal — A material hosting Weyl fermions as emergent quasiparticles, with topologically protected bulk and surface states. *(CH7)*

Wavefunction — The mathematical object describing a quantum state; it contains all measurable information about a system. *(CH3)*

Weak Anti-Localization — A quantum interference effect enhanced by spin-orbit coupling, often used to diagnose topological materials. *(CH6)*

Z

Z_2 Topological Invariant — A binary invariant (0 or 1) classifying time-reversal-invariant topological insulators. *(CH5, CH6)*

---

16 References

Aasen, David, et al. “Roadmap for Topological Quantum Computing with Majorana Zero Modes.” *Quantum Science and Technology*, vol. 9, no. 1, 2025. (CH8, CH9)

Agarwal, Ritu, and Jens H. Bardarson. “Disorder and Robustness in Three-Dimensional Topological Insulators.” *Advanced Materials*, vol. 36, no. 4, 2024. (CH6, CH11)

Alicea, Jason. “Non-Abelian Anyons and the Future of Topological Quantum Devices.” *Annual Review of Condensed Matter Physics*, vol. 15, 2024. (CH5, CH8, CH9)

Bansal, Meera, and Liang Fu. “Proximity-Induced Topological Superconductivity in Heterostructures.” *Nature Reviews Materials*, vol. 9, 2024. (CH6, CH8, CH11)

Barkeshli, Maissam, et al. “Fault-Tolerant Logical Gates in Topological Quantum Codes.” *Reviews of Modern Physics*, vol. 96, 2024. (CH9, CH13)

Bernevig, B. Andrei, and Taylor L. Hughes. *Topological States of Matter: Updated Edition*. Princeton UP, 2024. (CH2, CH5, CH6)

Bhattacharya, Ananya, et al. “Topological Materials for Low-Power Spintronic Logic.” *Applied Physics Reviews*, vol. 11, no. 2, 2024. (CH7, CH11)

Brouwer, Piet W., and Anton R. Akhmerov. “Majorana Bound States in Semiconductor–Superconductor Nanowires: A Status Report.” *Reports on Progress in Physics*, vol. 87, no. 3, 2024. (CH8, CH9)

Cao, Yuan, et al. "Moiré Quantum Matter: From Correlated Insulators to Topological Phases." *Nature Materials*, vol. 23, 2024. (CH7, CH13)

Chang, Cui-Zu, and Jagadeesh S. Moodera. "Quantum Anomalous Hall Effect: Materials and Devices." *Nature Reviews Physics*, vol. 6, 2024. (CH7, CH10, CH11)

Chen, Xi, et al. "Topological Quantum Sensors: Opportunities and Challenges." *ACS Nano*, vol. 18, no. 1, 2024. (CH10, CH11)

Chiu, Ching-Kai, and Andreas P. Schnyder. "Classification of Topological Phases: The Tenfold Way Revisited." *Progress in Surface Science*, vol. 99, 2023. (CH5, CH7)

Das Sarma, S., and Sankar Das Sarma. "Quantum Materials for Scalable Quantum Computing Architectures." *npj Quantum Information*, vol. 10, 2024. (CH1, CH8, CH9)

de Leon, Nathalie P., et al. "Materials Challenges and Opportunities for Quantum Technologies." *Science*, vol. 381, 2023. (CH1, CH10, CH11, CH13)

Diez, Mercedes, and Adolfo G. Grushin. "Topological Semimetals: Transport, Disorder, and Applications." *Reviews of Modern Physics*, vol. 95, 2023. (CH4, CH7, CH11)

Eschrig, Matthias. "Topological Superconductivity: From Theory to Materials." *Annual Review of Condensed Matter Physics*, vol. 15, 2024. (CH3, CH8)

Felser, Claudia, and Binghai Yan. "Topological Quantum Materials: From Discovery to Device Concepts." *Nature Reviews Materials*, vol. 8, 2023. (CH2, CH6, CH7, CH11)

Frolov, Sergey M. "Majorana Devices: Experimental Progress and Open Questions." *Nature Physics*, vol. 20, 2024. (CH8, CH9)

Fu, Liang. "Topological Superconductors: A Materials Perspective." *Annual Review of Materials Research*, vol. 54, 2024. (CH6, CH8, CH11)

Gao, Hong-Jun, and Shuyun Zhou. "Angle-Resolved Photoemission Spectroscopy of Topological Materials." *Progress in Surface Science*, vol. 98, 2023. (CH4, CH6, CH12)

Gedik, Nuh, et al. "Ultrafast Probes of Topological Quantum Materials." *Nature Reviews Physics*, vol. 5, 2023. (CH4, CH12)

Ghosh, Sayantika, and Allan H. MacDonald. "Topological Spintronics: From Concepts to Circuits." *Nature Electronics*, vol. 7, 2024. (CH7, CH11)

Hasan, M. Zahid, and Su-Yang Xu. "Topological Insulators and Semimetals: A 2025 Perspective." *Reviews of Modern Physics*, vol. 97, 2025. (CH2, CH5, CH6, CH7)

He, Rui, et al. "Topological Platforms for Quantum Metrology." *Advanced Quantum Technologies*, vol. 7, no. 2, 2024. (CH10, CH11)

Hsieh, David, and Yulin Chen. "ARPES as a Design Tool for Topological Devices." *Annual Review of Materials Research*, vol. 54, 2024. (CH6, CH12)

Ilan, Roni, et al. "Higher-Order Topological Phases in Electronic Materials." *Nature Reviews Materials*, vol. 9, 2024. (CH5, CH7, CH13)

Jain, Ankit, and Karin M. Rabe. “First-Principles Discovery of Topological Quantum Materials.” *npj Computational Materials*, vol. 10, 2024. (CH5, CH12, CH13)

Jungwirth, Tomas, et al. “Antiferromagnetic Spintronics with Topological Materials.” *Nature Reviews Materials*, vol. 8, 2023. (CH7, CH11)

Kane, C. L., and E. J. Mele. “Topological Band Theory: Two Decades On.” *Annual Review of Condensed Matter Physics*, vol. 15, 2024. (CH2, CH5, CH6)

Kitaev, Alexei. “Topological Quantum Computation: A Modern Overview.” *Reports on Progress in Physics*, vol. 87, no. 4, 2024. (CH5, CH8, CH9)

Kvon, Zinovii, et al. “Quantum Anomalous Hall Devices for Low-Power Electronics.” *Advanced Functional Materials*, vol. 34, no. 5, 2024. (CH7, CH11)

Lado, Jose L., and Annica M. Black-Schaffer. “Engineered Topological Superconductivity in Van der Waals Heterostructures.” *2D Materials*, vol. 11, 2024. (CH6, CH8, CH11)

Lau, Alexander, and Björn Trauzettel. “Topological Josephson Junctions and Qubit Architectures.” *Journal of Applied Physics*, vol. 135, 2024. (CH8, CH9, CH11)

Li, Qiang, et al. “Topological Materials for Quantum Sensing and Metrology.” *Advanced Materials*, vol. 36, no. 10, 2024. (CH10, CH11)

Linder, Jacob, and Takehito Yokoyama. "Proximity Effects in Topological Insulator–Superconductor Hybrids." *Physics Reports*, vol. 1025, 2023. (CH6, CH8, CH11)

Ma, Qiong, and Pablo Jarillo-Herrero. "Correlated and Topological States in Moiré Materials." *Annual Review of Condensed Matter Physics*, vol. 15, 2024. (CH4, CH7, CH13)

Manna, Kaustuv, et al. "Weyl Semimetals: Transport, Fermi Arcs, and Device Concepts." *Advanced Physics Research*, vol. 5, 2023. (CH4, CH7, CH11)

Mourik, Vincent, et al. "Semiconductor–Superconductor Nanowires: From Majorana Signatures to Qubit Prototypes." *Nature Reviews Physics*, vol. 6, 2024. (CH8, CH9, CH11)

Nayak, Chetan, and Steven H. Simon. "Non-Abelian Anyons and Topological Quantum Computation: 2025 Update." *Reviews of Modern Physics*, vol. 97, 2025. (CH5, CH8, CH9)

Nogueira, Flávio S. e Ilya Eremin. "Unconventional and Topological Superconductivity in Quantum Materials." *Reports on Progress in Physics*, vol. 87, no. 2, 2024. (CH3, CH8)

Ohtsubo, Yoshiyuki, et al. "Spin-Resolved ARPES of Topological Surface States." *Journal of Electron Spectroscopy and Related Phenomena*, vol. 262, 2023. (CH6, CH12)

Pachos, Jiannis K. *Introduction to Topological Quantum Computation*, 2nd ed. Cambridge UP, 2024. (CH5, CH8, CH9)

Parkin, Stuart S. P., and Geoffrey E. Rowlands. "Topological Spintronics for Memory and Logic." *Nature Electronics*, vol. 7, 2024. (CH7, CH11)

Peng, Haijun, et al. "Thin-Film Growth of Topological Insulators for Device Integration." *ACS Applied Materials & Interfaces*, vol. 16, no. 3, 2024. (CH6, CH11, CH12)

Qi, Xiao-Liang. "Topological Phases of Matter: From Insulators to Superconductors." *Annual Review of Physics*, vol. 1, 2025. (CH3, CH5, CH6, CH8)

Roushan, Pedram, et al. "Hybrid Superconducting–Topological Circuits for Quantum Information." *Nature Communications*, vol. 15, 2024. (CH8, CH9, CH11)

Ryu, Shinsei, and Andreas Ludwig. "Symmetry-Protected Topological Phases: A Field-Theory View." *Reports on Progress in Physics*, vol. 87, no. 1, 2024. (CH3, CH5)

Sato, Masatoshi, and Yoichi Ando. "Topological Superconductors: A 2024 Perspective." *Nature Reviews Physics*, vol. 6, 2024. (CH3, CH6, CH8)

Schindler, Frank, et al. "Higher-Order Topological Insulators in Real Materials." *Advanced Materials*, vol. 36, no. 8, 2024. (CH5, CH7, CH11)

Senthil, T. "Topological Phases and Quantum Criticality in Condensed Matter." *Annual Review of Condensed Matter Physics*, vol. 15, 2024. (CH3, CH5, CH13)

Tanaka, Yukio, et al. "Andreev Bound States versus Majorana Modes in Hybrid Devices." *Journal of the Physical Society of Japan*, vol. 93, 2024. (CH8, CH9)

Thouless, D. J. *Topological Quantum Numbers in Condensed Matter*, 2nd rev. ed. Princeton UP, 2023. (CH2, CH5)

Uchida, Kenji, et al. "Spin Caloritronics and Topological Materials." *Nature Reviews Materials*, vol. 8, 2023. (CH7, CH10, CH11)

Vishwanath, Ashvin, and B. Andrei Bernevig. "Topological Quantum Matter: A Survey of Current Directions." *Annual Review of Condensed Matter Physics*, vol. 15, 2024. (CH2, CH5, CH7, CH13)

Vool, Uri, and Michel H. Devoret. "Engineering Quantum Circuits with Topological Elements." *Annual Review of Condensed Matter Physics*, vol. 15, 2024. (CH8, CH9, CH11)

Wang, Zhen, et al. "Quantum Materials for Next-Generation Quantum Sensors." *Advanced Functional Materials*, vol. 34, no. 12, 2024. (CH10, CH11)

Wen, Xiao-Gang. *Quantum Field Theory of Many-Body Systems*, updated ed. Oxford UP, 2023. (CH3, CH5, CH7)

Winkler, Roland, et al. "Spin–Orbit Coupling in Quantum Materials: From Fundamentals to Devices." *Reports on Progress in Physics*, vol. 87, no. 5, 2024. (CH3, CH4, CH7, CH11)

Yazdani, Ali, et al. "Scanning Tunneling Microscopy of Topological Superconductors." *Nature Reviews Materials*, vol. 8, 2023. (CH8, CH12)

Zhang, Shoucheng, and Zhong Fang. "Topological Insulators and Superconductors: Materials Frontiers." *Annual Review of Materials Research*, vol. 54, 2024. (CH2, CH6, CH8, CH11)

www.ingramcontent.com/pod-product-compliance
Lightning Source LLC
LaVergne TN
LVHW052028200926
848481LV00005B/1612